The World Since 1945

Keith Robbins is Vice-Chancellor of the University of Wales, Lampeter, and currently Senior Vice-Chancellor of the University of Wales. His many publications include *Churchill, Eclipse of a Great Power: Modern Britain, 1870–1992, Polititicians, Diplomacy and War in Modern British History, Bibliography of British History 1914–1989*, and most recently *Great Britain: Identities, Institutions and the Idea of Britishness*.

The World
Since 1945

A Concise History

Keith Robbins

OXFORD

UNIVERSITY PRESS

OXFORD

UNIVERSITY PRESS

Great Clarendon Street, Oxford OX2 6DP

Oxford University Press is a department of the University of Oxford.
It furthers the University's objective of excellence in research, scholarship,
and education by publishing worldwide in

Oxford New York

Auckland Bangkok Buenos Aires Cape Town Chennai
Dar es Salaam Delhi Hong Kong Istanbul Karachi Kolkata
Kuala Lumpur Madrid Melbourne Mexico City Mumbai Nairobi
São Paulo Shanghai Singapore Taipei Tokyo Toronto

with an associated company in Berlin

Oxford is a registered trade mark of Oxford University Press
in the UK and in certain other countries

Published in the United States
by Oxford University Press Inc., New York

British Library Cataloguing in Publication Data

Data available

Library of Congress Cataloging in Publication Data

Robbins, Keith.
The World since 1945 : a concise history / Keith Robbins.
Includes bibliographical references and index.
1. History, Modern—1945– . I. Title.
D840.R53 1998 909.82'5—dc21 98–3706

ISBN 0–19–280314–X

3 5 7 9 10 8 6 4 2

Printed in Great Britain by
Clays Ltd., St. Ives plc

Contents

The World in 1945

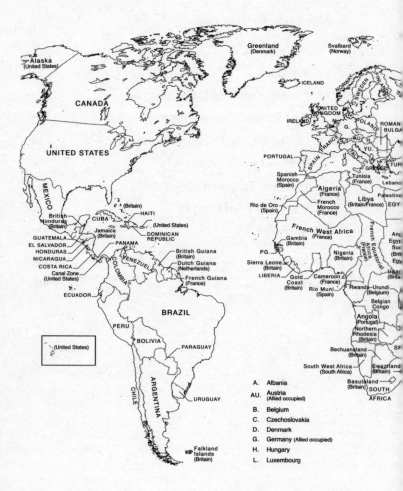

A.   Albania

AU. Austria (Allied occupied)

B.   Belgium

C.   Czechoslovakia

D.   Denmark

G.   Germany (Allied occupied)

H.   Hungary

L.   Luxembourg

UNION OF SOVIET SOCIALIST REPUBLICS

MONGOLIA

Sakhalin

AFGHANISTAN

CHINA

North Korea
(Soviet occupied)

South Korea
(US occupied)

Japan
(US occupied)

Syria
IRAQ
IRAN
Kuwait
(Britain)

TIBET

BHUTAN

Transjordan
Qatar
(Britain)

NEPAL

Macao
(Portugal)

Bahrain
(Britain)

Eritrea
SAUDI
ARABIA

Oman
(Britain)

India
(Britain)

Hong Kong
(Britain)

(United States)

TO

YE

Aden
(Britain)

THAILAND

Philippines

British North
Borneo
(Britain)

(United States)

French
Indo-China
(France)

ETHIOPIA

British Somaliland
(Britain)

French Somaliland
(France)

Italian Somaliland
(Britain)

Ceylon
(Britain)

Malaya
(Britain)

Brunei
(Britain)

Sarawak
(Britain)

Celebes

(United States)

(United States)

British East Africa
(Britain)

Sumatra

Borneo

New Guinea

Singapore
(Britain)

Dutch East Indies
(Netherlands)

Portuguese
Timor
(Portugal)

Territory of
Papua and
New Guinea
(Australia)

(Britain)

Tanganyika
(Britain)

Java

(Britain)

Nyasaland
(Britain)

Madagascar
(France)

(Britain/France)

Mozambique
(Portugal)

AUSTRALIA

(France)

(Britain)

N.   Netherlands

PG.   Portuguese Guinea (Portugal)

SR.   Southern Rhodesia (Britain)

S.   Switzerland

TO.   Trucial Oman (Britain)

YE.   Yemen

YU.   Yugoslavia

Tasmania

NEW
ZEALAND

The World in 1998

A.	Albania	BU.	Bulgaria
AR.	Armenia	CAR.	Central African Republi
AU.	Austria	CR.	Croatia
AZ.	Azerbaijan	C.	Czech Republic
B.	Belgium	D.	Denmark
BO.	Bosnia–Herzegovina	DR.	Dominican Republic

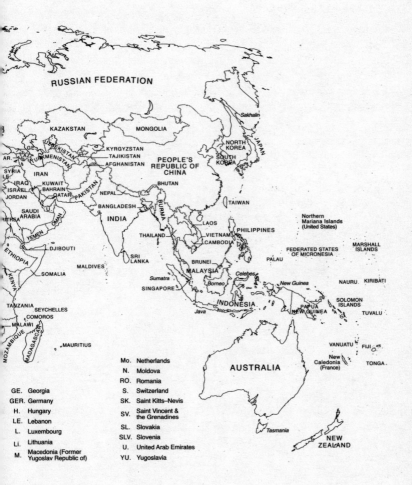

RUSSIAN FEDERATION

KAZAKSTAN
MONGOLIA
UZBEKISTAN
KYRGYZSTAN
GE.
AR.
TURKMENISTAN
TAJIKISTAN
SYRIA
LE.
AFGHANISTAN
PEOPLE'S
REPUBLIC OF
CHINA
NORTH
KOREA
JAPAN
Sakhalin
SOUTH
KOREA
IRAN
KUWAIT
IRAQ
BAHRAIN
ISRAEL
QATAR
JORDAN
PAKISTAN
BHUTAN
NEPAL
SAUDI
ARABIA
OMAN
BANGLADESH
TAIWAN
ERITREA
YEMEN
INDIA
BURMA
LAOS
THAILAND
VIETNAM
PHILIPPINES
Northern
Mariana Islands
(United States)
MARSHALL
ISLANDS
ETHIOPIA
DJIBOUTI
CAMBODIA
MALDIVES
SRI
LANKA
BRUNEI
FEDERATED STATES
OF MICRONESIA
PALAU
SOMALIA
KENYA
MALAYSIA
Celebes
SINGAPORE
Sumatra
Borneo
New Guinea
NAURU
KIRIBATI
TANZANIA
SEYCHELLES
COMOROS
INDONESIA
SOLOMON
ISLANDS
PAPUA
NEW GUINEA
TUVALU
MALAWI
Java
MOZAMBIQUE
MADAGASCAR
MAURITIUS
VANUATU
FIJI
New
Caledonia
(France)
TONGA

Mo.   Netherlands
N.   Moldova
RO.   Romania
S.   Switzerland
SK.   Saint Kitts–Nevis
SV.   Saint Vincent &
      the Grenadines
SL.   Slovakia
SLV. Slovenia
U.   United Arab Emirates
YU.   Yugoslavia

GE.   Georgia
GER. Germany
H.   Hungary
LE.   Lebanon
L.   Luxembourg
Li.   Lithuania
M.   Macedonia (Former
      Yugoslav Republic of)

AUSTRALIA

Tasmania

NEW
ZEALAND

Introduction

No individual can embrace the full complexity of the world since 1945. No single person can enter 'from the inside' all of its complex structures and cultures. There is no detached vantage point which permits an author to see the world 'as it really is' removed from the inescapable limitations produced by his own location in time and place. What constitutes 'due weight' is itself culturally determined. So, this historian confesses himself to be British and male, not able fully to shake off a perspective derived from education and employment in a small group of islands off the coast of Europe which has had, even in the late twentieth century, a 'disproportionate' place in world history.

He first went to school in 1945, a year in which his school atlas disclosed that a large part of the world was coloured red and was in some sense British. His atlas now discloses a very different picture. Yet 'what the world is like' is not a simple matter of representation. Even cartography has an irreducibly subjective element. Every map 'projects' its own concept of how the world is structured and the relationships it contains. In subtle ways, it transcends the physical and social realities it describes. So, locked in individual and national consciousness, produced by a complicated interplay of memory and image, are 'mental maps' which 'make sense' of the world. Location on a map may be one thing, location in the mind may be another. It is an important point to bear in mind when, as this book largely does, we approach the world on a continental basis. Not all continents are 'equal' and not all interact with each other to the same degree or in the same manner.

The historian of the world has also to wrestle with time as

well as space. The year 1945 is a date in a Christian time-frame and so is the millennium. The whole world, however, does not operate within this time-frame, though it cannot ignore it. To use it in this book is itself a limitation, though one without deliberate dogmatic intent. Few countries in the modern world seek to emulate the Frenchmen for whom the Revolution consti- tuted a new beginning—'Year One'. Yet it is obvious that most societies identify themselves against different time-markers. As the French historian Braudel remarked of his own country, each 'current event' brings together movements and processes of dif- ferent origins operating to different rhythms. How much more is that the case when a history of the world is involved! There is something artificial in supposing that half a century since 1945 holds the same universal significance. Yet the chapter divisions adopted in this book do encapsulate certain phases of world development. There is a global pattern. The world did dance to a particular music of time, even if some states and societies with- in it did so more conspicuously and dramatically than others.

The author has lived through the entire period of this narra- tive, mainly in a country which has grown increasingly uncertain to what 'world' it belongs. It follows that memory, sometimes vivid, complicates scholarly study. He has also travelled quite widely in different parts of the world, and in different decades, though never with a systematic comparative purpose in mind. Such experience can increase understanding, though it may deceive by its superficiality and randomness. Any author, in short, who attempts to write world history must inevitably make uncomfortable and inescapably contentious choices of topic and treatment. In this particular case, the task is made more difficult still by the need, dictated by the series, to write succinctly about matters which are often complex. The risk of oversimplification is present in every sentence. Questions are sometimes raised but not always answered, or at least not with the fullness that a longer book would allow. The Further Reading list, besides acknowledging the scholarship of others without whom the book could not have been written, is designed to allow readers to take matters further across a whole range of topics.

So, out of many possible 'world histories' what 'world history' is being attempted? It is emphatically an international political history. The focus is firmly on global political interaction. The book provides the reader with an account of the main political developments since 1945. There is, however, a tension between some attempt at global 'coverage' as a desirable goal and the recognition that some countries, at particular junctures, are 'more equal' than others in their impact on world affairs. They therefore command more space. In one sense a world history can only lay claim to being universal if the reader learns where even the smallest states—many of which are not mentioned at all—'fit in', but world history as interpreted here cannot be the sum of the history of *all* its components. And, sadly, it is countries and regions which see conflict and war which seem doomed to receive more attention than those where it is absent or minimal. No student of international history, however, can be unaware that the origins of conflicts and wars are frequently multifaceted. Their complexity is touched on in this book but rarely is it possible to present the issues as all the 'actors' and their subsequent interpreters have seen them.

Of course, world history might properly be written differently. World matters of great importance which are only touched on lightly in this book—economic development, financial integration, social transformation, religious pluralism, demography, sport, to name only some—could *each* have been made the central hub of different books. One might identify a world of great cities—London, New York, Tokyo among them—which have a specific relationship with each other. It becomes wearisome, though still necessary, to stress that more attention could have been given had length not been constrained. That said, while it is recognized that some kind of 'world society' exists, replete with 'transactions'—personal, cultural, intellectual, economic, religious, scientific—outside the formal framework of states, it is without much shame that what is described remains fundamentally a 'world of states'. In this sense, as certain other (American) writers on international history would urge, the state has indeed been brought back in. There is a refusal, however, to take a dogmatic stance on the hoary issue of whether foreign policy or domestic politics has 'primacy' in the behaviour of states. There are 'linkages', but except where they are most conspicuous they are not systematically alluded to or identified here. Indeed, almost by definition, if world history has an essence it lies in the word 'connection'. It is a conviction which is at the heart of this book.

The theme which does underlie the volume is at once vague and profound: the world conceived as unity and conceived as diversity. It notes the huge range of contacts across the world in almost all spheres of activity. It observes a sense of 'one world' which emerges, albeit transiently and uncertainly, in so many contexts. A scenario of global homogenization has mingled, at times, with a nightmare of global destruction. Yet, alongside the aspiration to create some kind of more stable world order has been the reality of continuing war and conflict. And global homogenization has been seen as a threat to be resisted because it brings with it large-scale social and cultural dislocations. Hence, a renewed emphasis on difference and individuality. These two broad tendencies have existed side by side since 1945. Neither appears, at the time of writing, unambiguously to have triumphed.

1

Towards One World?
The Year 1945

Taking a World View

In April 1961 the Soviet cosmonaut Yuri Gagarin became the first person in space. He was the first human being to orbit the Earth and thus look at 'the world' from 'outside'. Even at this moment of triumph, however, there was a paradox. His achievement has to be seen in the context of a 'space race' between the Soviet Union and the United States. Even as states thrust men beyond the world, they did so in competition with each other. Cost and other factors might lead to collaboration in the future, but in its early stages space exploration seemed to confirm division rather than unity. It was apparently only in the increasingly popular world of 'science fiction' that 'Earthlings' united to confront the aliens of outer space. It is the tension between creeping universalism and tenacious particularism which forms the central theme of this book.

Two decades before Gagarin, in August 1942, Wendell Wilkie, American publicist and presidential candidate, took off from an airfield in New York in a four-engined bomber to see what he could 'of the world and the war'. Forty-nine days later, he landed in Minneapolis, Minnesota, having circled the globe on a route which crossed the Equator twice. He travelled a total of 31,000 miles. It was an extraordinary fact, they believed, that to cover this 'enormous distance' Wilkie and his companions were in the air a total of only 160 hours. He interviewed the British General Montgomery among sand dunes on the Mediterranean; he chatted in coffee-houses in Baghdad; he spent five hours sitting next to Stalin; he had long talks with Generalissimo Chiang Kai-shek in China. He concluded, in his widely read *One*

World (1943), that to win the peace it was necessary to plan on
a world basis so that all nations might be free, politically and
economically. The United States had a vital role, he believed, in
this process. Indeed, the world demanded the full participation
of a self-confident America. A new era of history was about to
dawn. The sense that there was at least potentially 'one world'
was widespread if inchoate in the literature of the time. The
tyranny of distance, which had so long kept peoples and states
apart, was diminishing daily. It would be possible, within decades, to travel the globe in considerably more comfort and
greater speed than was possible for Wilkie in a four-engined
bomber. It is easy to see why, perhaps for the first time in human
history, it seemed to some contemporary idealists to be both
possible and necessary to 'plan on a world basis'.

Prospects for Peacemaking

Half a century later, however, after decades of conflict, these
sentiments may well appear naïve and gauche, but they were
none the less widely echoed. 'Realists', however, even at the
time, remained sceptical. Looking back, not only to the war that
was ending, but to the inter-war period and the earlier attempt,
in 1919, to make a fresh start after a major war, they saw little
prospect of an imminent transition to permanent peace. The new
League of Nations could claim some success in helping to resolve
disputes between small states, but it soon became apparent that
it was not an embryonic world government. By the 1930s, the
initial assumption that all the great powers had a mutual interest
in the maintenance of peace was seen to be flawed. Germany,
Italy, and Japan, to name only the most significant states, were
all prepared to go to war to realize their objectives. It was simply
not the case that 'the world' would rally in unity to defeat a
single intrepid sinner. If, therefore, after 1945, there was to be
another attempt at world management, the omens were not very
encouraging.

   In comparison with 1914–18, the Second World War was
more truly a global conflict. There was, therefore, in theory at

least, an opportunity for all the major belligerents to be involved in creating a new world order after 1945. The First World War admittedly had remained fundamentally a European war, settled by the major European belligerents and, only latterly, by the involvement of the United States. The Second World War, however, extended significantly beyond Europe, and in effect embraced two conflicts: the war in Europe which began in September 1939 with the German invasion of Poland and the war in Asia which began in July 1937, when Japan attacked China. Of course, over time, these two conflicts intersected, but their distinct origins ensured that the Second World War was more than simply a European struggle projected onto a world stage. It was meaningful to speak of a *world* whose character would be fundamentally shaped by the experience of war. Although many areas escaped actual fighting—North and South America, much of Africa, most of the Indian subcontinent—in practice war had a major impact on all states, belligerent or not. It would have been odd, therefore, if 'the world' had emerged from such an upheaval into an effortless tranquillity.

There was another fundamental issue which could not be ignored. What was the relationship between domestic politics and international policy? Was it the case that democracies were inherently pacific, whereas 'totalitarian' regimes were inherently aggressive? Could a stable and acceptable world order only be envisaged if Anglo-American understandings of democracy became prevalent worldwide? The 1919 assumptions of the peacemakers that the new Europe would eagerly embrace such understandings had quickly faded. Mussolini's new 'Fascism' in Italy, and its imitations elsewhere, together with Hitler's later National Socialism in Germany, were contemptuous of feeble parliamentarism. They had purported to offer a new dynamic way to the future. 'Fascist' leaders, in or out of power, claimed to speak for a national 'community'. They considered 'struggle' to be essential and 'peace' an enfeebling delusion. In addition, the Bolshevik Revolution of 1917 set itself apart from the 'bourgeois' Anglo-American world-view which had predominated in 1919 peacemaking. The new Soviet regime offered itself

as an example to the working class of the world, and of Europe
in particular. Were there grounds, therefore, for supposing in
1945 that the latent conflict between 'bourgeois' and 'Bolshevik'
had been transcended merely because the Soviet Union and
Anglo-America had ended the war as comrades in arms? Did
not Washington and London deceive themselves in supposing
that the democratic character of their governments gave them a
'bias towards peace' and made them disinterested in the arbitra-
tion of world affairs?

Viewed as inter-state conflict, the Second World War had
indeed come to an end, but it was more than that. 'Resistance'
in occupied Europe had been plagued by ideological rifts and
suspicions. In some instances, rivals seemed as much concerned
to establish internal supremacy in relation to each other as to
engage the forces of the occupier. Exiled governments saw their
ability to bring about a political restoration on their own terms
slipping away. Even local Communists were not altogether
enamoured of the comrades who would return home after a war
spent in Moscow. Western governments had made contentious
and difficult decisions. In the conspicuous case of Yugoslavia,
for example, there was support for Tito's Communist partisans
on the grounds that his forces caused most disruption. Nor were
such ambiguities confined to the war in Europe. They were very
evident in China. To the intense irritation of Stilwell, the American general sent to galvanize the Chinese war effort, Chiang
Kai-shek seemed on occasion as much concerned to maintain
the position of the Guomindang regime which he headed as to
fight the Japanese forces occupying large areas of China. The
Guomindang, by this juncture, was the somewhat corrupt
'Nationalist' Party of the 1911 Chinese Republic. There was a
strong prospect that, once Japan surrendered, a final struggle
with the Communists would ensue in China. Both sides jockeyed
for position. In this sense, in very different parts of the world,
there was still the strong possibility of continuing or renewed
fighting. The relationship between internal and external considerations in the behaviour of states was constantly shifting.

Legacies, Hopes, and Fears

It is not necessary, however, for present purposes, to attempt even an outline sketch of the history of the Second World War itself. Such accounts are readily available elsewhere. Yet no assessment of how the world 'settled down' after 1945 can properly be made without some understanding of its multifaceted legacy. Emotionally and psychologically, it was inconceivable that memories could be banished and a 'fresh start' made at once. Millions had died, many far from their own homes. Enmities, once aroused, remained potent. The propaganda and rhetoric which had accompanied armies and stimulated expectations still lingered. In addition, at many levels, close relationships had been established between states on a scale scarcely conceivable in 1939. It was not possible, therefore, to envisage a straightforward return to the world of 1939 in Europe or of 1937 in East Asia. Too much had happened in the interval to make such a return to the previous status quo feasible, even supposing that it was desirable.

An important case in point was the British Empire. In 1939, through its empire, Britain looked incontestably a Great Power, though even then in reality the fact of its worldwide spread gave a deceptive appearance of strength. 'Appeasement', as pursued by British governments in the 1930s, however, in part had reflected an underlying anxiety—Britain was 'overextended' and could not protect the Empire against all potential opponents. Even the victorious outcome of a war would prove crippling. Perhaps 'Pax Britannica' was inexorably passing and the United States would inevitably surpass the United Kingdom in economic, industrial, and military might, indeed perhaps had already done so. If so, Britain had no option but to emphasize a 'special relationship' and behave as a junior but still potent partner. Influential sections of British opinion, however, were by no means reconciled to this fate in 1945.

The relationship between the British Empire and the United States had indeed become very significant in determining the outcome of the war and the future of the world. Even before

Pearl Harbor, rhetorical steps had been taken to proclaim, in August 1941, an 'Atlantic Charter' which embodied 'certain common principles in the national policies of their respective countries on which they base their hopes for a better future for the world'. Churchill, with a British father and an American mother, suggested during the war that 'a better future for the world' did indeed rest on the British–American partnership. Yet Churchill was also worried by the evidence of American hostility towards the British Empire and, as time passed, by the way in which the increase in American strength diminished Britain's capacity to bargain. Roosevelt, for his part, despite a personal intimacy with Churchill, had no intention of subordinating American interests. Significantly, it was in Washington, not London, that in January 1942 the United States, the Soviet Union, the United Kingdom, and China, together with twenty-two other allied countries—the 'United Nations'—pledged themselves not to make separate peace treaties. There was, however, an absence of unity about their immediate objectives, a division which reflected their different pathways into global conflict. For example, a section of American opinion, particularly on the West Coast, thought of the war primarily in terms of Japan and the Pacific region. The United States ought not to be sidetracked into the European struggle as a first priority: Japan should be defeated first.

In short, on the return of 'peace', there were two fundamental ways of looking at the world. One was to assume that the war had done its job: Germany, Italy, Japan, and their clients, the disturbers of the previous peace, had all been comprehensively defeated. Hitler's 'new order' in Europe and a Japanese 'new order' in East Asia were no more. They should never unsettle international order again. Once that was done, however, world history would evolve smoothly because that was what the victorious powers wanted. On the contrary, others countered, no such assumption could be made. 'World order' was always changing, a matter of infinitely subtle shifts and balances. No wartime coalition would continue to work together indefinitely in peacetime. To believe so would be to accept the flawed assumptions of 1919. Italy and Japan, after all, had been among the 'Allies' of the First World War; but by the 1930s, from a British perspective, they were so no longer. Such commentators considered that to accomplish 'one world', if it could ever be achieved, would be an arduous and lengthy task. It looked more likely that wars and rumours of wars would be as prevalent after 1945 as they had been before 1939.

These two conflicting assumptions have been stated boldly. They were elaborated and refined in all the victorious governments of the world. Diplomats and professors all had their say. They were, at least in the Anglo-American world, anxious to avoid the utopian optimism allegedly characteristic of 1919. It was necesssary, above all, to be realistic. However, such a stance did not altogether preclude the expression of hope. The folly of supposing that one world war would ensure that there would never be another was evident, but 1939–45 might just be special. It had given the customary fillip to weapons technology; it had further obliterated distinctions between civilians and combatants; it saw whole cities burned out by air attack; and so on. Millions of people came to death in a manner more gruesome even than those who had gone up the line on the Somme in 1916—if one can make such fine comparisons. Total estimates for the number of dead in the Second World War vary between 45 and 50 million. Two specific ways of dying, however, need further attention because, in different ways, they informed the mood and assumptions of 1945—through the Holocaust or 'Final Solution' and through the atomic bomb.

In 1945, approaching Poland and Germany from their respective directions, the Russian and Anglo-American forces came across the death camps whose names soon became common currency—Auschwitz, Belsen, Buchenwald, and others. The questions which arise from the systematic slaughter of some 6 million Jews—one-third of the world Jewish population in 1939—continue to reverberate down to the present. The majority were murdered in Poland and the German-occupied parts of the Soviet Union. Perhaps some 300,000 European Jews survived the camps and death marches. How could killing become such a matter of routine? What logic was it that supposed that the destruction of a people could be justified on 'scientific grounds'? Were the policies pursued by the Third Reich 'modern' or fundamentally 'reactionary'? What, if anything, could have been done to prevent such bestiality? Who knew what and when? How deep was anti-Semitism in European society? Should the Pope (to take only one figure) have 'spoken out' to more effect? Such questions could be multiplied as the post-1945 world struggled to come to terms with the enormity of what had occurred. The debate amongst historians across the world has deepened as they have examined the grim picture that has been steadily filled out through the recollections of survivors and the publication of ghetto diaries. No short summary can adequately 'explain' a catastrophe which still hangs over the late twentieth-century world. It is generally agreed, however, that Hitler envisaged a future society whose functioning would be based upon the 'racial recovery' of the German people. Racial purity was the heart of the matter and, while Jewish people were the primary targets, gypsies and the mentally and physically handicapped would also have to be eliminated to achieve a new society.

Even so, argument rages as to how such a strategy came to emerge and how far it was accepted/imposed within Germany. Some reparation to Jewish organizations was made in the post-war decade and some trials and executions of perpetrators took place. Nevertheless, the scar remained and could not be easily healed. Controversy concerning the 'Holocaust' still revolves around the extent to which such a descent into barbarism is latent within all advanced societies or was the outcome of a singular regime 'without precedent or parallel'.

It is apparent that there were many other atrocities in the war, for example the massacre of Polish army officers in the Katyn forest near Smolensk in 1940. It is now clear that this action was carried out on the direct orders of Stalin and the Soviet Politburo. And, in the scale of deaths attributable to Stalin, such deaths rank fairly modestly. The Soviet Union in 1945 tended to soft-pedal the killing camps that its forces came across lest attention turn to the Soviet slave labour camps—the Gulag population. There were perhaps 1 million deaths per annum during the war years in these camps, though this figure is disputed. Whatever precise total is suggested the essence of the problem remains: is it sensible or feasible to place the scale of slaughter, wherever it occurs, in some kind of hierarchy of evil? Can the motive behind mass-murder ever be extenuating? Is there a difference between mass-liquidation in pursuit of a 'classless society' and its employment to create 'racial purity'? Is iniquity a matter of numbers? To stress the uniqueness of the Holocaust runs the risk of regarding other wartime (and sadly, as was to prove to be the case, post-war) mass killing as merely 'persecution' and, by stressing that it was a 'special case', make it seem a freak phenomenon. To 'normalize' it, however, runs the risk of eliminating some of its distinctive aspects and appearing, however misleadingly, to downplay its significance. Historians can and do place their emphases differently, partly because their craft yields no simple verdict on the springs of human behaviour and the sources of evil.

The dropping of the atomic bombs in August 1945 took the world into a new era. It was as overarching in its implications for the post-war world as was, in a different respect, the Holocaust and its legacy. The news of nuclear fission had been published in February 1939 in the British science journal *Nature*. In the years that followed, British and American scientists, alongside scientists exiled from Europe, worked in great secrecy on the 'Manhattan Project'—in some fear that a German nuclear programme was well advanced (though in fact it had taken a wrong turning). The first bomb was successfully tested in New Mexico in July 1945. 'Little Boy' and 'Fat Man' were dropped a few weeks later. In Hiroshima around 140,000 people died and in Nagasaki around 75,000, not to speak of longer-term consequences. It was against this background, after complex exchanges, that Emperor Hirohito called upon the people to 'endure the unendurable' and accept defeat. Ever since, debate has raged as to whether there was any point—leaving morality on one side—in President Truman causing the bombs to be dropped. Did he have a political lesson to give to the Soviet Union? Yes, to a certain extent. Could Japan not have been brought to surrender by other means? A 'peace party' of a kind did emerge in leading circles, but only late, and it must be doubtful whether Emperor Hirohito could have intervened sooner than he did to bring about peace and save his country from the atomic bombs. It is still sometimes vigorously argued, and was the immediate 'excuse', that the use of the bombs saved hundreds of thousands of lives, both Allied and Japanese. Stimson, the US Secretary of War at the time, produced in 1947 the figure of over a million American lives saved; this became an orthodoxy, but one now considerably dented. Other much lower figures were being quoted at the time—though, of course, any figure is speculative. It is also sometimes still argued—though equally vehemently dismissed—that dropping the bombs probably ended world wars for ever. They had to be dropped to show how terrible they actually were.

When all these matters were reassessed in July/August 1995 by historians in all the countries concerned, varying emphases were still apparent. Some historians argued that, once the bomb worked, there was an overwhelming consensus to use it. It was evident in 1995 that 'the world', in the form of press and media coverage, was not yet ready for an analysis of these episodes which acknowledged a complexity of motives in both Washington and Tokyo at this juncture. The salient fact remains, however, that for the world of 1945 these weapons existed, and would in all likelihood be further developed and become even more devastating. The world could soon destroy itself. It was certainly a new world, as the atomic scientists were well aware. And, in evaluating strategic and political options, there was a growing feeling in the immediate post-war decades that morality could not in fact be 'left on one side'.

Notwithstanding this dismal picture, there was in 1945, and remained in the English-speaking countries, a conviction that it had been a necessary war, even a good one: the Hitler regime was truly evil. It was Hitler who had wanted the war. It was Hitler who came close to conquering Europe. It was Hitler who might have gone on to conquer the world. In such a context, the raids of the RAF and the USAAF on Cologne, Hamburg, Dresden, and Berlin, to name only four German cities, were deemed to be justified. In other parts of the world, too, there were Allied actions which subsequently did not appear beyond reproach. Nevertheless, on balance, there was no doubt in Washington and London that a righteous cause had triumphed. Such satisfaction obscured the fact that the United States might never have involved itself in the Second World War in Europe had it not been for Pearl Harbor.

Victory inescapably entailed belief in the superiority of broad Anglo-American political values and understandings of democracy. It was not, as had sometimes been alleged pre-war, necessarily inefficient and incompetent. The British 'victory' in 1945 led many British commentators to feel that the British parliamentary and party system offered a model for the world. The assumption that democracies were inherently pacific had a considerable history in Anglo-American thinking about peace and war. It was now suggested that the sooner the world became 'democratic', more or less in a British or American manner, the more peaceful and progressive it would become.

Such convictions faced difficulties. In the first place, the Soviet leadership did not share these Anglo-American assumptions. It read the history of the twentieth century, and particularly of the war itself, differently. It had a strong conviction that the Anglo-Americans underestimated the massive contribution which the Red Army and the Russian population as a whole had, at very heavy human cost, made to the victory in Europe. For example, over 600,000 of Leningrad's inhabitants died during the 900-day siege of the city. Some 10 million of the 13.6 million German casualties and prisoners lost in the war were sustained on the Eastern Front. Perhaps the Anglo-Americans had even deliberately delayed the launch of a 'Second Front' in Western Europe. From a Soviet perspective (i.e. Stalin's), it was the Soviet Union which had won the war and was entitled to its reward. The 'democracy' which the Soviet Union was now going to support in Eastern Europe was more democratic than most of the pre-1939 regimes in that area, even when viewed from an Anglo-American understanding of democracy. And, of course, the concept of a 'people's democracy' had, in Soviet eyes, an ideological logic of its own which rendered it superior to 'bourgeois' versions of democracy. Moscow suspected that the Western 'peace-loving democracies' would have been happy if Hitler had left them alone and directed his fire against the Soviet Union from the outset. These very democracies were in fact agencies of a capitalism which was by definition aggressive. Some of these perceptions seemed accurate to sections of opinion in Britain. It was inconceivable, therefore, that the Soviet Union either could or should transform itself. If that was accepted, and there seemed little alternative, such an admission meant that world history after 1945 could not demonstrate worldwide acceptance of the 1941 Atlantic Charter.

In the second place, it was not only in the eyes of the Soviet Union that assumptions by the British and the Americans about the merits of their democracies did not seem so justified. It was a particular problem for the British—even in relation to the Atlantic Charter. How was devotion to democracy—Britain took pride in being 'the mother of parliaments'—to be reconciled with the exercise of control over conquered colonial peoples? Colonial 'partnership' was not democratic government. Here is one further example of the domestic/external duality to which attention has already been drawn and which will be a recurring feature of this book. After 1919, and again in 1935, steps had been taken to increase Indian participation in the government of India. During the war, however, the British faced American criticism of their continuing colonialism. Roosevelt had no interest in helping the colonial powers to hang on to 'the archaic, medieval Empire ideas'. Gandhi had told him in 1942: 'If India becomes free, the rest will follow.' In fact, from 1942 onwards, the question was no longer whether Britain would withdraw, but when and in what circumstances. However, there appeared to be deadlock between the Congress and the Muslim League at the all-India level and increasing evidence of conflict at the local and communal level. It was, to say the least, doubtful whether Britain would be able to control the process of change. It was a graphic illustration of the extent to which already frayed pre-1939 assumptions about the relative strength of colonial powers and colonial peoples could not be sustained.

There was a strong anti-imperialist strand in the Labour Party which formed the new British government in 1945, but in practice the Attlee administration had no intention of winding up the Empire immediately. Herbert Morrison, Labour's Deputy Leader, spoke of the government as being 'great friends of the jolly old Empire'. Intra-imperial trade was vigorously promoted: slightly more than 50 per cent of British exports went to the Empire in the first post-war decade. Plans for 'Colonial Development' were enacted, which were arguably designed to be of as much benefit to post-war Britain as to the colonies (mainly African) themselves. And, it seemed, there was still scope for settlement with a long-term future. The European population of Southern Rhodesia, for example, more than doubled between 1945 and 1955. In this sense, it is misleading to identify 1945 as the year in which there was an abrupt and total shift in the mindset of European colonial powers.

Organizing the United Nations

The question before the victorious powers was whether the world could be 'managed' without a multitude of small conflicts and possibly one cataclysmic one. One answer was to focus again on a world organization. Roosevelt, from 1943 onwards, pressed forward his notion of a Big Four, who would be the policemen of the world, acting, naturally, in the interests of small powers. It was conceivable that the latter might take exception, so it was desirable to develop the existing 'United Nations' into a formal organization in which their voice could be heard. Here, in essence, was what was to become the United Nations Organization, a body which would have both a Security Council (for the Great Powers who really mattered) and a General Assembly (for the remainder). That said, however, there was a great deal of debate in detail on the nature, scope, and resources of the new body, culminating in the San Francisco conference beginning in April 1945, before the Charter was agreed in June.

Inevitably, some states were most anxious that their recent opponents could be adequately contained. That was more important than lofty utopias. There was particular scepticism in Britain about American enthusiasm for a 'World Council', and Churchill initially distrusted any universal body. He preferred to think primarily in terms of regional organizations—for the Americas, Europe, and Asia—which would be suited to deal with their own problems. It would be absurd to have every nation poking its fingers into every other nation's business. If problems could not be resolved at this level, then there should be a supreme council made up exclusively of the Big Four. However, he had to back down. There remained, however, a good deal of general talk about the world being organized into pan-regions. Indeed, still after the war, in November 1945, Ernest Bevin, the new British Foreign Secretary, suspected that 'instead of world co-operation we are drifting into spheres of influence'.

As far as the new world organization was concerned, all sorts of ideas were ventilated—a United Nations Force, the abolition of alliances, among them—but they failed. In the end, with modifications, the United Nations Organization was a revamped League of Nations. As in 1919, so in 1945, statesmen and diplomats predictably sought to devise a body with the past rather than a future in mind. The United Nations depended on the willingness of *states* to work within it. There could be no new instant 'one-world' history. World history would be what its *states*, and the Great Powers in particular, were prepared to allow it to be. The Security Council of the new organization consisted of five permanent members and (until 1965) six other member-countries serving for two-year periods. To this body was entrusted primary responsibility for the peace of the world. Its decisions, however, required unanimity—each permanent member had the right of veto. The General Assembly, on the other hand, could pass resolutions with a two-thirds majority.

The 'Big Five'

The drivers of world history, therefore, were identified as the 'Big Five': Britain, China, France, the Soviet Union, the United States. At the Yalta conference in 1945, the second wartime summit meeting of Stalin, Roosevelt, and Churchill, Stalin made it clear that they should 'never allow any Allied action to be submitted to the judgement of the small powers'. It was the Soviet understanding that the three governments (Britain, the Soviet Union, and the United States) had dealt with each other as equal parties and there had been no case where one or two of the three had attempted to impose their will on the other(s). That was the way things should continue.

The 'Big Five', however, might readily be reduced to the 'Big Three', even the 'Big Two'. The 'Big Three' consisted of the Americans, the British, and the Russians. It was only at Yalta that it was agreed to give France a permanent seat on the Security Council. Chiang Kai-shek made what may be described as a guest appearance at the November 1943 Cairo conference with Churchill and Roosevelt, but that was the only occasion on which he was present at a summit. It is obvious, therefore, that the 'Big Five' were not equally 'big'. Indeed, a certain 'bipolarity' already existed: the United States and the Soviet Union. Churchill himself acknowledged that after July 1944 'it was America who made the big decisions'. Some have placed American ascendancy even earlier, though in the nature of things precise dating is impossible. Britain still had an important role to play, but it was subordinate. The elevation of France was a gesture. Battered, disorientated, divided France scarcely merited the description 'Great Power'. Charles de Gaulle, however, in exile, had made it his mission to ensure the revival of France. He upset those on whom he depended to ensure that 'France' was heard. He had some success and even though, in the event, he did not himself guide its immediate destiny, France would seek its own independent path in world affairs. Finally, China's admission was also a gesture—a place had to be found for the largest 'independent' Asian country, even though its condition was parlous.

This 'Big Five' in 1945 could be categorized in different ways in world perspective. Britain and the United States, though they had their disagreements, were closest culturally and linguistically, though on different continents; together they stood for that rather uncertain entity 'the English-speaking World'. On the other hand, for the British it was not comfortable to be present at a time when 'Pax Britannica' was being replaced, it seemed, by 'Pax Americana'. Britain and France (both still also external powers) represented 'Europe'. Representing 'Europe', however, was not something which Britain and France had clear or convergent convictions about; indeed most British opinion was scarcely 'European' at all. Such unity as shared imperialism brought was complicated by the recent past of the French Empire and British attitudes towards it. In addition, remembering previous alliances in earlier decades, it might be necessary for France to cultivate a relationship with the Soviet Union across the ideological divide as a means of escaping from the domination of the 'Anglo-Saxons'.

The inter-war evolution of the British Empire into a Commonwealth that was still British might also be significant. France had nothing to compare with the close, though occasionally fraught, relationships that existed between Britain and the 'old Dominions'—Australia, Canada, New Zealand, and South Africa. They had come through the war together, but geography could strain unity—as events in South-East Asia had demonstrated where Britain and Australia were concerned in 1942. Field Marshal Smuts of South Africa, however, suggested publicly that 'the British group' might yet have a vital role: it could constitute 'the area of stability between the two Power poles'.

Britain, France, and the United States could be taken to exemplify 'the West', whereas both the Soviet Union (at least its eastern territory) and China represented 'the East'. Even here, however, care is necessary. Chiang's Nanjing capital, before the Japanese invasion, was self-consciously 'Western' and the American influences on his entourage, and his need of American support, have already been noted. It was only through Britain, in a sense, that the southern hemisphere had some kind of guaranteed access to the Security Council, but that did not amount to much. The United States and the Soviet Union both proclaimed a hostility to imperialism. Opinion in the State Department advised that war between the two countries was in the highest degree unlikely. Their geographical location meant that there was no place where friction could automatically arise. Indeed, there was influential American opinion which suggested that a breach between the USA and the USSR was a British game which Washington ought not to play. Lastly, Britain, China, France, and the United States, defined negatively, were non-Communist states, indeed anti-Communist, to greater or lesser degree, whereas the Soviet Union was a Communist state. In the end, it was this last divergence which showed every sign of becoming the most significant divide within the 'Big Five', but for a brief moment it seemed one way, though not the only way, of looking at the configuration of world power in 1945. A great many people, even in high places, did not really know which way the world was going to turn.

Power

The Big Powers, pre-eminently the USA and the USSR, certainly had power. They both had armies of some 12 million men, the Red Army being a little the larger of the two. What was most significant, however, was the projection of American power overseas. In 1945 there was not a single US army division at home—sixty-nine divisions were in Europe and twenty-six in Asia/the Pacific. The United States had an impressive array of ships and aircraft, many more than the Soviet Union. It also had the enigmatic power which the atomic bomb represented. The expansion of the American economy during the war was spectacular. Its gross domestic product had grown by some 70 per cent and constituted roughly a half of the world's total production. Its oil reserves were massive. Now was the time to remove those protective tariffs, preferences, and autarkic tendencies (the pursuit of self-sufficiency) which many economists argued had caused the global economic crisis of the 1930s. If that was indeed the case, and it was widely believed, then it was time to fashion a more open world trading order. The fact that such an order would be in the American interest was as incidental as the British enthusiasm for Free Trade in the nineteenth century.

More generally, the United States buzzed with modern communications—radios and telephones. It had Hollywood. In short, in the image of the world beyond its shores, America represented modernity. What America was in 1945 offered a foretaste, guardians of 'old world' culture believed, of what the whole world would become at some stage in the not-too-distant future. The venerable English historian G. M. Trevelyan discerned an age which had no culture except American films and football pools. However, the allure of America remained. After all, in all its ethnic diversity it was itself a microcosm of the world itself: *e pluribus unum*. But if the capacity of the United States was formidable, the achievements of the Soviet Union also seemed remarkable. Vast internal obstacles had been overcome, at a price, to relocate production and support the Red Army. The Dean of Canterbury was only one of many commentators in Britain and elsewhere to laud *Soviet Strength* and *Soviet Success*.

Power, in all its manifold aspects, might be what mattered in the transition beyond 1945. Even in 1941, it was a British Foreign Office view that the American President only paid lip-service to the Atlantic Charter, and was determined to 'put the USA definitely on top, and see that she stays there'. In 1945, of course, Roosevelt was dead and indeed, of all the major war leaders—Churchill, Hitler, Mussolini—only Stalin made the direct political transition from war to peace. Perhaps, after all the rhetoric and good intentions, there was no clear road to 'One World'. 'It seems to me', wrote the new British Foreign Secretary Bevin in November 1945, 'that what we are dealing with is power politics naked and unashamed.'

2

Cold Division
c. 1945–c. 1953

The Domination of the World

In March 1953 Stalin died. His death is indeed a turning point.
In the years after 1945, if any one man had the whole world
potentially in his hands, it was this diminutive but perhaps
demonic figure. That was how matters were often perceived in
'the West'. Early in 1946 Frank Roberts, a British diplomat in
Moscow, wondered whether 'the world is not now faced with
the danger of a modern equivalent of the religious wars of the
16th century, in which Soviet Communism will struggle with
western social democracy and the American version of capitalism for the domination of the world'. And, while Stalin lived,
this was what was happening. There were two alternative systems
and the peoples and states of the world had to choose this day
whom they would serve.

Freezing Over

There has inevitably been elaborate and enduring debate on the
world's path from 1945. Was this division inevitable? Did it flow
from legitimate anxieties? Naturally, there is no simple answer
to these questions. Some writers, both at the time and subsequently, have argued that there is no real problem to address.
Suggesting that it would have been absurd to take the rhetoric
of 'One World' seriously, they contend that international order
depends, paradoxically, not on some supposed 'natural' harmony but on there being 'friends' and 'enemies' who can be held
in balance. In 1945, after the defeat of Germany and Japan,
there was necessarily a power vacuum which had to be filled.

Friends and enemies had to be established afresh. The Soviet Union and the United States, from this perspective, merely clustered clients about them, seeking to secure the boundaries of their influence by demonizing each other. Ideology—the 'Free World' versus the 'Communist World'—was in no sense the cause of conflict but merely the almost incidental outcome of an inescapable geopolitical situation. It was the British geographer Mackinder who had decades earlier advanced the proposition that the ruler of Eastern Europe commanded what he called the 'Heartland', and the ruler of the Heartland commanded the 'World-Island', and the ruler of the World-Island ruled the world. So, checks and balances against such a domination were needed and between 1945 and 1950 were duly put in place. There is, on this analysis, no call to apportion blame: the division of the world simply had to happen.

Such geopolitical calculations, however, have proved too abstract for other writers, particularly for historians, who have stressed, without a-priori assumptions about the inevitability of world division, the behaviour of particular individuals and states. Such investigation, however, has itself been conditioned by time and place. American authors in the quarter-century after 1945 largely saw the Cold War as a brave response by free men to the threat of Communist aggression. During the Vietnam War, however, dissenting American writers, critical of American involvement, thought that it proved the fundamental imperialism of the United States since 1945. Assessments of the 'Cold War' in its successive phases, in short, frequently reflected contemporary anxieties and the political sympathies of authors. Its ending, without it ever becoming a 'real' war, has led some commentators to suggest that the Cold War was a kind of elaborate global game. It was a device used by American administrations to buttress 'bourgeois/capitalist values' and equally a Soviet device to prevent 'genuine' revolution in Europe. It is on somewhat flimsy foundations, however, that the 'world strategies' of both Washington and Moscow have been identified. Confronted by these divergencies, some writers have latterly, although somewhat artificially, sought to sift out 'primary' and 'secondary' causes, and then to rank them. No such hierarchy is presumed in the discussion that now follows.

Fear of Stalin, and behind him the 'totalitarian' society which he controlled, was undoubtedly widespread and needed little orchestration. Benign wartime 'Uncle Joe' soon seemed sinister after 1945, even, for example, to elements in the British Labour Party initially well-disposed to the Soviet experiment. Despite admiration for the Soviet war-effort, it was ultimately impossible to overlook the brutal nature of his rule. Some commentators, however, have drawn a contrast between his domestic ruthlessness, grudgingly admitted even by some fellow-travellers, and what they have claimed was his cautious pragmatism in foreign policy. It is this distinction which has become standard in certain accounts of the years 1945–53: Stalin, tyrant though he was, had a legitimate concept of Soviet security which was defensive in essence. It was not even the case, they suggest, that the Red Army advanced westwards as far and as fast as it could. Soviet forces, for example, might have advanced more swiftly into Hungary and then on to Berlin. They might have advanced deeper into northern Norway and even into Denmark. To make these observations, however, and to leave matters there, underplays the degree of genuine alarm in Western Europe.

At the time, in view of what it had suffered, there was some recognition in the West that the Soviet Union had reason to seek a 'sphere of influence' or even 'hegemony' in Eastern Europe. Such language, however, is notoriously imprecise. Over what area might a 'sphere of influence' extend and what did 'hegemony' entail? A kind of Soviet hegemony had been prefigured in the secret protocol to the Hitler–Stalin pact of August 1939, a protocol only admitted to exist, incidentally, during the Gorbachev era in the Soviet Union. A minority of Western observers argued further that it was only a 'sphere of influence' which Stalin wanted, taking the view that it was perfectly understandable that Russia/the Soviet Union should seek to guard itself against another Napoleon/Hitler. Stalin, in short, did not aspire to 'Pax Sovietica' on a world scale. The Soviet Union had been drained by the war and was in no condition to fight another.

What it needed was a breathing-space. On any 'rational assessment', it was claimed by those who took such a view, and by some subsequent historians, the USSR was no immediate danger to anyone outside the reach of the Red Army's occupation forces. The notion of a 'communist world conspiracy' was an American fantasy. The source of the 'Cold War', on this analysis, lay in Washington's wilful exaggeration of Soviet intentions. Moscow was essentially reacting 'defensively'.

So was Truman to blame? Henry Wallace, his initial Secretary of Commerce, certainly took the view that the Soviet Union had as much cause to fear the United States as the United States had to fear the Soviet Union. In personal terms, of course, the new American President was an unknown quantity in Moscow. Roosevelt, one suspects, had been a puzzle to Stalin, and on occasion he certainly appeared naïve in his grasp of Soviet intentions. He had, for example, rebuked Churchill for his suspicions: 'You have 400 years of acquisitive instinct in your blood and you just don't understand how a country might not want to acquire land somewhere if they can get it.' Yet he himself did not disclose the American development of the atomic bomb. The new President from Missouri seemed, by contrast, alarmingly direct. Molotov, the Soviet Foreign Minister, received the benefit of 'the straight one-two to the jaw' concerning compliance with what had been agreed at Yalta. Within six months, however, Truman pronounced himself 'tired of babying the Soviets'. Henry Wallace, who wanted to 'trust a bunch of adventurers in the Kremlin Politburo', had to go. What caused such apparent stiffening, apart from the fact that, after the 1930s, all politicians distanced themselves from discredited 'appeasement'?

Soviet propaganda, in a simple-minded way, saw Truman as the puppet of Wall Street. The bosses, although ultimately doomed, were still capable of aggressive action to defend the system. The 'industrial-military complex', as it later came to be called, was not going to forfeit its new-found prominence. It was to these interests that the President was allegedly beholden. He directed a 'capitalist world conspiracy' which was in process of gaining momentum. Such statements do not take us very far.

The reality was that in 1945–6 the United States stood at the crossroads in terms of a world role. Domestic opinion pointed in different directions. Isolationism had revived from 1944 onwards and there were powerful forces wanting, as they supposed, to put 'America First' once more. Lend-Lease, passed with difficulty in 1941, was abruptly terminated by Truman in August 1945 in response to Congressional pressure. The British had anticipated at least one year of aid after the war ended. They were also to find themselves frozen out of that collaboration which had played so important a part in developing the atomic bomb. Above all, American servicemen wanted to go home—over 12 million were demobilized between October 1945 and June 1946. Roosevelt had let it be known at Yalta that all American forces would be out of Europe within two years. Such tendencies suggested the consolidation of 'Fortress America' rather than the adoption of a new post-war role as 'Leader of the Free World'. On the other hand, there was a strong sense, welling up from 'concerned' religious and humanitarian groups, that the United States had a mission to put the world back on its feet. Paradoxically, however, despite the vast overseas projection of the United States during the war, the complexity and diversity of the world was often little understood back home. There remained considerable ignorance even of the geographical location of countries whose problems were now brought to the attention of the American people.

Yet, once the United States had involved itself globally, retreat into isolation was scarcely feasible. It was a fact that Truman was the first man in history able to exercise an 'atomic diplomacy', though we now know that the available atomic bombs could neither be assembled nor transported. In so many parts of the world it had been American power which had determined the outcome. If it was abruptly and rigidly withdrawn, the circumstances and conditions which had caused that intervention might simply (and swiftly) return. If Western Europe had been able to look after itself (Japan raised different issues), the story might have been different, but it appeared that it could not. And, above all, there was still the 'German question'.

Europe

The United States and the Soviet Union might meet in Berlin but, sooner or later, 'Europe' would have to be responsible for its own destiny. Such language, however, was remote from the actual circumstances which prevailed in a continent. It appeared in a state of suspended animation, perhaps on the brink of an uncontrollable breakdown of the whole social structure. Once the 'purification' of society was complete by the punishment of collaborators and murderers (if it ever could be complete), a new beginning had to be made. What were the bases on which 'European Civilization' could be reconstructed? It was inevitably in Europe, in Amsterdam, that the new World Council of Churches held its First Assembly in 1948, reflecting on 'The Church and the Disorder of Society'. People, particularly in Europe, had lost any spiritual cohesion. Where was the way back? New Christian Democratic parties tried to find a new synthesis between religious insight and social and economic policy. The Vatican contributed to this debate, but there were those who felt that Pius XII had not himself exercised unambiguous leadership in the world of European atrocities. 'Existentialism' arose out of wartime contexts where men and women had had to make their own decisions in the absence of agreed societal norms. They would have to continue to do so in peacetime too.

Recollection of the harshness of the times, however, releases the historian from the notion that contemporaries had nothing to do but discuss the abstract basis of world order. 'Freedom from want everywhere in the world'—one of the 'Four Freedoms' announced in Roosevelt's annual message to Congress in 1941—had been identified as the grand objective of the United Nations Food and Agriculture Organization (FAO), formally set up in October 1945. In the summer of 1946 it was reported that in Europe 100 million people were being fed only at a level which seriously damaged their health. Housing, domestic equipment, tools, footwear, but above all food were desperately short. 'Food, clothes, and fuel' were apparently the 'main topics of conversation' even with the British royal family in January 1946. George VI told his Prime Minister that his family was 'down to the lowest ebb' where clothes were concerned. If that was the situation in Buckingham Palace, millions across Europe were at an even lower ebb. They were close to starvation. It was a British publisher, Victor Gollancz, in *In Darkest Germany* who drew attention to the calamities overtaking German cities—though his pleas on their behalf largely fell on deaf ears. The imperative simply to survive was even more important for many millions than 'freedom'. 'Displaced persons' trudged wearily across Central Europe. If they had lost their way, so too had their continent.

In large part, this catastrophic situation, which many commentators thought likely to endure even for decades, was a reflection of the final stages of the war. Unlike the position in 1918, Germany had been invaded and its fate was in the hands of the victors. They all shared a determination that Germany, under whatever regime, should never be in a position again to disturb the peace of the world, but differed as to how this should be ensured. 'Unconditional surrender', agreed back in 1943 by Roosevelt and Churchill at Casablanca, had in the event led to a situation in which Germany had been so comprehensively defeated, and its leaders latterly so bent on their self-destruction, that there was nothing left. All sorts of options had been considered, confronted by the possibility of such an outcome. In September 1944 the US Treasury Secretary, Henry Morgenthau, had put forward a plan that Germany might be 'pastoralized', though it was not adopted. Others favoured splitting Germany up into small states. There was general agreement that somehow Germany had to be 'cleansed' of the National Socialist virus that had infected it.

In the event, there was no immediate and comprehensive peace settlement—though by February 1947 it was possible to sign treaties with states formerly allied to Germany. However, at Potsdam in August 1945 certain specific decisions were reached by Truman, Stalin, and Attlee, amongst them that the Oder–Neisse line would constitute the German–Polish frontier. The four occupying powers—Britain, France, the United States, and the Soviet Union—wrestled in their own way with the paradox of forcing a people to be free. Germany was supposed to be still a single economic unit, but Stalin was notably determined to strip his zone of surviving assets which would help rebuild the Soviet economy. The British, looking back to the early 1920s, were more of the opinion that their own prosperity, and that of Europe as a whole, could not be achieved if Germany were left as a stricken economic giant. The Western occupying powers began to encourage the local revival of German political parties. In September 1946 Secretary of State Byrnes told an audience in Stuttgart that American forces would remain in Germany for the foreseeable future. In January 1947 the British zone was merged into the American. By the end of the year, there was clearly no possibility that the Four Powers involved would agree on a common approach to the German economy. 'Two Germanies' seemed ever more likely as the D-Mark was introduced into the Western zones.

These 'temporary' expedients settled into an acceptance by the Four Powers of *de facto* partition. The deterioration in West/East relations did not obliterate deep suspicions of Germany and the thought of re-establishing it as a single entity did not attract grenadiers from any quarter. Each power, for different but not incompatible reasons, could acquiesce in—and even privately welcome—this 'unplanned' division. It was, perhaps, only because of Stalin's subsequent enthusiasm for prising the Western allies out of Berlin—the city being itself divided into zones—that an arrangement between the occupying powers for the containment of Germany which seemed, at least in the immediate term, so satisfactory, became itself a source of friction and suspicion. And, as that tension increased and time passed, so did the obvious temptation for the Great Powers to enrol embryonic

German institutions into their respective camps as partners/
clients in the 'Cold War'.

The future of Germany was a particular issue, but it was also
an aspect of the general European question. It was widely felt
that pre-1939 Europe could not simply be restored. The decade
of the 1930s had been, in general, a disaster. The air was alive
with talk of 'modernization' and 'planning' with the objective of
'full employment'. The precise means by which change was to be
accomplished varied from country to country but there was a
general swing to the left (if the Communist and Socialist vote is
added together). The governmental impact was less, of course,
because the left was not in fact one—a situation which made
possible the emergence and consolidation of various Christian
Democrat groupings from Italy to the Netherlands. The right
and the old Radical Party in France substantially lost ground to
the Communists and Socialists. Labour won its first absolute
majority of seats in Norway and in Great Britain in 1945.

However, there were even more fundamental questions which
some groupings and individuals felt that Europe needed to
address. A Nazi 'New Order' had been quite unacceptable, but
there could be a different kind of new order. It was argued that
too great a fetish had been made of the 'nation-state'. The
pursuit of 'autarky' by some countries had distorted economic
development. It was time not only to formulate new individual
constitutions but to think in terms of 'Europe' as an entity. The
dogma of national sovereignty should not hinder beneficial
integration. European countries had brought disaster on themselves by war and it was now incumbent on a new generation of
statesmen to devise means which would make it impossible in
the future.

The goal could possibly be a 'United States of Europe'.
Americans, understandably used to the idea that the United
States of America came close to perfection, thought this an
admirable notion. So did Churchill in a well-publicized speech
in Zurich in 1946 in which he advocated Franco-German reconciliation as the cornerstone of such a structure, taking it for

granted that Britain could applaud and assist, but could not join such an enterprise. It was indeed obvious that Britain would stand outside. However, it might be relatively easy, too, for Italy to be reincorporated into respectable society under such an umbrella. What the 'Benelux' countries were doing on a small scale could serve as the model for greater European integration—their 'union' conceived in exile in 1944 was consolidated by a customs union in January 1948. A way should be found to exercise a kind of joint sovereignty over joint resources. It was not until May 1950, however, that a specific, though limited, scheme came forward. Schuman, then French Foreign Minister, proposed that a 'supranational authority' should supervise the coal and steel production of France and West Germany, together with that of such other Western European countries as wished to join. The result was the European Coal and Steel Community agreed to in April 1951. France, West Germany, Italy, and the Benelux countries certainly did not sacrifice their national objectives in this arrangement but nevertheless evolved a complex set of regulations which to some extent transcended them. 'The Six', and France and West Germany in particular, established an embryonic 'European' identity and interest—though the need to evolve a structure which would 'contain' Germany remained a strong consideration for the non-Germans.

Beneath the rhetoric, however, there was ambiguity. National sentiment remained strong and governments spent more money than they had ever done in the past in asserting their cultural individuality. Travel remained restricted. A new event like the Edinburgh International Festival in 1947 was supposed to show that high culture could cement international harmony. That had yet to be proved. On the non-Communist left, expressed in different forms, was the belief that Europe could offer the world a 'Third Way' between Soviet Communism and American Capitalism. Elements, though only elements, in parties of the centre and the right were also attracted by a somewhat nebulous 'European' identity and the notion of a United States of Europe. The difficulty for both was that they perceived their security to depend upon a continuing American presence. Indigenous Communist parties were strong in France and Italy and added another dimension to the 'Cold War'. In the November 1946 elections to the French National Assembly, the Communists—the most Stalinist in Western Europe—emerged as the largest single party.

Conceivably, in the future, a United States of Europe might offer a means of balancing American world influence. For the moment, however, it was the possibility of American withdrawal rather than the continuing American presence which caused most alarm amongst the non-Communist but divided majorities of Western Europe. Inevitably, however, the 'Europe' which was in the air in Western capitals could involve only part of the continent. Some kind of 'European Union', if formalized, would reveal to the world how divided Europe was. Eastern/Central Europe could not be part of it. In March 1946, in another famous speech, Churchill declared in Missouri that an 'Iron Curtain' had been lowered in Europe from Stettin in the Baltic to Trieste in the Adriatic. 'Europe', of course, had always been a tantalizing concept. The 'Iron Curtain', however, emphasized a new continental fault-line, one that might solidify Eastern and Western Europe in an enduring fashion.

In Eastern Europe, Stalin did not formally annex, as he had done in the case of the Baltic states and part of Poland before the war. Even Finland remained outside the Soviet Union. In October 1944 he and Churchill under a 'percentages' accord allocated each other degrees of influence in South-Eastern Europe, but it did not stick. Instead, in the Soviet sphere, coalitions or quasi-coalitions were established—though in Poland, Romania, and Bulgaria they did not last long—in which Communists shared power with non-Communist parties. Non-Communists did share power with Communists initially in some cases in Western Europe (though on a rather different basis). Life in Eastern Europe became very uncomfortable, however, for liberal and peasant parties and, under various labels, mergers between Social Democratic and Communist parties were achieved. The Red Army was in the background and 'advisers' from the Soviet Union were active. Soviet domination in Poland and Czechoslo-

vakia was accepted as a buttress against German 'irredentism'—
millions of Germans had fled or were expelled from Eastern
Europe at the close of the war—an unpleasant fact but one
which nevertheless was to mean that Eastern Europe was to be
less troubled by minority issues than had been the case before
1939. There was, however, sometimes tension between Communists who had stayed in their own countries during the war and
those who came back with the baggage of the Red Army. In
social and economic terms, the countries followed the same
broad pattern—nationalization, central planning, land reform,
state education—all within an ideological framework which was
described as Marxism-Leninism-Stalinism. This 'squeeze' on
political enemies was in a sense not dissimilar in West and East,
except for the crucial difference that elections in the West were
substantially more free than those in the East.

This process was watched with alarm in the West, where it
was suspected that Stalin would use or threaten force to extend
such a system beyond its initial base. It would seem, in fact, that
he did not urge the French or Italian Communist parties to
attempt to seize control, at least not at this juncture. When
Communist power was consolidated in Czechoslovakia in February 1948, however, it was taken to be an ominous sign in the
West: Communists would take complete control whenever and
wherever they were in a position to do so. A year earlier, Britain
had declared itself unable militarily to sustain the position in
Greece (where civil war raged) and Turkey (under Soviet pressure to allow access to the Mediterranean). It seems probable
that it was a move deliberately designed to put pressure on the
United States to take up the burden. In March 1947 Truman
declared that at that moment in world history nearly every
nation had to choose between alternative ways of life. The
United States would support free peoples who were resisting
attempted subjugation by armed minorities or by outside pressures. It was a pledge, 'the Truman Doctrine', whose importance
spread far beyond the Eastern Mediterranean. What was evolving was a 'strategy of containment' which also had an economic
dimension.

In June 1947, Secretary of State Marshall informed a Harvard graduation ceremony that the United States, conscious that the entire fabric of the European economy had been upset by the war, would do what it could to restore stability and hope. In Britain, in early 1947, it snowed solidly for seven weeks—not a regular insular phenomenon. The Chancellor of the Exchequer commented in his diary that the best place to be was in bed. The British did not know how fortunate they were. It was mass starvation which threatened in Germany and elsewhere in Central Europe. That was the context in which 'aid' was vital, but it was for the European powers themselves to formulate their needs through an Organization Committee on European Economic Co-operation (OEEC). There was a commitment, however, that substantial American support would be forthcoming. The 'Marshall Plan', as it was elaborated (with some difficulty) over the next few years, aimed to create a prosperity on the American model through advances in productivity. Success would limit Communist advance, reduce class tensions, and set European states on the path both to flourishing democracy and to participation in a multilateral system of world trade. It was also a grand design for European integration, something the British resisted. The language was inspiring, but no one knew whether the Marshall Plan would work and how many dollars would be made available. Even if it did succeed, there might still be a perpetual 'dollar gap'. In the event, between 1948 and 1952, when the Recovery Programme ended, $13.2 billion was made available in grants and credits, with the largest amounts going to Britain, France, Italy, and West Germany, in that order. This generosity was not without its benefits for American industry. The OEEC remained in existence after the European Recovery Programme came to an end. So did the European Payments Union set up in 1950, which made possible payments in any of the members' currencies and thereby facilitated trade.

On the whole, Marshall's initiative was welcomed in Western European capitals, though some politicians and diplomats did fear that Western Europe was becoming a kind of satellite of the United States. There was particular concern in France about the fact that Germany (i.e. in practice the Western zones) was to be a beneficiary. A restored Germany in turn revived old French fears. The Soviet Union and its satellites, however, would have nothing to do with Marshall Aid. Their abstention, therefore, further divided Europe, as did the Soviet Union's announcement in September 1947 of the formation of the Cominform, an agency for co-ordinating the main Communist parties of Europe, east and west. However, Communist attempts failed to bring down by strikes and demonstrations the unstable coalition governments of France and Italy (and thus scupper Marshall Aid which they accepted). Two years later, as a kind of riposte to the Marshall Plan, the Soviet satellites were forced to join Comecon (Council for Mutual Economic Assistance), but its real initial purpose was to enforce an economic boycott directed against Tito's Yugoslavia.

It was the status of Berlin which led, more or less directly, to the military equivalent of American aid. In July 1948 Moscow cut off all road and rail traffic between West Berlin and the Western zones of Germany. Allied rights in this respect were ill-defined but had become contentious, probably because Stalin saw such pressure as a way of dissuading the Western powers from sponsoring 'West Germany'—as has been noted, they had announced the establishment of a single currency, the D-Mark. Alternatively, if he could not prevent that, he might be able to eliminate the troublesome example of relative prosperity represented by West Berlin in the heart of what might be 'East Germany'. Truman was determined not to give way, but equally rejected any proposal to force a passage. In the event, between July 1948 and May 1949 (when the Soviet blockade ended, together with the Allied counter-blockade of the Soviet zone), Berlin was supplied from the air. US B-29 bombers arrived in Britain 'just in case'. In April 1949 the Western powers promulgated new statutes which created the Federal Republic of Germany with full self-government except for certain reserved matters.

In March 1948, Britain, France, and the Benelux countries signed the Treaty of Brussels which provided for mutual action in the event of aggression, though the potential aggressor was not identified. It was a sign that these states were transferring their fears from Germany to the Soviet Union, though anxieties about Germany remained. In June 1948 the 'Vandenburg Resolution' allowed the United States to enter into alliances with non-American powers. In April 1949, the United States, Canada, Denmark, Iceland, Italy, Portugal, Norway, and the Brussels Treaty powers signed the North Atlantic Treaty, which provided for mutual defence. In this new alliance there was no doubt that the United States held the upper hand but Europeans were expected to play their part—and perhaps might need German involvement to play it effectively. The organization's title, too, is significant. The 'North Atlantic' did not abound in people. It was an ocean which linked governments in a 'world' which had never previously existed, notwithstanding the innumerable links between particular American communities and particular European countries. It remained to be seen, in the longer term, whether it would be an enduring 'world' or whether the very success of the United States in both reviving and defending 'its' Europe might jeopardize NATO's viability. What was broadly accepted as 'defence of common values' might come to appear an unacceptable exercise of American hegemony.

That was for the future. In the short term, the impetus behind NATO sprang from concern about the disparity, at least numerically, between Soviet forces and those of Western European countries. There were only some 100,000 US troops in Europe at this juncture. Confronted by what seemed an alarming scenario, even the British were prepared to commit forces 'permanently' to the Continent. Over the next few years—Greece and Turkey joined in 1952—NATO developed an effective integrated command structure. Increasingly, too, there was a possibility, though not yet the reality, that the German Federal Republic might be allowed to rearm and thus contribute to the defence of 'the West'.

The broad structure of 'Europe', west and east, was therefore established between 1945 and 1953 and looked increasingly 'permanent'. Ireland (which left the (British) Commonwealth in

1949), Spain, Sweden, and Switzerland stood outside this military division, but almost every other European state was 'aligned', completely or in part. The statute of the Council of Europe, signed in London in May 1949, committed its members to supporting freedom and the rule of law: it was a body, therefore, which by definition could not extend eastwards. There, 'show trials' and instances of oppression and coercion caught the headlines in the West. They are occasionally explained away, not convincingly, by suggesting that Stalin genuinely feared a US military attack on Eastern Europe. However, in March 1950 a new factor had come into the equation. It was announced that the Soviet Union possessed the atomic bomb (its first tests had been carried out in August 1949), something likely to deter the United States, even supposing that Washington planned such an attack—which it did not. A more likely explanation for this 'insecurity' is that it was impossible, in a crisis, for Stalin to judge how viable these new regimes actually were. In 1948, for example, Marshal Tito of Yugoslavia, refusing the desired co-ordination, was expelled from the Cominform. He sought to be Communist but 'non-aligned'. Some thought at the time that there would be more 'Titos' who would refuse to toe the line. They were wrong. Tito's freedom of manœuvre derived from circumstances: he had not been put in power by the Red Army.

The division between East and West, between the 'free world' and the 'Communist world', therefore ran through the heart of Europe. Arguably, that was where the ideological cleavage was most apparent, but by 1953 it had long ceased to end there.

Japan and China

The defeat of Japan was followed by a period of occupation which lasted formally until April 1952. As in the case of Germany, the victors were determined to ensure that Japan could never again dominate East Asia by military means. The Japanese military machine was dismantled and the police decentralized. Indeed a new Constitution in 1946 contained an article which declared that the Japanese people renounced war and the threat of force for ever. This Constitution confirmed the symbolic role of the Emperor and was accompanied by various measures of land and labour reform designed to further the 'democratization' of Japan. The existing economic basis of Japanese military strength had to be destroyed and could not be permitted to revive. As also in the case of Germany, however, the imperatives of repentance, reparation, reconciliation, and regeneration, simultaneously urged, existed uneasily together. Within a couple of years, it became necessary to talk about 'the recovery of Japan'.

The troops stationed in the country were American, with the exception of a modest British Commonwealth contingent. Unlike the situation in Germany, there was no zonal division and no direct role of any substance for the Soviet Union, China, Britain, or Australia, though eleven nations nominally supervised the occupation. The Supreme Commander Allied Powers, General Douglas MacArthur, grappled with the complexities of Japanese society still in a state of shock and economic distress. By 1949 he pronounced that his policy was shifting from the 'stern rigidity' of a military operation to the 'friendly guidance' of a protective force. To some, this shift was no more than a recognition of realities. The United States would not go on financing the vital imports needed to prevent disease and unrest. Japan had to regain some economic strength. Likewise, to seek to 'rectify' Japan's recent past—for example, by seeking to put the Emperor on trial—would have required a very substantial military presence, perhaps indefinitely. That was not desirable.

It is not sufficient, however, to consider this matter solely in a Japanese–American bilateral context. In 1949 the Chinese Communists made dramatic progress in the civil war, entering Beijing in January, Nanjing in April, Shanghai in May (a 35-mile-long wooden 'Shanghai Wall' proved of no avail), and Canton in October. The People's Republic was formally proclaimed in Beijing in October 1949. Chiang Kai-shek had notionally resigned as President in January and, as his military position collapsed, he withdrew with as many troops as he could manage to the island of Formosa (Taiwan), where in March 1950 he again proclaimed himself President of the Republic of China. This outcome was not generally predicted in 1945/6. Chiang's army was then some three times as large as that of the Communists and better equipped. In 1946, there were periodic attempts to avoid full-scale fighting, with the Americans trying to act as mediators. At first, in 1947, things seemed to go well for Chiang. He captured Yanan, then the Communist capital, in February 1947, but it was a less significant event than might seem. In addition, his army was plagued by internal divisions and poor morale. Chiang wanted to assert his authority over as wide an area of China as he could and as quickly as he could, but found himself overstretched. By the end of 1947 and into 1948, the Communists were moving over from guerrilla warfare to set-piece battles on a major scale, though they still faced forces superior in both numbers and equipment. The decisive battles of the civil war were fought between November 1948 and early January 1949. The lengthy Battle of Huai-Hai at the end of 1948 is widely taken as decisive. Nationalist losses have been put as high as half a million. Their forces inflicted insignificant casualties. Thereafter, even what passed for élite corps melted mysteriously from the field of battle. All the while, inflation was rampant and was accompanied by almost universal corruption. The Guomindang movement as a whole had lost whatever energy and sense of purpose it had once possessed. By contrast, the Communist Party seemed to have won the propaganda war, conveying an impression of invincible energy and purpose. China was being reborn at last.

The Truman administration reacted cautiously to these developments. General Marshall's mediation efforts in 1946 were partly compromised by the obvious fact that the United States was giving some support to Chiang—there were even US Marines, though non-combatant, in North China into 1947. On the other hand, both in 1946 and subsequently, a great deal more might have been done to assist Chiang. However, the Congress was assured after 1947 that the Truman Doctrine, whatever it might mean in Europe, did not presage United States intervention in China to support, in the words of the Doctrine, 'a free people resisting attempted subjugation by an armed minority'. As 1948 passed, China was manifestly slipping into a Communist future. Some elements in American society came to believe that China had been 'betrayed'.

What did these dramatic events mean? One simple interpretation was that they represented a major advance for 'world Communism'. There could be no doubting the Marxism of Mao Zedong, even though, as in Russia after 1917, the Chinese Communist Party had itself to leap over that stage in history which theory might have identified as 'bourgeois'. Its military struggle against the Guomindang had been accompanied by a violent attack on landlords and rich peasants. There was a strong egalitarian impulse. Hundreds of thousands of people were executed as 'counter-revolutionaries' as the party set about the enormous task of creating a united country, disciplined according to its ideals. Its formal structure replicated in essence what obtained within the Soviet sphere. There was a formal government headed by Mao Zedong with Zhou Enlai as Premier; but real power at all levels rested with the Party, which was itself Mao's instrument. In early 1950 Mao signed a treaty of mutual assistance with the Soviet Union.

Yet China was China. Even though its insights had potentially universal application, Marxism was indubitably a European ideology in origin. Chinese Communism could be expected to have its own characteristic features and emphases as it bedded down in a country which was by reputation intensely self-contained, even arrogantly xenophobic. In course of time, therefore, new China might play a major part in world history but, if so, it would be likely to be in its own right. It would not be Moscow's inferior partner. Stalin had signed a Treaty of Friendship and Alliance with Chiang Kai-shek in August 1945. However, in Manchuria—occupied by Soviet forces after the declaration of war against Japan in that same month—partiality was shown to the CCP. Even so, there were signs that the Russian and Chinese Communist parties did not necessarily have the same interests. In April 1950, Secretary of State Acheson privately claimed that he was seeking to drive a wedge between

China and the Soviet Union. The task did not seem impossible. Scraps of evidence were sifted in Washington and elsewhere, seeking to establish Chinese intentions. Some American opinion clearly took the view that 'the world' was indivisible. Unless the United States 'won' in Asia it would also ultimately 'lose' in Europe. Others were more sceptical, wishing to 'wait and see', neither recognizing the new government (which the British did in January 1950, largely because of the special circumstance of their presence in Hong Kong) nor expressing outright hostility.

Korea: Civil War/Global Conflict

However, on 25 June 1950, the armed forces of North Korea launched a successful surprise invasion of the South. The peninsula, annexed by Japan in 1910, had been divided into these two zones in 1945. Soviet and American troops respectively had remained until 1948/9 while fruitless negotiations had taken place to establish a unified, independent, and democratic Korea. Regimes in Pyongyang under Kim Il Sung and in Seoul under Syngman Rhee were then set up. Both claimed authority over the entire peninsula. Both provoked each other by threats and propaganda. It was assumed in Washington that Stalin had not opposed, even if he had not initiated, this attack. It is a question much considered of late by historians in the light of fresh though still incomplete evidence. It now seems at least clear that Kim Il Sung could not have acted without Stalin's encouragement and equipment—Kim was in the Soviet Union for most of April 1950 (and in Beijing in May). It may be that it was the pattern of events in Japan, previously described, which led Stalin to see Korea as a counter, and perhaps there was a fear that Rhee might indeed strike north. For his part, Kim preferred to work more closely with Stalin than Mao, without becoming a puppet of either. There was an assumption that an invading army would be assisted by Communists in the South. However, in all probability, Stalin was persuaded that a swift victory for Kim was possible, which would minimize international complications. The United States would not react militarily. There would be no danger of world war. It was on these bases that support was given to the North Korean offensive, support which extended to involving Soviet officers in planning the offensive.

Korea had hitherto not been a major concern of Washington. It even lay outside the American 'defensive perimeter' as conceived by Acheson in early 1950. The reaction to the invasion, however, was a striking example of the extent to which governments were thinking globally. It was the parallel with Germany which seemed exact. Two consequences followed. The invasion of South Korea had to be repelled, in part for its own sake, but also because of the signal it would send that a strike across the North German plain would be similarly resisted. Even more importantly, it gave fresh impetus to plans already in existence (the American National Security Council Memorandum 68, of January 1950) for substantially enhanced military expenditure by the United States. By the end of the year, NATO foreign ministers had endorsed an integrated defence structure and four divisions of American ground forces were committed to Europe. General Eisenhower returned to Europe as Supreme Allied Commander with his headquarters in Paris. Over the next couple of years, the NATO structure was further consolidated. US defence expenditure rapidly increased and it was made clear that Britain and other allies had little option but to follow suit. It was Eisenhower's mission to ensure the survival of Western civilization.

Immediately, however, that civilization's survival was held to depend upon dispatching North Korean forces back across the 38th parallel in Korea. The United States had to decide whether the issues at stake required the involvement of its forces in a conflict which could in turn involve the Soviet Union and China. Dulles argued that to sit by while Korea was overrun would start a disastrous chain of events which would probably also lead to world war. There was another view, however, that the Korean incident had been engineered in Moscow in order to embroil the United States with Communist China. But might there also be a Chinese invasion of Taiwan? There was nervousness in Europe that the United States would become involved in war in Korea, and that Moscow would exploit this fact to increase pressure in Europe. To do nothing, however, might equally give encouragement to Stalin in Europe—and perhaps make Japan vulnerable in the longer term.

Here, surely, was a matter for the 'world body', the United Nations. It happened, however, that since January 1950 the Soviet Union had not taken part in meetings of the UN Security Council, on the grounds that the wrong Chinese regime was present. On 27 June the Security Council carried by seven votes to one (Yugoslavia) a resolution which condemned the inva sion, called on North Korean forces to return to the 38th parallel, and recommended member states to assist South Korea. The US General MacArthur, a man of immense prestige and self-confidence, though not personally known to the American President, speedily concluded that the situation in the South was grave and could only be retrieved by the commitment of US ground troops. It was important to Truman, however, that the US role in Korea should be seen as a 'police action' under the authority of the United Nations, though in practice it was to Washington rather than to the UN Secretary-General Trygve Lie that the 'UN command' reported.

MacArthur's force of American and South Korean troops, with contributions also from a total of fifteen states, succeeded in retrieving a desperate situation in the South by early October, when a daring landing at Inchon turned the tide. Should they cross the 38th parallel? Was this the opportunity to unite the peninsula? However, despite the fact that Syngman Rhee had obtained a Ph.D. from Princeton under Woodrow Wilson, his regime was hardly an exemplary democracy. To take such a step, moreover, ran the risk of precipitating Soviet and/or Chinese intervention. Was it not better to demonstrate a clear UN success in repulsing an invasion and return to the status quo ante, unsatisfactory though it admittedly was? In all the capitals concerned—particularly Washington, Moscow, Beijing, London, and New Delhi—therefore, options and hypotheses were explored. There were, unsurprisingly, substantial divisions of opinion as to what would happen if an offensive north occurred. The confidence of MacArthur hindered a more sober assessment.

UN forces did advance towards the Yalu River, the frontier between North Korea and Chinese Manchuria, a move endorsed by the UN General Assembly in October. However, the prospect of American troops on his border alarmed Mao, despite assurances that they would remain only until Korea had been re-unified. Mao was determined to assert China's international importance; indeed there was always a likelihood of some kind of Chinese intervention once Kim's initial gamble had failed. History showed, according to Beijing, that the existence of the Korean People's Republic was closely intertwined with the security of China. Kim now looked for Chinese support. A huge Chinese 'volunteer' army sent MacArthur reeling back deep into South Korea. A new and potentially more dangerous war had begun. It was with great difficulty that UN forces regained, more or less, the 38th parallel. However, in April 1951 MacArthur was sacked when he publicly demanded the authority to bomb China, if need be with nuclear weapons. A stalemate ensued. Peace talks began in July 1951 and were to drag on for a further two years before an armistice was concluded, though it left unresolved the future of a devastated Korea itself.

Kim Il Sung's peninsular adventure, which led to the death of nearly 4 million people, therefore had world consequences probably beyond his expectations. The Chinese intervention appeared to confirm that the Beijing regime was 'thoroughly locked into collaboration with Moscow', as the leading American Korean negotiator put it, though that conclusion was not invariably drawn in Britain. China, it was claimed, was evidently now assertive beyond its own borders—though Mao could scarcely have been expected to welcome American forces on the Yalu. Dean Rusk, Assistant Secretary of State, suggested that the 'Peiping regime' might be 'a colonial Russian government'. In 1951, China also extended its authority over Tibet and this was taken to be a further indication of Chinese expansionism. China had shown what its conventional forces could achieve—albeit with the assistance of fighter aircraft supplied by the Soviet Union. Yet even China, with its huge manpower, was vulnerable to 'nuclear blackmail' and wanted to show, in short order, that it could develop its own weapons and thus become a true World Power. It could not be doubted that China had 'emerged'.

It was the United States which presided over the response in Asia, a response which extended far beyond the indefinite commitment to South Korea. Still acting on the assertion that the Chinese mainland government was 'not Chinese', Washington committed itself to a far greater extent than before to the government—all too Chinese in the eyes of indigenous Taiwanese—in Taiwan. Chiang Kai-shek, ardently supported by the American 'China Lobby', was restored to favour and his administration on the island recognized by Washington as the legal government of China. In addition, there was fresh urgency concerning the future of Japan. Were Japanese Communists perhaps originally expecting to be able to destabilize Japan, helped from a Communist Korea? It was time, therefore, from both the Japanese and the American standpoints, to reopen the question of a peace treaty which would restore Japanese sovereignty. It was signed at San Francisco in September 1951, to come into operation the following spring. However, neither China nor the Soviet Union, together with other Asian countries, were signatories. A week earlier the United States, Australia, and New Zealand had signed the Pacific Security Agreement, which provided for mutual assistance if any of the signatories were attacked.

The extent to which Japan remained within the American orbit was emphasized by the simultaneous signature of a bilateral treaty which provided that the United States should maintain its own armed forces in or about Japan with a general responsibility for 'the maintenance of international peace and security in the Far East'. It was possible, on the request of the Japanese government, that these forces could be required to put down large-scale internal disturbances. Prime Minister Yoshida felt increasingly more confident about internal security, especially since some 75,000 Japanese 'policemen' were trained to replace American troops being redeployed in Korea. The Japanese government, for obvious political reasons, had no wish itself to be drawn into the Korean conflict.

Fractured Freedom: The Indian Subcontinent

The future of the Indian subcontinent, and with it Sri Lanka (Ceylon) and Burma, was immediately on the agenda after 1945. During the war and in elections at its end, the Muslim League led by M. A. Jinnah grew in importance. He could claim nearly every seat in Muslim areas and when he demanded a six-province Pakistan he could not be ignored by either the British or the Indian National Congress. Congress, however, continued to resist what it regarded as the Balkanization of India. The loss of life, injuries, and homelessness which resulted from the intercommunal violence of the 'Great Calcutta Killing' of August 1946 was an indication of what could lie ahead. The Attlee government wrestled with the problem, but it is, of course, misleading to suppose that it could dictate events. The British, confronted by increasing signs of intercommunal violence, wanted to be able to withdraw in an orderly manner. In the end, in August 1947 (after a British announcement in February that Britain would withdraw by June 1948 at the latest), two states emerged, India and Pakistan (with the latter consisting of two widely separated parts). Whether advancing the date of British departure was an act of folly or wisdom continues to be debated. Even more fundamentally, it may be questioned whether by August 1947 Britain had any power to 'transfer'.

It was a solution which no one really wanted but seemed eventually the only feasible outcome. Historians will continue to differ on the extent to which British policy contributed to this outcome and the extent to which the decision reflected intractable differences within India itself. Certainly, afterwards, there remained many loose ends and the fate of Kashmir, in particular, bedevilled relationships between the new states. The outcome, in detail, was not satisfactory to any of the parties concerned. There was a considerable upheaval of population, with packed trainloads of refugees crossing the frontiers in both directions (perhaps 5.5 million moved each way across the West Pakistan/ India border). There was savage slaughter, leading to the death of some 1 million people. Even so, a substantial Muslim minority remained in India. In that sense, Pakistan was not *the* Muslim state in the subcontinent. On the other hand, to leaders of the Congress, the existence of Pakistan was an affront to the 'secular' theory of the new India which aspired to evoke the loyalty of Hindus, Muslims, Sikhs, Christians, and other religious groups. It was by no means clear that it could do so.

The rulers of the new India believed that they could stay outside the power blocs of this period. In important respects India would value its British inheritance in politics and its understanding of democracy, but its freedom had also been won from the British. There were, indeed, elements in the Congress who felt that membership of the Commonwealth was itself still a sign of continuing subordination. India had to speak as the most populous voice of new Asia and be even-handed, not partial, in its relationships with the Soviet Union, the United States, and China. It had a very individual voice which it wished to bring to world history. Commentators wondered, however, whether there was *one* individual voice which was 'India'. The rich variety of its languages and peoples was both strength and weakness. It might not be long before the country fell apart though, perhaps paradoxically, not while a British-educated, English-speaking élite—epitomized by Prime Minister Nehru— still guided its affairs. And the controversial fact that the English language was given an extended, though supposedly temporary, lease of life perhaps pointed to the ambiguities in India's identity.

Emergent South-East Asia

In South-East Asia the transition to independence was equally fraught with difficulty and conflict. An Indonesian Nationalist Party had existed in the inter-war period. Its leading figure was Achmad Sukarno, who had been imprisoned and exiled by the

Dutch. During the Japanese occupation his status was much enhanced, enabling him to claim to be President of Indonesia in 1945. He had an effective army at his disposal. However, it was not until the end of 1949, after intermittent fighting and temporary agreements, that the Dutch recognized Indonesian sovereignty. There had been a widespread belief in the Netherlands that without control of the Indies it would be impossible to build up the Dutch economy again. A federal state had originally been envisaged but in fact Java dominated—a source of tension over the next few years. The United States granted independence to the Philippines in 1946, though it signed a 99-year lease for air and naval bases in the following year. A revolutionary movement, the Hukbalahap, threatened the stability of the state but was contained.

In 1945 Ho Chi Minh declared Vietnam independent but the French were determined to re-establish their authority in Indo-China. Although over the next few years they devised new structures in an attempt to gain acceptance, and declared Laos and Cambodia to be autonomous (but within the French Union), they found themselves in protracted fighting. The British restructured government in the Malayan peninsula, creating the Federation of Malaya in 1948. It was followed by a Communist insurgency and protracted jungle warfare which still continued in 1953. The insurgents, however, were largely drawn from the Chinese community and their defeat was imminent. In these and other instances, therefore, considerable instability and uncertainty remained.

What did 'independence' actually mean in a part of the world which was escaping from pervasive European political, economic, and cultural hegemony? There was much debate about the nature of the political movements involved. That they were 'anti-colonial' was self-evident, but were they 'nationalist' or 'Communist'? The United States might at one stage be disinclined to support the suppression of 'nationalism' in Indo-China but later support the suppression of 'Communism'. And what did the European concept of a nation or indeed of Communism—Ho Chi Minh was a founder member of the French

Communist Party—mean in South-East Asia? Could one say which islands and peoples should or should not be included in 'Indonesia' or in the Philippines? What was the future of the Chinese in Malaya or the Tamils in Ceylon? Were the Karens and other ethnic minorities of Burma not peoples rightly struggling to be free? And, perhaps looked at in a longer term, could 'South-East Asia' have a distinctive place in world history or, with the actual or imminent removal of direct European control, might it not be a region, as in a longer past, squeezed between the new giants of China and India? Such questions were frequently asked at the time and neither then nor subsequently has it been possible to answer them categorically. Contemporaries asked them urgently. Subsequent history suggests, however, that categorization into 'Communist' or 'Nationalist' oversimplifies. Alongside both 'Western' straitjackets were indigenous religious and cultural outlooks which had at least as much significance as Western-imported ideologies.

Africa

In 1945, the entire continent of Africa could only supply four states as founder members of the United Nations—Egypt, Ethiopia, Liberia, and South Africa. It was thus marginal to the politics of the world and in 1953 that could still be said. However, in every part of the continent changes were taking place which would shortly end the colonial era. In British West Africa, specifically in the Gold Coast (the later Ghana) and Nigeria, commissions of inquiry set up in response to the emergence of political movements and some economic unrest led to constitutional change and increased African participation. In 1952 Kwame Nkrumah became Prime Minister of the Gold Coast. In British East and Central Africa constitutional change was complicated by the presence of relatively small British settler communities who either possessed (Southern Rhodesia) or aspired to possess (Kenya) considerable self-government. One solution, though opposed by African opinion, was to federate the two Rhodesias and Nyasaland as the Central African

Federation—and this came into controversial existence in 1953. An East African Federation (Kenya, Uganda, Tanganyika) had been mooted but came to nothing. In Kenya itself, following increased violence in the Kikuyu country, the 'Mau Mau' emergency was declared in 1952 and in the following year Jomo Kenyatta was convicted of managing 'Mau Mau'.

South Africa evolved its own policies. The country had taken part in the Second World War under the leadership of Jan Smuts. His long experience of world politics (he had served in the Imperial War Cabinet in the First World War) climaxed in his participation in wartime conferences at Cairo and Algiers and in taking part in the drafting of the United Nations Charter. To some extent, however, his 'world' perspective cut him off from the mood of South African white politics. In 1948 the National Party under Malan, largely Afrikaner in composition, defeated Smuts. It formalized and gave ideological justification for apartheid: there should be separate provision for blacks, coloureds, and whites. South Africa would remain a democracy but only whites (once a franchise for coloureds had been eliminated) could participate. In these circumstances, bearing in mind embryonic developments elsewhere in Africa, the new government's desire to be seen as the southern outpost of the struggle against worldwide Communism was awkward for Washington. In the early 1950s, there were further legislative enactments of the apartheid system, though the racial laws evoked some 'passive resistance'. The Afrikaner-dominated South African government was not deterred and, not setting great store by the British connection, was indifferent to criticism from within the Commonwealth.

The speed with which British governments appeared to be moving towards self-government in Africa proved embarrassing to the other European powers. Neither the Belgians (Congo) nor the Portuguese (Mozambique, Angola, Guinea) contemplated any such step at this stage. For France, the position was more complicated. From 1944 onwards, after a conference at Brazzaville, an alternative strategy was sketched out. Africans would have a greater say in the affairs of a 'French Union' which would be an effective partnership—with a role for African politicians in metropolitan France as well as a continuing role for France, at least in equatorial Africa. It remained to be seen whether this could work. North Africa, however, was another matter. Algeria had been 'integrated' into metropolitan France, though it was not like any other part of France in that it was only a minority of its Arab population who had been given the vote, and then only on the condition that they abandoned Muslim traditions. In 1945 a demonstration at Setif was suppressed with loss of life. The incident was the start of a nationalist campaign complicated by the presence of a substantial French community, Berber aspirations, and a section of the Arab population which had been 'Frenchified'. In Tunisia and Morocco also, France found itself confronted by both 'modern' and 'traditional' opposition, to neither of which it appeared willing to make concessions.

Muslim World?

The future of the Maghrib was also part of a wider issue. Was there an 'Arab world', itself part of, though central to, a 'Muslim world' which was in process of regeneration? In Libya, administered by Britain after 1945, a united kingdom became independent in 1951. In 1952, after an army coup, King Farouk of Egypt was forced to abdicate and a programme of 'national liberation' was set in train. British forces were still present in the Suez Canal Zone. Elsewhere in the 'Middle East' change rapidly followed the end of the war. France conceded independence to Syria and Lebanon. Transjordan became a kingdom, changing its name to Jordan in 1949. The most dramatic change, however, was the creation of the state of Israel in 1948. Britain, which had administered Palestine under mandate from the League of Nations since 1918, gave up the struggle to find a solution to the competing aspirations and claims to legitimacy of Arabs and Jews. The Holocaust in Europe made it difficult to resist the notion that a Jewish state should exist, but should it exist at the expense of Palestinian Arabs? It was a question put immediately to the test of war from which Israel emerged victorious against Arab forces from Egypt, Jordan, and Syria.

The creation of Israel complicated where the 'Middle East' stood in the world. Israel's survival appeared to depend upon 'out of area' support, in finance and equipment, from the United States in particular. In this sense, however much Jews perceived Israel as 'home', their neighbours perceived them as an outpost of 'the West'. Israel's existence strengthened a sense of Arab solidarity by creating a common 'other'. In 1945 an Arab League had been founded, with an Egyptian Secretary-General, to promote the 'Arab world', but its focus was uncertain. Individual Arab states still pursued their own distinct interests. It was also problematic whether pluralist democracy, emanating from Europe/America, was compatible either with Islamic tradition (a rather vague expression which perhaps hid considerable plurality) or with the interests of ruling families in Saudi Arabia or elsewhere.

And British influence, although eroding, had not yet evaporated, particularly in the Gulf but also elsewhere. It was evident, however, that the oil wealth of the region, acknowledged for decades but as yet only minimally exploited, made the Gulf of potentially much greater significance than it had been for centuries. It was also evident, given the increasing centrality of oil in the economies of foreign countries, that they would watch over the region's politics. The United States was likely to fill the British place. In 1951, in Iran, the Prime Minister, Dr Mossadeq, announced the nationalization of the Anglo-Iranian Oil Company, though he was not able to secure his own political position for long.

Iran, of course, was not part of the Arab world, but it was part of a Muslim world which now stretched to independent Pakistan and Indonesia. The separate Sunni and Shia communities complicated the position, but in theory at least there was a single *Umma* (world community of Islam). It appeared that the world of Islam could be more prominent than it had been for centuries. A World Muslim Conference was held in Karachi in 1951, attracting delegates from thirty countries. The re-emergence of Islam, too, might raise questions for Turkey, equally not an Arab country. Kemal Atatürk's inter-war revolution had seen its transformation, at least to external appearance, into a lay state. Neutral during the war, until the very last moment, it had subsequently moved firmly in a 'Western/ European' direction. Elections in 1950 had even seen the success of the opposition party under Menderes. The dispatch of Turkish troops to Korea and membership of NATO further confirmed Turkey's occidental orientation.

Latin America

The countries of South and Central America seemed, comparatively, on the periphery of determining world events. Their influence on any other part of the world was minimal. Brazil, for example, had declared war against Germany and Italy in 1942 and sent a modest expeditionary force to Italy in 1944— the first South American republic to send fighting troops to another continent—but this was not a prelude to a world role. Nevertheless, with a population of some 50 million at this juncture it was a country capable of exercising great influence, although Portuguese-speaking, in Latin America. Its economy, however, was heavily susceptible to the price-volatility attached to coffee and rubber production. The commitment of Brazilian forces abroad did not indicate a profound commitment to democratic values. Its president, Vargas, who had been in power since 1937, was in effect a dictator. He stepped down in 1945 but took office again in 1951 after a fair election. The economy deteriorated. He committed suicide in 1954. Mexico likewise declared war on Germany and Japan but without major effect, except in so far as it bound the country commercially even closer to the United States.

The independence of South America from Spain and Portugal in the nineteenth century had left only a residual and largely inconsequential connection with the world beyond. The successor states had prided themselves, often, on the progressive character of their constitutions, but the social and political reality was different. The region was perceived outside, with some justice, to be endemically unstable—military coups, revolutions, assassinations, and civil wars. It was still the case, almost without exception, in the decade after 1945 that a small social élite held the reins of power: the great part of the population was poor and illiterate. Revolution was a permanent possibility in a context where a mediating middle class was weak. In Argentina, Juan Perón, aided by his wife Eva, dominated the country's politics in an authoritarian manner, though he was formally elected as President in 1946. After her death in 1952, Perón fell into a conflict with the Catholic Church. He was forced into exile in 1955. However, he still had a substantial body of support—a fact which was to complicate Argentine politics for decades to come. In Brazil and elsewhere, there were increasing signs of social unrest and political instability; civil war broke out in Colombia in 1948. There was no strong hemispheric sense—indeed border disputes between some of South America's ten independent states could still flare up. Brazil's capacity to 'lead' South America was complicated by the fact that its language was Portuguese. Such a continent was not poised to assume a world role—only Colombia responded to United States pressure and sent a small force to fight in Korea.

Ever since the enunciation of the 'Monroe Doctrine' in 1823, the United States had accepted a special responsibility, as it saw it, for the western hemisphere. The Panama Canal remained another important world artery and the United States still had the lease on the territory immediately on its banks. Only in the north-east of South America and in the Caribbean did the British, French, and Dutch have a toehold. The circumstances of the war made the European powers even more beholden to the United States, and their colonies likewise soon aspired to greater self-government. The United States was the inspiration behind the establishment of the Organization of American States (Canada stood outside) at Bogotá in 1948. The Secretary-General of the new organization came from South America but the secretariat was based in Washington. The expectation that there would be a kind of Marshall Plan for Latin America was not realized. The extent to which this world of the Americas was apparently sealed off from outside influence was sometimes commented on by Soviet commentators, who wondered why Americans took such exception to Soviet spheres of influence in Europe. It was not only 'influence' that Washington exercised. In Guatemala in 1950 an election was won by Jacobo Arbenz, whose land reform programmes upset the dominant United Fruit Company and were perceived in Washington to lead to Communism. The tenth inter-American conference at Caracas in 1954 could not be brought to share this interpretation of events. The United States conspired with disaffected Guatemalans who then mounted a successful invasion which overthrew Arbenz. It was a clear sign that Washington still regarded the area as its own 'back yard'.

Balance Sheet

The American diplomat George Kennan, advocate of 'containment', reasoned that there were only four centres of industrial and military power in the world which mattered from the standpoint of American national security besides the United States itself: the Soviet Union, Great Britain, Germany and Central Europe, and Japan. The steps taken in the five years since 1947 appeared to be creating a world which could balance the Soviet Union and perhaps, in the longer term, place it in a position of inferiority. Such steps, however, in the case of Germany and Japan, did entail at least the economic restoration of two recent enemies more rapidly than had been anticipated in 1945.

Nevertheless, in the United States itself, there remained an anxiety, bordering on hysteria, which was little swayed by abstract considerations of geopolitical balance. There were indeed some spies and traitors at work in the United States, notably in conveying information that assisted the Soviet atomic bomb project. It was therefore predictable that at the time of the Korean War suspicions of an internal 'red menace' mounted and the dangers were magnified. It was Senator Joe McCarthy who claimed in February 1950 that there were 205 Communist sympathizers working in the State Department. He would track them down by Congressional committee. 'McCarthyism' smeared many unjustly, but if it is compared with Stalin's own paranoia in his final years its crudeness appears mild. The Soviet government was becoming less brutal, but there may still have been half a million political murders between 1945 and 1953.

These suspicions of 'the enemy within' were a reminder of the fact that the apparent division of the world was not simply a matter of armies and alliances. There remained in the 'free world' covert or overt sympathizers with Communism and in the 'Communist world' there were those who wished that they lived in 'open societies'. And at what point, if at all—as was debated in Australia in 1950, for example—was an 'open society' justified in banning a Communist Party? Communist countries did not purport to be 'open societies' and had no hesitation in restricting, and normally eliminating altogether, the right of expression and dissent. That there was hyperbole, disinformation, exaggeration, and distortion in the respective images held of each other by these 'worlds' may be conceded, but there were indeed fundamental differences. It is, therefore, an undue relativization to suppose that in the power politics of the period all that mattered was power. It remained true, however, perhaps by the early 1950s it was becoming increasingly true, that bipolarity did not fully encompass the world's complex identities, alignments, and interests.

Doom and Gloom?

The world between 1945 and 1953 had therefore certainly not become 'one'. Talk about the cultivation of 'world loyalty', to be found in hopeful British wartime pamphlets, seemed impossibly utopian. It might be true, as the 1944 British *Liberal Plan for Peace* had put it, that a turning point had been reached in the history of mankind which required that its 'collective good sense' should 'get a grip' upon the course of events, but that was easier said than done. Indeed, in the study of international relations in the English-speaking world there was a determined emphasis on 'realism' in world affairs. Perhaps the most influential text of the period, by the American Hans Morgenthau, *Politics among the Nations* (1948), saw little sign of a system of supranational ethics influencing the actors on the international scene. A 'world public opinion' restraining the international policies of national governments was a mere postulate. The reality of international affairs showed hardly a trace of it.

Indeed, between 1948 and 1953, US defence expenditure quadrupled and Soviet more than doubled. Yet the resilience of the US economy and the economic recovery being experienced in Western Europe and Japan by the early 1950s equally did not correspond to the forecasts of doom which had also been made at the end of the war. Indeed, while global disparities in economic achievement became more apparent, 'the world' had emerged much more positively from its second conflict than it had from its first. The immense loss of life was apparently being redressed, without undue encouragement from governments, by an apparently elemental human desire to reproduce—though such new births could not simply 'compensate' for the deaths that had occurred. The population of the world in 1950 was estimated at some 2,516 million. It was still satisfaction at recovery from war rather than anxiety about the implications of growth which predominated.

It appeared too that economic 'lessons' had been learnt. In July 1944 at Bretton Woods it was agreed to establish an international stabilization fund, the International Monetary Fund (IMF) together with the World Bank (technically the International Bank for Reconstruction and Development), and these bodies came into existence in 1947. Member states contributed a quota and in return could negotiate a loan if they found themselves in debt. Stability was supposed to be introduced by the setting of fixed parities for currencies. The complexities of these arrangements cannot be pursued further here, but they were again symbolic of an aspiration to think globally. In some quarters, too, there was the belief that the more international trade there was, the less the likelihood of war. Domestically, too, within states there was a general tendency, though not universal, towards a 'mixed economy' and its concomitant, a 'welfare state'. The state, private business, and organized labour all had a role to play in economic development. Internationally, there was the same general recognition of the importance of trade and the need to stimulate it by the liberalization of tariffs. After a conference in Geneva in 1947 there was a General Agreement on Trade and Tariffs (GATT) which would keep these matters under regular review.

Despite the prominence given to creating the United Nations Organization, with its headquarters in New York, the 'world body' did not actually keep the world under control. In this sense it disappointed ardent idealist internationalists. Reference has earlier been made, in discussing the Korean War, to the role of American and other foreign troops. No mention was made, however, of the fact that, technically speaking, it was a United Nations force under the command of MacArthur. In practice this operation did not mean that 'the world' was united against a solitary aggressor, though the membership of the United Nations at this time was predominantly 'Western'-orientated. The 'success' of the United Nations in Korea, therefore, was only one for those states who were at the time dominant within its structures and mechanisms. It did not show that the organization could 'police' the world, though it did demonstrate that states found it helpful to have the authority of the United Nations to support their actions. It began to look as though it was through its specialized agencies—the International Labour Organization (originally 1919), the United Nations Educational, Scientific, and Cultural Organization (UNESCO—1946), the World Health Organization (WHO—1948), the United Nations International Children's Emergency Fund (UNICEF—1946), to mention only some—that a sense of 'one world' might emerge and it would be at a level below that of high politics.

It was another American writer who at this time suggested a shift away from an exclusive focus upon power relations in a world of states. Quincy Wright in *The Study of International Relations* (1955) suggested that scholars should conceive the human race as a single community which, while still divided in numerous ways, was in fact becoming integrated in a 'world society'. It was the numerous non-governmental 'transactions' which should also be studied. The concept of a 'Commonwealth' was in theory at least an example of a kind of community which operated on a different basis from normal inter-state alignments. It embraced both Britain itself, the 'British' countries of settlement—Australia, Canada, New Zealand, and South Africa—and newly independent countries with different cultural backgrounds. Membership was voluntary and it was held together as some kind of global entity by a host of such non-governmental 'transactions' as Wright referred to.

Other aspects of 'world business' resumed. The Olympic Games were held in London in 1948, a dozen years after they were last held, controversially, in Berlin. The World Cup (football) resumed in Brazil (1950). New 'world events' emerged—a basketball championship and Formula One Motor Racing (both 1950) added to their number. These and other such instances were 'non-governmental events'. There was an assumption, perhaps mistaken, that events of this kind provided a harmless release for those ineradicable rivalries between nations which otherwise issued in war. However, as yet, the extent to which such 'world events' actually impinged on the population of the world was minimal. The Berlin Olympic Games had been the first to be televised, but cinema newsreels remained the dominant visual mass medium. Even in the United States, mass television remained in its infancy. In Britain it was the coronation of Queen Elizabeth II in 1953 which both boosted the sales of television sets and made a wider public aware of the extent to which a national event could come into the home. That 'world events' could similarly be 'captured' was closer at hand than many appreciated. Perhaps a new sense of 'world history' might then emerge.

3

Confrontational Coexistence
c.1953–1965

Funeral

In January 1965 great men, and just a few great women, including the Queen of Tonga, came to London to represent 'the world' at the funeral of Sir Winston Churchill, the last Englishman who would be truly a world figure. Churchill had not in fact been in office for a decade; nevertheless his death, twelve years after Stalin's, had a certain symbolic significance: the Second World War was being buried. The congregation in St Paul's cathedral represented states both great and small, old and new. Famous and familiar names mingled with newcomers to world politics: men moulded by their experience of wartime power, and a new generation only now coming into significant office. This mixture characterized political leadership in the world between the death of Stalin and the death of Churchill. Indeed, in the case of Churchill himself, during his last period as Prime Minister (1951–5) he was seeing the world as a man who had come of age politically half a century earlier. At the end of his life, he could no longer feel at home in what it had become. The transition to a new generation of leaders, not surprisingly, did not take place in every country at precisely the same time. As the following summaries demonstrate, it was their experience of war which still loomed large in the thinking of the Great Powers' leadership between 1953 and 1965.

Big Five

In the Soviet Union, the succession to Stalin could not be other than fraught. There was no established procedure and competing claimants jostled for position. Against Beria, feared for his control of the security police, there was, however, a passing unity. He was shot on the pretext that he was a 'British spy'. Malenkov became Prime Minister, though he was eased out in February 1955 to be replaced by Bulganin. It became clear, however, that it was Khrushchev, the First Secretary of the party (from 1953), who became the dominant figure until he in turn was deposed at the end of 1964. He also served as Premier from 1958. Molotov, brought back again briefly as Foreign Minister in 1957, made way for Gromyko, veteran of wartime conferences and the United Nations Security Council. He had also served briefly as Soviet ambassador to Britain. There was nothing cosmopolitan about Khrushchev. The only border he had thus far crossed was that between the Ukrainian and Russian Republics in the Soviet Union. He had spent the war immersed in Ukrainian affairs and had been closely involved in military matters. He approached the outside world with all the suspicion of the underground miner which he had once been. But he was not a Stalin.

Also in 1953, Eisenhower became President of the United States. He was elected in 1952 as a Republican, but his popularity transcended party politics, as was shown by his re-election for a second term. Classically Midwestern, he was the first American soldier-president in nearly a century and knew Europe at first hand, both at the end of the war and again in a NATO context in 1951. He had risen to 'a position of world leadership without parallel in history', as the contemporary author of *America's Man of Destiny* put it in 1952. His successor, in 1961, John F. Kennedy, confidently East Coast, had commanded a torpedo-boat in the Pacific but at 44 he too saw himself as leader of a new generation. Foreign policy, he asserted bluntly in 1960, was a matter for the President. Apparently, the banner of freedom could be unfurled everywhere. Before the war he had seen Britain through the unsympathetic eyes of his father, then United States ambassador in London. He had reflected independently on *Why England Slept* during this critical period. His assassination in 1963 brought another wartime US Navy man to the White House, the Texan Lyndon Baines Johnson. In 1964 he was elected by the biggest percentage of the vote hitherto obtained by a president.

In 1953 Charles de Gaulle sat peacefully in his study in Colombey-les-Deux-Églises, writing his memoirs and awaiting a summons to save France, a call which some observers were confident would never come. Since 1945, when the new French Fourth Republic rejected the idea of a strong American-style Presidency, he had played no personal part in French politics, though he had a movement which looked to him, the Rassemblement du Peuple Français. He watched what he regarded as the feeble ineffectiveness of the Fourth Republic with dismay. Its Prime Ministers, in their swift and unmemorable succession, had prematurely acquiesced in France's subjection to the 'Anglo-Saxon' world. In 1965, however, when he paid tribute to his old comrade/opponent, Winston Churchill, he did so as President of a new Fifth Republic in France, with the powers of office he had been denied twenty years earlier. De Gaulle was apt to reflect profoundly on France and its place in the world. He had not forgotten her humiliations and was determined to question the initial post-1945 world order and France's place within it. Under his leadership after 1958 the war years, and their legacy, gained fresh and unanticipated resonance in world politics.

In Britain Churchill's successors, Eden and Macmillan, had come and gone by 1965. Both before and during the war, Eden had acquired a considerable knowledge of the world in his role as Foreign Secretary (1935–8, 1940–5) but his downfall in 1956/7 suggested that he had failed to adapt to new realities. His successor, Macmillan, like Churchill, had a British father and an American mother. During the war, he had held the post of Minister Resident in North Africa, a post in which he had come into close contact with General Eisenhower. By 1963, when Macmillan resigned as Prime Minister, and as Algeria fought its way to imminent independence from France, it was difficult to conceive that a British politician had ever been resident in North Africa. Harold Wilson, the new British Prime Minister, was only 48 in 1964. He had been a wartime Civil Servant and only entered the House of Commons in 1945. Since Wilson's elevation stemmed also from a Labour victory for the first time since 1951, a fresh start was being made. In proclaiming, as he did, that Britain was a World Power or nothing, however, Wilson seemed determined to maintain the orthodoxy that he had inherited.

In China, East Asia's one 'Big Five' member, there appeared to have been little change in the perspective at the top. In 1953, and still in 1965, Chiang Kai-shek was President of the Republic of China, and his government retained its seat on the United Nations Security Council. He was, however, in reality only established on the island of Formosa/Taiwan, although he continued to make rhetorical claims to mainland China. In the People's Republic, Mao was no longer quite the figure he had been in 1953. In 1959 he gave up being head of state, though he retained the chairmanship of the party. In a sense, he was living in Beijing 'in retirement', though he did not wish to use his leisure to come to St Paul's cathedral for Churchill's funeral! Commentators, unduly ignorant about old Chinese men, sometimes suggested that he would simply fade away, without making any further mark on his country's or the world's history.

However, whether the 'Big Five' countries of 1945 still represented the actual configuration of power and influence in the world of 1965 is another matter. By 1960, the membership of the United Nations had doubled, and it is in the dozen years under review in this chapter that a new 'non-aligned' world, itself the product of accelerating European decolonization, makes its mark. Soviet–American competition still centred on Europe, though it also now entailed a much more complex engagement with disparate issues worldwide. It is inevitable, therefore, that it is with the world as seen from Washington and Moscow that this chapter must begin.

Bipolar Confrontations: Eisenhower, Kennedy, and Khrushchev

Few supposed that the death of Stalin would immediately transform the world scene. The contest between the Soviet Union and the 'Free World' had developed a momentum of its own which even the death of one sinister figure could not stop. Rivalry seemed to extend to every type of human activity in which competition was possible. At the 1956 Melbourne Olympic Games, the Soviet Union gained 37 gold medals whilst the USA gained 32; Australia came next with 13. At Rome in 1960 the Soviet Union won 43 and the USA 34; Italy came next with 13. Both countries were clearly ahead of the rest of the world. What happened at the Olympics was an illustration with wider significance: there were only two competitors who really counted in world affairs.

Nevertheless, for both of the 'superpowers', it was time to take stock and reflect on a destiny that was less 'manifest' than had once appeared. It was only in the space of a dozen years that the United States had moved from non-belligerency to globalism, but there was little disposition to reverse. What opportunity, if any, did the death of Stalin open up? The emphasis of the Eisenhower administration appeared to move from mere containment to active liberation (though whether that meant anything in practice will shortly be discussed). The United States, it was stated, could never rest until 'the enslaved nations of the world' had freedom to choose their own path. Only if such freedom were achieved would it then be possible to live permanently and peacefully with Communism—though surely no nation so liberated would actually choose Communism. The achievement of freedom would in fact be synonymous with the end of Communism. It was time to talk of 'rollback'. Eisenhower's Secretary of State, John Foster Dulles, believed that 'brinkmanship' was a necessary art, as he intended to demonstrate.

Dulles was the epitome of Protestant rectitude. He believed that the United States was in a fight on the world's behalf, and he intended to win. The particular tone of this rhetoric was peculiarly American and grated somewhat on more cynical European ears. At this time the writings of the British historian Arnold Toynbee were much in vogue in the United States. His probing of the rise and fall of civilizations in *The Study of*

History could be gratifyingly reduced to a simple thesis: challenge and response. The United States now had a challenge and
it was responding. Abroad, the American call to freedom was
both infectious and bewilderingly naïve: so also was 'the American way of life' as it now manifested itself across the world.

The singularity of the United States became ever more apparent. It was neither a state nor a nation as Western Europeans
understood those terms, but rather a sprawling diversity of
continental proportions, forced to find its unity in exaggerated
abstractions. It had gone through a savage civil war less than a
century earlier in which many more Americans killed each other
than lost their lives in the Second World War. It was a country
where there was no embarrassment about patriotism, where the
Stars and Stripes fluttered at every conceivable opportunity. It
was a country which in 1961 sent its young people out into the
world in a 'Peace Corps' to help and be helped, 7,000 of them in
forty-four countries. 'What the world most needs from this
country', declared Sargent Shriver, Kennedy's brother-in-law, 'is
better understanding of the world.' 'We had heard of America,'
declared a tribal chief in Sierra Leone concerning Peace Corps
Volunteers in his country, 'but now we know what it means.'

Even so, it was not a country at ease with itself. There was
unintentional irony in the above comment from an inhabitant of
a land which ex-slaves had been expected to transform at the
end of the eighteenth century. In 1954 the United States Supreme
Court ruled that racial segregation in schools was unconstitu-
tional. The following year, in Montgomery, Alabama, Dr Martin
Luther King began a boycott of local buses, demanding an end
to segregation. The Supreme Court gave support in a 1956
ruling. Over the following years, in Little Rock, Arkansas, and
elsewhere, inter-racial tension mounted and required federal
intervention. The Southern Christian Leadership Conference
pressed for civil rights. The United States was entering on an
anguished decade in which, for its black population, it had to
translate the rhetoric of freedom into reality.

The gravity of this crisis suggested to some outside observers
that America's distant enthusiasm for 'enslaved nations' was

hypocritical. For others, the internal struggles were a demonstration that the United States was a kind of laboratory for the world. It was grappling with ethnic diversity within its own society, and its at least partial success in doing so offered a model and inspiration to the world. Certainly, the United States maintained its attractions as a land of opportunity for millions of Europeans, amongst whom could even be numbered university professors. The identification of a Communist enemy at large in that world no doubt helped to bind Americans together at home, though enthusiasm for world freedom was more than a domestic political strategy. Always alert to the plight of 'moral man' and 'immoral society', however, it was the influential American theologian/commentator Reinhold Niebuhr who grasped *The Irony of American History* (1952) at this juncture. Here was a country teeming with committed Christians, tempted to play God with the world, with the aid, if need be, of nuclear weapons now many times more powerful than those dropped on Japan in 1945. It was a country which came to believe itself justified in playing by new rules, faced with what it considered an implacable enemy whose avowed objective was world domination. It could sabotage and subvert because the cause was just. The Central Intelligence Agency, directed by the brother of the Secretary of State, recruited some of the brightest and best to master the use of dirty tricks. There was, in short, nothing simple about 'power and the pursuit of peace'. The burden of freedom carried by the United States was immense but it threatened to distort and destroy the country's own cherished institutions and values in the process. It was Eisenhower himself, in his farewell address in January 1961, who spoke of the need, in the councils of government, to guard against unwarranted influence, sought or unsought, on the part of the 'military-industrial complex'. Here was another ironic aspect of America's place in the world.

Inside the Soviet Union, taking stock after the death of Stalin necessarily had a different character. The notion of an ongoing public debate was inconceivable in Soviet society. It was also the case, however, that the 'Soviet Empire' was more compact and yet more fragile than the 'empire' of the United States. The

Warsaw Pact was concluded in 1955 to co-ordinate the military
forces of the Soviet Union and East European states, inevitably
under a Soviet commander-in-chief. Contiguity dictated that
anything that happened within the Soviet Union would have
repercussions on the 'bloc' and vice versa. The Soviet Union
itself covered a vast area with an ethnically diverse population,
and was ostensibly a federation. Stalin himself, after all, was a
Russianized Georgian. Any attempt, even minimal, to unpick
the Stalinist past risked not only unravelling the ties that bound
the 'satellites' to Moscow but also the very structure of the
Soviet state itself. Stalin's latter-day demonization of the 'capitalist world' had been much more a necessary means of keeping
this structure together than was the demonization of Communism by American politicians. It had not escaped his attention
that even during the 'Great Patriotic War' there were Soviet
peoples whose instincts were not wholly patriotic. There had
been German attempts, meeting with some success, to utilize
anti-Soviet feeling by forming units composed of non-Slav
peoples—for example, Armenian and Azerbaijani legions.
General Vlasov, captured by the Germans in July 1942, had
tried to form an anti-Soviet Russian Liberation Movement,
though his efforts to persuade the Germans to shape their policy
to encourage anti-Soviet activity did not meet with much success.

    After Stalin's death, thousands of prisoners were released from
the Soviet labour camps between 1953 and 1956. The new
leadership, however, had a major problem. Who in its ranks
could truthfully say that they (and by extension the party as a
whole) had not shared responsibility? At length, at the first post-
Stalin Party Congress (1956), in secret session, Khrushchev
denounced Stalin's 'cult of personality' and the ensuing grave
perversions of party principles. It was no doubt in his own
interest to take this popular step, being much less implicated in
Stalin's deeds than some of his rivals for power. The speech was
not published in the Soviet Union but its broad contents were
known both abroad and within the Soviet bloc. The text
appeared in the West in June 1956. It was apparent that while
Stalin's pathological criminality was attacked, an attempt was

being made to set limits to the discussion. It was necessary somehow to believe that the Central Committee of the Communist Party had been impervious to what had been going on. A distinction between Lenin and Stalin was emphasized, five years later, by the removal of the latter from the mausoleum in Red Square in Moscow. The Party Congress of that year saw further ideological refinements—the state was now held to express the will of the whole people and not simply of a particular class. In addition, far-reaching agricultural reforms were envisaged, together with extensive changes in the criminal code. How much further Khrushchev could go, or wanted to go, in 'de-Staliniza-tion' was problematic. Dissident writers were still arrested.

Even before the 'Secret Session' speech, there were indications of the difficulties any relaxation or reinterpretation might cause. Three months after Stalin's death, there had been demonstrations outside the Soviet Union, first in East Berlin but then also elsewhere in the German Democratic Republic (as the Soviet-backed regime now called itself). Ironically, it was the pace of economic change determined upon by its leader, Ulbricht, somewhat against Soviet advice, which played a major part in creating a crisis. Soviet troops and tanks intervened, with some loss of life, to restore the status quo. Elsewhere in Eastern Europe, partly owing to Soviet influence, Communists who had earlier been purged made a comeback. In Hungary, Imre Nagy returned in 1953, though only temporarily, as Prime Minister. In Poland, Gomułka was released from 'protective custody' in 1955. In June 1956, with loss of life, the Polish army put down a strike in Poznań, but a few months later Gomułka was General Secretary of the Polish Communist Party. In both of these cases, and in Hungary again in 1956, Soviet ministers were directly involved in the changes and Soviet soldiers and tanks were in the offing. While it might be necessary to shuffle individuals in order to produce some stability, the leading role of the party could not be questioned. It was when that did happen in Hungary that the most serious crisis unfolded.

Nagy, once more Prime Minister, announced at the end of October 1956 the abrogation of one-party rule and its replacement by a government based on democratic co-operation among the coalition parties of 1945. Stalinists were condemned and it was announced that talks would begin, to bring about the withdrawal of Soviet troops from Hungary. At first some sort of compromise seemed possible, but in early November tanks were sent into Budapest. Fierce fighting took place there and elsewhere. Might prevailed, but it was almost a year before the government was able to exercise its previous authority. Nagy was executed in 1958. Kádár, who had at one stage denounced Stalinists as agents of despotism and national enslavement, now fought to stave off the 'counter-revolutionary threat'. Some 200,000 Hungarians fled to the West.

A kind of raw stability was therefore restored—but the shock to the Soviet system had been considerable. In 1955, when Khrushchev visited Belgrade and patched up relations with Tito, it seemed that a recognition of a modest plurality of paths to Socialism was possible. After 1956, in varying degrees, throughout the Eastern European states, there was some flexibility so long as the fundamentals were not jeopardized. Soviet forces were always in the background but to a large extent the post-1956 leaderships were permitted to make their own judgements. It seemed that there were enough people—characterized by the Yugoslav dissident Djilas as *The New Class*—who had a vested interest in keeping the system intact. So, for a time, there appeared to be a degree of local freedom of manœuvre. Romanian leaders, for example, refused to take sides in the quarrel between Moscow and Beijing and ostentatiously visited non-Communist capitals in Western Europe. Even so, although it now contained some modest variety, the Soviet bloc was still intact—as a visit by Brezhnev to Bucharest in 1965 reminded the Romanian leadership.

In fact, the notion of 'rollback' had little practical utility. The American President might authorize an increased budget for Radio Free Europe, and the eastward dispatch of 300 million balloons with inspiring messages, but in June 1953 there was no support for the East Berlin demonstrators. Eisenhower did not 'roll back' Communism in Korea but rather signed an armistice in July 1953 which maintained the status quo as it had been before fighting broke out. Republican administrations had no enthusiasm for high levels of government expenditure and reduced the size of the armed forces. Eisenhower required a 'New Look' and as a result total US defence expenditure dropped in 1954–6 from a high point in 1953. There was a reliance on nuclear weapons transported in big bombers. The threat of massive retaliation would deter an aggressor. The United States would not again have to fight in a ground war as in Korea. The possession of nuclear weapons not unnaturally caused both sides problems. History offered little guidance. There were those who believed that their existence had prevented the outbreak of conventional war and those who believed that their existence would bring disaster to the human race.

In 1956, at the Party Congress, Khrushchev hinted that nuclear weapons made war impossible as a deliberate act of policy, though there remained the awful possibility, as weapons proliferated, that nuclear war would begin prematurely. The size of the Soviet bombs had increased considerably by this juncture. In 1958 he suggested that they might lead to the elimination of almost all life, especially in countries with small but dense populations—which presumably excluded the Soviet Union itself. It was suggested by Soviet ideologists that Marxist-Leninist parties now had to prevent the extermination of peoples as a result of thermonuclear war. Socialism could progress, perhaps only progress, in conditions of peace. At much the same time, Eisenhower had likewise come to the conclusion that nuclear war would destroy the world. Capitalism could progress, perhaps only progress, in conditions of peace.

This odd symmetry suggested a summit. The conclusion in May 1955, after years of bickering, of the Austrian State Treaty seemed another favourable sign. All occupying forces were to be withdrawn and the country accepted permanent neutrality. In July 1955, Soviet, American, British, and French heads of government met in Geneva, with a follow-up meeting of Foreign Ministers in the autumn. There was much talk of the 'spirit of Geneva'. Bulganin accepted Eisenhower's declaration that the

United States would never take part in an aggressive war. Eisenhower grinned, something Dulles disliked. Proposals for arms limitation and inspection were tabled, though they made little progress. At the October meeting, suspecting that the new Soviet style was merely a ploy, Dulles berated the Soviet Union for its oppression of Eastern Europe. The conference broke up without specific agreement, but the two sides now seemed to be talking more constructively.

The 1956 Hungarian revolution presented 'rollback' with an opportunity, and some urged Eisenhower to take it, but he declined either to threaten to use nuclear weapons or to drop arms to aid the rebels (who may, however, have been misled by the rhetoric of freedom). Indeed, it is possible that Khrushchev had received an assurance of American non-involvement before Soviet troops moved back into Budapest for the final onslaught. There might conceivably have been a different outcome had it not been for the simultaneous Suez crisis (to be discussed subsequently). Certainly, Khrushchev had an unexpectedly favourable moment for intervention. Even so, Soviet suppression split West European Communist parties. The only lesson that could be drawn in Eastern Europe itself was that 'liberation' by the West was pretence. The division of Europe might hold for all time.

'Peaceful coexistence' therefore came to seem inescapable for the re-elected Eisenhower and the increasingly loquacious Khrushchev. The term itself was used by the latter at the 1956 Party Congress. A war with imperialism would be the most destructive war in history. Khrushchev gleefully told Western leaders that they were doomed to go under, leaving the Soviet Union master of the world. The Socialist system was infinitely superior—as was apparently demonstrated by his admirably precise statement that Soviet industrial production had increased 1,949 per cent since 1929. The possibilities of the Socialist system were unlimited, as the rest of the world would soon realize. 'Peaceful coexistence', therefore, did not mean the end of competition; indeed the pursuit of influence and prestige throughout the world could become more intense, not less, precisely because a war between NATO and the Warsaw Pact in Europe had become almost inconceivable. There were, as will be seen, ample opportunities for such global rivalry, either directly or by proxy.

Even in Europe, there could still be moments of crisis which looked like a replay of earlier clashes. In November 1958 Khrushchev reopened the question of Berlin against a six-month deadline. He wanted to end the position of the Western powers and declare West Berlin a Free City which would in practice be economically integrated into the East German state. The contrast between West and East Berlin was indeed a contrast between two worlds—West Berlin was a deliberate showpiece of 'the West' in comparison with the drab East. It was through Berlin that East Germans in tens of thousands fled to West Germany. Eisenhower was not impressed by the proposal but neither was he anxious to raise the temperature. Khrushchev accepted an invitation to visit the United States in 1959 and see the capitalist world for himself. Although he was deprived of a trip to Disneyland, the visit was a success. There was talk of a solution being found which would protect the legitimate interests of all concerned.

This apparent progress fell apart when the ensuing summit, which had taken a long time to arrange, collapsed before it began. On 5 May 1960, on its eve, Khrushchev dramatically announced that an American U-2 spy plane had been brought down inside Russia. Eisenhower's reputation for honesty was in ruins, and Khrushchev crowed. No progress could be made on Berlin. That would have to wait for another American President. In deciding not to continue the summit, it may be that Khrushchev was under pressure from elements in Moscow who felt that he had been unduly impressed by the prize cattle Eisenhower had given him in the United States! At any rate, nothing further could be done. Eisenhower and Khrushchev had both gone as far as they politically could in moving on from the world of 1953. By 1960, perhaps the world as a whole had become too volatile for bipolar 'management' of its affairs to be viable.

The new young President, John F. Kennedy, was not likely to accept such a conclusion. He was not old enough to be able to resist a challenge. He wished to reinvigorate his country and the ringing tone of his inaugural address had both a domestic and foreign audience in mind. Every nation should know that the United States would pay any price and bear any burden to assure the survival and success of liberty. He claimed that freedom was under the most severe attack that it had ever known, that the tide of events was moving against the United States. If the United States failed, then freedom failed. However, since freedom could not be promoted by nuclear war, it would have to be advanced by the infectious vitality of his country. Kennedy, and those around him, had abundant vitality. There would be a struggle for hearts and minds beyond Europe and, in this respect, the march to the 'New Frontier', accompanied though it was by a sustained increase in defence expenditure, mirrored Khrushchev's message in 1956. The condition of the world which was to benefit from the attention of the superpowers will be discussed shortly. Meanwhile, the issue of Berlin had not gone away and it was Europe, therefore, which was still the foremost locus of East–West tension.

Kennedy met Khrushchev at a summit in Vienna in June 1961 and was confronted by a renewed demand that a German peace treaty be signed, that the occupation regime be ended, and that West Berlin become a Free City. In the summer of 1961, as both sides rattled their sabres, Moscow resumed nuclear testing (suspended by the Soviet Union, the United States, and Britain since 1958). Its most powerful device was supposed to be 3,500 times more powerful than the bomb dropped on Hiroshima. The late-Eisenhower 'spirit of Camp David' seemed to have evaporated. In August 1961 a concrete-and-barbed-wire barrier sealed off East from West Berlin and dramatically reduced the number crossing into the West. This 'Berlin Wall' may have begun as a temporary improvisation but over time it came to symbolize yet further the reality of a lasting division between West and East. The occupying powers acquiesced in this new situation, but their forces in the city were not subjected to harassment. A new stalemate had been reached, but the international temperature had risen. Coexistence had become indubitably confrontational.

In October 1962 there was worldwide apprehension, but it was
not triggered by Berlin, nor by any other of the traditional
flashpoints of the post-war era. It was instead the island of Cuba
which brought the world closer to nuclear conflict than it had
ever been.

In the past, Cuba had never been thought likely to be the
fulcrum of world history. The Caribbean island had been ruled
by Fulgencio Batista as head of a regime which had lost whatever reforming ambition it might once have possessed. Fidel
Castro, formerly a law student, launched an abortive revolution,
with a small force, in 1953. Imprisoned, but then exiled, he
returned to Cuba in December 1956. Two years later, his guerrilla movement and its allies marched into Havana and took
over power. A programme of land reform and other changes
was embarked upon. He wished to transform Cuba into a
developed and independent nation. Central planning was essential for this task, and Soviet advisers and technicians arrived to
help. Castro, a strikingly charismatic figure, drew on 'anti-
Yankee' feeling to boost his position. There had been some
initial sympathy for him in the United States, but it soon
evaporated in the face of show trials, executions, and confisca-
tions. Cuban emigrants to the United States fuelled American
hostility. In April 1961 a force of exiles, with American support,
carried out a disastrous invasion, as it proved, at the Bay of
Pigs. Its failure increased Castro's standing and led him to seek
closer ties with the Soviet Union. He announced that he had
been a Marxist-Leninist since his student days. Despite this
portentous revelation, however, the Cuban revolution had a
flavour all its own. What had happened on a poor small island
in the Caribbean came to have a magical significance which
extended even to Europe and beyond. Was the Cuban revolution
not a universal prototype?

In 1962, however, there were moments when its fate seemed
rather to portend universal destruction. Plagued by internal
difficulties and fearful of another American-backed invasion,
Castro had agreed to accept Soviet missiles on Cuban soil. Their
presence was detected by an American U-2 spy plane and

President Kennedy demanded their withdrawal. He imposed a 'quarantine' line around the island. A Soviet convoy, which included a freighter carrying more warheads, was heading towards it. The ultimate disaster of nuclear war appeared as close as it had ever been. In the event, the Soviet convoy turned around. A couple of days later, Khrushchev announced that he would remove the nuclear missiles from Cuba if NATO missiles were withdrawn from Turkey, a condition the United States rejected. Further negotiations followed, and by the end of November Khrushchev had agreed to withdraw Soviet bombers and rocket personnel from the island. In the end, although Castro could at least now have some confidence that the United States would not attempt another invasion (Khrushchev had extracted a pledge from Kennedy), it was galling that the whole affair had been settled without him. The extent to which the world was in fact 'settled' by Washington and Moscow was made plain. And the settlement appeared to be a triumph for Kennedy's firmness. As it was famously put by his Secretary of State, Dean Rusk, 'Eyeball to eyeball, they blinked first.' As for Cuba itself, ironically, a revolution which had sought to escape from economic 'colonialism' now found itself increasingly locked into a dependency on the Soviet Union.

After Stalin: Making Western Europe

It also seemed to some Europeans in the early 1950s, particularly on the left in France, that Western Europe was a kind of dependency of the United States. The leadership and support offered by Washington had thus far proved vital to its survival, but the American protective role neither could nor should be relied upon indefinitely. It was time again for 'Europe' to consider its own destiny. The previous section has demonstrated the extent to which the world was bipolar. Nevertheless, there were stirrings and aspirations towards 'one Europe', a structure, it was supposed, which might eventually enable the old continent to regain the pivotal place in world affairs which had been forfeited by its own internecine conflicts. Equally, however, that past still hung heavily over the present. Even if the global conflict suppressed old European rivalries, it did not altogether eliminate them even within Western Europe (and when reference was made to 'Europe' it was only its western part which writers usually had in mind, a very partial Europe). The extent to which Britain and France, in particular, wished still to maintain some kind of world role of their own further complicated the picture. In 1953, whatever the portents, they both remained substantial imperial powers bent on controlling at least the pace if not the fact of decolonization.

It was the Suez crisis, three years later, which brought home the limits of their independent capacity and provided a dramatic example of shifting power realities. In 1952 a group of young officers had overthrown the monarchy in Egypt. The young man who eventually headed the revolution was Gamal Abdul Nasser. Two years later, under pressure, the British agreed to a phased withdrawal of the forces they stationed in the Suez Canal Zone— the largest British garrison in the world. The new regime was upset by the way in which 'Anglo-Egyptian' Sudan became independent in January 1956. In July 1956 Nasser announced the nationalization of the Suez Canal Company. The revenues from the canal were to be used to build a dam at Aswan on the Nile. His action was denounced in Britain as high-handed and unjustifiable. While diplomatic efforts to find a settlement proceeded, the British and French governments were in touch with the Israeli government. Israel attacked Egypt on 25 October. Displaying impeccable impartiality, so it was said, London and Paris required the belligerents to withdraw from the Canal Zone; the reality was that Israel, Britain, and France had agreed on this course of action in advance. Only the Israelis complied, whereupon a Franco-British air bombardment began, followed by a parachute drop on Port Said.

The reaction to their joint action surprised Britain and France. The threat of rockets from the Soviet Union was perhaps predictable, but it was the response of the United States which caused them both anger and dismay. Washington voted against Britain, France, and Israel when the issue came before the

United Nations. Pressure on Britain's gold and dollar reserves followed. Canada was openly hostile, as were India and Pakistan. Only Menzies of Australia gave Britain the kind of backing which might traditionally have been expected from the Empire/Commonwealth. It is worth adding, in parenthesis, that as far as Australia was concerned this gesture should not be taken to indicate that Australia's place in the world was simply and self-evidently always at Britain's side. In this same year, Melbourne had hosted the Olympic Games and rejoiced that the country seemed briefly the centre of the world. Australians were not sure, however, whether that was where they wanted to be. Remoteness had its advantages. New migrants, even heroic Hungarians, should leave 'old-world hatreds' behind them. The blood spilled in the water-polo final between the Soviet Union and Hungary seemed to many Australians an unnecessary European vendetta. While the emotional and practical significance of the Suez Canal was a different matter, Menzies already seemed somewhat old-fashioned in his attachment to 'home'.

In the event, on 6 November the British government ordered a cease-fire. The entire affair humiliated Britain and France. It now seemed clear that neither country could mount a substantial overseas expedition contrary to American wishes. At least temporarily, the British–American 'special relationship' was in tatters. It was also the case, as will be considered subsequently, that the consolidation of Nasser's position inaugurated a new phase in the politics of the Middle East. The 'informal empire' there, which Britain still maintained, was under challenge. Suez was the fiasco which further contributed to a French loss of morale and made 'Europe' a more attractive option than might otherwise have been the case.

It was self-evident in these years that talk of 'Europe' as if it were some kind of political reality in practice excluded most states which could claim to be European. Even 'Western Europe' had a dubious identity. Franco's Spain and Socialist Sweden, for different reasons, were but two states which could not 'belong'. Some might doubt whether Britain was in Western Europe, though the Republic of Ireland, also insular and even further west, seemed sure that it was. The new Coal and Steel Community could be taken to presage a wider pooling of sovereignty on the part of a European 'core'. Run by 'good Europeans' with different ideological and national backgrounds, the ECSC was producing a fifth of the world's steel production by 1959. Such an achievement was taken at the time to be an indication of virility and vitality.

Whether it was either feasible or desirable to go further in the direction of European unity was another matter. It was evident by now that Britain would not provide the engine of integration. A 'continentalized' world (with Britain in 'Europe') held little attraction for a British leadership wedded to the notion—the blip of Suez apart—that the Atlantic united rather than divided. Eisenhower, a few years earlier, had somewhat sadly noted that Churchill was still supposing that an American President and a British Prime Minister could direct world affairs on their own from some rather Olympian platform. International complexities, however, in his opinion rendered any hope of establishing such a relationship 'completely fatuous'. The British, though, did not give up easily. And, as regards 'Europe', official suspicion of 'supranationalism' remained entrenched. It was not necessary to go beyond 'intergovernmentalism' in developing either economic or defence structures. The issue of the hour was the possibility of a European Defence Community, first floated in 1950, and argued over for years until the French Assembly failed to ratify the project in August 1954: the deputies sang the 'Marseillaise' in relief. A 'European' command structure had been envisaged, chiefly as a way of achieving a German contribution to European defence without the creation of a German general staff. In the wake of this failure, it was the British who emerged with a solution through an extension of the Brussels Pacts. It was an outcome which confirmed London in the merits of an intergovernmental approach.

However, very shortly afterwards, the 'Six' (France, Federal Germany, Italy, and the Benelux countries) embarked on the 'rebirth of Europe' at the Messina conference of June 1955. The Spaak committee presented its report in 1956. British policy oscillated between participation and abstention in these discussions. It became steadily more apparent that a full-scale customs union was coming into view. British expectations that German 'free traders' would triumph over German 'integrationists' proved misplaced. The scope for British sabotage diminished. The Rome Treaties creating the European Economic Community (EEC) and the European Atomic Community (Euratom) were signed by the Six in March 1957. The treaties gained large majorities in the parliaments of the signing countries, though for somewhat different reasons. In Federal Germany (sovereign since 1955) participation was a sign of growing confidence, politically and even more economically. In France, the Assembly was no longer in a mood to sing the 'Marseillaise' so resolutely. Other participants all believed that the EEC would boost further that economic prosperity and 'consumerism' which had arrived (though not universally) with such unexpected rapidity. The need to 'tie in' Germany remained fundamental, though not explicit. The EEC was perceived in the Soviet Union as a 'capitalist conspiracy' (its role in the Cold War was undeniable) and in Asia as 'protectionist'.

This 'New Europe' was a paradoxical creation, fusing together in uneasy combination free market, 'social market', and 'indicative planning' enthusiasms. Its structure was complex, reflecting the need to accommodate so many diverse interests: an independent Commission selected by the national governments; a Council of Ministers; a Parliament (not as yet directly elected); a Court of Justice. The scope, function, and composition of these bodies did not remain static over subsequent years. It was incontestable that the unfolding enterprise was not only novel in the history of Europe, it was unique in the world. It excited enthusiasts by the very fuzziness of its structures, processes, and goals, since what was being set adventurously in motion was neither federal, confederal, nor unitary, as conceived in classical constitutional terms. It contained states still strong in their heritage and tradition but now housed them within a novel framework. No one knew, however, where a balance between cultural diversity and uniformity, between commercial and eco-

nomic harmonization and national policy objectives, might ultimately be struck. Indeed no one knew if it could be struck
anywhere with any degree of permanence since the whole structure, sometimes dismissed as a plaything of technocrats, might
collapse. For its part, half-hoping that it would collapse, the
British government took the lead in forming the European Free
Trade Association in 1960. Britain, together with the Scandina-
vian countries, Austria, Portugal, and Switzerland, attempted to
create a free trade zone which would leave national sovereignty
inviolate. The potential of this association was limited, admittedly largely because of the weakness and diversity of the
participating powers. It was a delusion that Britain could by this
means win back the 'leadership' of Europe.

Even so, it was evident, particularly after 1958 when de Gaulle
came to power in France, that the degree and nature of the
integration that was necessary or desirable still troubled the Six
themselves. The tension can be illustrated by two events in 1965.
On the one hand, a treaty was signed in April to bring together
the superior institutions of the ECSC, the EEC, and Euratom
into a single Commission and Council of Ministers; but in July,
on the other hand, the French government announced a boycott
of all EEC meetings, apart from those concerned with routine
management of existing questions, as a sign of its determination
to resist a slide towards majority voting. Two years earlier, in
January 1963, when Britain did make a first application to join
the European Economic Community, it had been de Gaulle who
stood in the way of success. The previous months had shown
how Britain and France both did and did not see the 'world' in
the same way. In November the two countries agreed to develop
a supersonic airliner—Concorde. In December, however, meeting Kennedy in the Bahamas, Macmillan prevailed upon the
American President to supply Britain with Polaris missiles in
place of the defunct British Skybolt system. Whether there could
or should be a 'European loyalty' was and remained problematic. The formation of a European Economic Community had
certainly made it possible to bring the Federal Republic into
'Western Europe', as Chancellor Adenauer desired. Such an

orientation undoubtedly satisfied many Germans, but others still hankered after German unification. A 'European identity' also appealed to some, in Germany and elsewhere, as a bulwark against the Americanization of the continent, though in practice, in almost every sphere of life, that process was pervasive, though not complete. Books were written on how to confront 'the American challenge', but despite them, the 'Frankfurter sausage' was in inexorable transition to a 'hot dog'. Mr Elvis Presley, himself nothing but a hound dog, was stationed in Germany in the US army between 1958 and 1960, but his singing had already captured Europe, and indeed the world. And it was not even necessary to understand English to be able to rock and roll.

Towards a Post-Colonial World

The reconfiguration of Western Europe, which seemed in important respects to be happening, was in part a response to the transformation that was taking place beyond its frontiers. Governments and peoples had to accommodate themselves to the ending of an era in which Europeans had seen themselves as lords of humankind. They had buttressed their conviction of superiority by their achievements in administration and education. Rule had in the last resort rested on force but it had been tempered by a degree of consent, or at least acquiescence, on the part of the governed. If the 'modernization' of Europe seemed virtually inseparable from its Americanization, so the 'modernization' of the world had for long seemed inseparable from its Europeanization, at least at an élite level. Between 1953 and 1965, for Britain and France in particular, steps were taken which made clear how ubiquitous was European decolonization. The ending of the British Raj in 1947, noted in the previous chapter, was a clear sign of what was to come. After 1965 there still remained certain intractable imperial problems, but that was what they were, a residue. In the intervening years, the pass of colonial 'liberation' had been sold beyond recovery.

The 'transfer of power' is not simple to summarize. How and why it took the particular form it did in country after country depended upon a multiplicity of factors. There had been many ways of being a colonial power, and to speak of a single British system or even of a single French system is to oversimplify. Imperial powers had accommodated their rule to different circumstances. The societies which they governed were likewise highly diverse in their economic and social development and in their ethnic composition, religious beliefs, and cultural achievements. The impact of the French and British overseas was also necessarily affected by the duration of their control and whether territories had been merely governed or had been settled. To speak of 'decolonization' in these circumstances, as though it were a single process leaving in its wake common legacies, is misleading. Decolonization was a central aspect of world history at this juncture, but, rhetoric apart, it was not a simple, uniform process.

Explanations must therefore also vary in particulars. Terminology carries its own loaded message. To speak of 'decolonization' perhaps implies that the initiative was metropolitan. In London or Paris decisions were taken by governments and officials according to their perception of the national interests of the imperial power. Indian independence was indeed a precedent but did not necessarily constitute a reason for immediate replication elsewhere. Ripeness was allegedly all in determining when to hand over power. Predatory exploitation had for so long bewilderingly coexisted with paternalistic concern to form the imperial ethos that mixed emotions and motives were inevitable in determining the timing of independence. Surely it was necessary to move in steady stages so that 'good government' was ensured? By the late 1950s, however, particularly in Britain, there was a new mood emerging. The luggage of imperial responsibility began to be jettisoned in favour of an unsentimental calculus. Cost–benefit analysis suggested that it was time to wind up the imperial enterprise as quickly as possible. Even if empire in the past had been essentially exploitative—an orthodoxy which was being subjected to some challenge—it was now a burden. New Europe did not need it.

To speak of 'liberation', however, is to lay the emphasis on the role of subjected peoples in ejecting colonial rulers. Wars or the threat of wars, strikes, and civil disobedience together made life so uncomfortable for the colonial powers that they had no alternative but to bring forward the date of their withdrawal and retreat in as much good order as they could manage. Subjected peoples were as one in demanding the end of the colonial order, and their leaders merely gave voice to pervasive 'national' aspirations. Empire had always depended upon violence. It was now ending by violence or its prospect.

Elements of both narratives can be found in most contexts—in varying proportions. Which seems most persuasive can depend as much upon the location and perception of the observer as upon objective fact. Astute British manipulators of imperial retreat may indeed have believed that they were managing decline consummately—as the Governors departed and the flags were lowered. Men of violence in Cyprus or Kenya, in Indo-China or Algeria, may have believed that victory was theirs. Neither side saw the whole picture.

British Retreat

On the whole, however, as far as Britain was concerned, the transition to independence was accomplished with a considerable degree of good will and mutual regard. In 1957 Malaya became independent, a state expanded in 1963 to become Malaysia by the incorporation of Sabah (British North Borneo), Sarawak, and Singapore. Four hundred miles separated Eastern and Western Malaysia and there was something paradoxical in the creation of a state whose elements were linked in a sense by their passing British connection. In addition, relations between Malays and Chinese could be difficult—and in 1965 Singapore broke away and became an independent state. The possible fragility of post-colonial states was further demonstrated by the 'confrontation' which developed between Malaysia and Indonesia from 1963. Indonesia, itself 'artificial', found Malaysia even more so.

This one example pinpointed the difficulty in supposing that the withdrawal of European control in itself entailed the creation of a peaceful post-colonial world. Pakistan, separated between east and west by over 1,000 miles of Indian territory, looked increasingly precarious as a state. In addition, the future of Kashmir remained a perpetual source of tension—and in 1965 actual war—between India and Pakistan. And even in 'European' Cyprus, independent in 1960, it was questionable whether the Greek and Turkish communities would work together. The transfer of power in Africa seemed likely to raise even more questions about the applicability of European concepts of 'nation' and 'state' and the durability and relevance of the frontiers that had been carved out by the European powers. Ghana (the Gold Coast) became the first British African territory to become independent, followed by Nigeria (1960), Sierra Leone (1962), and Gambia (1965). Kwame Nkrumah, Prime Minister and subsequently President of Ghana, saw himself as 'Africa's Gandhi'. In the Convention People's Party, he had successfully organized the first mass-appeal party in black Africa. His appeal extended far beyond his own country in Africa and for a time he was the charismatic symbol of 'Pan-African' aspirations. In East Africa, the idea of federation having been abandoned, Tanganyika (1961), Kenya (1963), and Uganda (1964) followed suit. In the West Indies, too, federation was abandoned, leading to the independence of Jamaica and Trinidad. In 1963 the Central African Federation was dissolved after a decade of increasingly unacceptable existence in the eyes of its African populations. Zambia and Malawi became independent in 1964. What would follow in Rhodesia was unclear. Prime Minister Smith, a white settler, declared unilateral independence in 1965.

The speed of these and other transitions was remarkable, but generally welcomed. Macmillan, in a famous speech to the South African Parliament in 1960, had spoken of the 'wind of change' blowing through the African continent. It was not a message which had immediate consequences in South Africa itself. Indeed, on the contrary, following a referendum which supported the proposal that South Africa should become a republic, the country decided in 1961 to leave the Commonwealth. The policies of apartheid were strengthened.

There appeared to be a confidence, in public at least, that the crafted constitutions which accompanied independence would endure. It was tempting to believe that a strong British institutional legacy would remain. All the countries alluded to above had become members of the Commonwealth of Nations on gaining independence—the adjective 'British' now being redundant. In 1965 the decision was taken to set up a Commonwealth Secretariat so that its activities could be 'owned' and organized collectively by all its members. The Commonwealth, in other words, should not be an adjunct of Britain either administratively or more generally. In a year in which its two senior Asian members were fighting each other, it could not be assumed that the Commonwealth was necessarily 'united for peace'. Those who welcomed its survival and wished it well for the future argued that the world needed it. There was no other grouping which possessed its distinctive capacity to transcend geographical, ethnic, and, to some extent, ideological barriers in a world now increasingly divided along these lines. It was a 'world' of its own. Its 'senior' members—Australia, Canada, and New Zealand—still attached importance to the Commonwealth, but, however stable and prosperous they were, they were not major world players. Whether indeed the Commonwealth possessed sufficient coherence—other than in a sort of 'British' past, an inevitably diminishing element—remained to be seen. In Britain itself, the passage of the Commonwealth Immigration Act 1962 was an indication that in the new circumstances there was little sense of 'commonality'.

French Retreat

The British, somewhat smugly, believed themselves to have handled their decolonization more satisfactorily than had the French. The 1954 Geneva Agreement recognized a partitioned Vietnam, with capitals in Hanoi and Saigon. It brought to an end eight years of fighting in which French forces had attempted to maintain France's position. Their defeat at Dien Bien Phu earlier in the year was a blow to French military prestige generally and to the Fourth Republic. It reinforced the determination to maintain the French position in Algeria with its large settler population. The bitter war there began in November 1954 and ended with the Évian Agreements signed in March 1962. Atrocities and cruelties abounded as the war spread from the eastern part of the country to Algiers itself. The army and the settler community, determined on maintaining *Algérie française*, precipitated the crisis in 1957–8 which led to the collapse of the Fourth Republic in France in May 1958 and the advent of de Gaulle to power. The supposition that de Gaulle shared this commitment proved false. After subtle manœuvres on his part, the Algerian population chose complete independence in a plebiscite. His actions permanently endangered his life. A section of the French population, swelled by returning settlers, was never reconciled to the loss of Algeria. In Morocco and Tunisia, where there was no comparable settler population, independence had been conceded a few years earlier. So it had also been in French West and Central Africa, though France continued to play a much more explicit role in the evolution of these territories than Britain attempted in its former African colonies. Some commentators, indeed, suggested that the expression *plus ça change, plus c'est la même chose* characterized French withdrawal.

More generally, with certain publicized exceptions, decolonization was not a total and complete rupture with the past. 'Informal' empire which had often preceded 'formal' empire now reappeared. Educational and commercial networks remained intact and still led back, in many cases, to London and Paris. A generation of black West African leaders—an Houphouët-Boigny or a Senghor—were French in language and cultural orientation. The dream of 'Euro-Africa', held off and on since 1945, was not entirely dead. Ruling élites in contiguous African independent states spoke different European languages. Events in the Congo (Zaïre/Democratic Republic of Congo) after the precipitate and complete Belgian withdrawal in 1960 suggested that political order was precarious. Aspirants to political power sought outside backers and it seemed likely that the Cold War would come to the Equator. Relations between the regions of Nigeria deteriorated. In 1963, in Addis Ababa, the Organization of African Unity (OAU) was established with the twin object-ives of eradicating colonialism—the Portuguese remained in Mozambique, Angola, and Guinea—and maintaining solidarity among the new African states. For all their limitations, it was accepted, at least in principle, that the inherited boundaries were sacrosanct. At one level, the OAU was another example of the contemporary 'continentalization' of the world. In practice, the African world was too fragmented and poorly infrastructured for that aspiration to become a reality, at least in the short term.

A Non-Aligned World?

From 1955, an attempt had been made to create another 'world', predominantly Afro-Asian. What would hold it together would be the common experience of and opposition to colonialism, either in the past or still in the present. Its adherents would be 'neutral' or 'non-aligned' in a Cold War world where the prin-cipal antagonists sought, and sometimes bought, allegiance. Hosted by President Sukarno of Indonesia, representatives of twenty-nine Asian and African countries came to a conference at Bandung to support this goal. The youngest (and newest) leader present was Nasser of Egypt. One Greek Orthodox priest was present—in the person of Archbishop Makarios of Cyprus. The heavyweights, however, were Zhou Enlai from China and Pandit Nehru from India. There was an aspiration that Afro-Asia would be an 'area of peace' in the world. It was an attractive prospect but one not easily achieved. The united front against colonialism, over the ensuing decade, admitted of various interpretations. In 1965, a second Afro-Asian conference, due to be held in Algeria, had to be abandoned. The Algerian govern-ment had just been overthrown. However, stresses and strains had been apparent from the outset, in particular as Sino-Indian relations, buoyant at Bandung, deteriorated rapidly.

It was in the decade up to his death in 1964 that Nehru, Prime

Minister of India since independence, made his greatest impact on world affairs. India, he claimed, exemplified the essence of non-alignment. It was neither Communist nor a lackey of the United States. Its constitution proclaimed that it was a secular country, albeit one in which religious convictions were held with passionate intensity. India remained a pillar of the Commonwealth but had denounced the British Suez expedition of 1956. Obeisance was made to notions of non-violence inherited from Gandhi, but the government did not eschew all force. Nehru rightly supposed that there was no other great state like India. No other power could be the lofty arbiter of its affairs which the world needed. He had the command of language necessary for the task. Unfortunately, Chinese actions in Tibet, initially accepted, subsequently caused concern in New Delhi. Border issues in the Himalayas led to skirmishes between the two countries in 1961–2. This deterioration—blamed not altogether convincingly by India on China—scarcely heralded the promised 'area of peace' in Afro-Asia.

The idea of a third bloc, however, extended beyond Afro-Asia. President Tito of Yugoslavia, a specialist in the requirements of non-alignment, saw the movement as an ideal vehicle for his own concerns. A conference of 'non-aligned' nations was held in Belgrade in 1961 and again in Cairo in 1964. It was undoubtedly the case that as new states emerged on the world stage they sensed a certain kinship with each other and shared a disinclination to accept the choices which existing world politics seemed to offer.

The meeting in Cairo was testimony to the status of Nasser. The 'Middle East' had indeed changed substantially over the preceding decade, though not quite as radically as Nasser would have wished. The Baghdad Pact (1955), signed originally by Turkey and Iraq with the notion of forming a 'northern tier' against Soviet expansion, and later joined by Britain, Iran, and Pakistan, had offended much radical Arab opinion. Its Muslim members spoke in November 1956 about the 'rising tide of subversion' in the Middle East. In January 1957 the United States President proclaimed the 'Eisenhower Doctrine', which offered economic aid and assistance to any country requiring help against armed aggression by any country controlled by international communism. Traditional Arab leaders did not rush to accept it. To have done so might only have precipitated their downfall. It was supposed that Syria was on the point of being taken over by 'Communists'. In 1958, revolution in Iraq over-threw the monarchy and led to the country's departure from the Baghdad Pact. Just beforehand, Syria and Egypt proclaimed a somewhat precarious 'United Arab Republic'. American and British troops landed for a short period in Lebanon and Jordan to buttress the respective regimes. Elsewhere, British forces successfully assisted the Sultan in Oman. In the event, too, the United Arab Republic had little substance and Syria broke away within a few years. Indeed, what was characteristic of the region as a whole was its endemic instability. Kuwait became independent in 1961 and its existence was immediately threatened by Iraq. Civil war broke out in Yemen.

As so often in the past, it was geography which helps to explain the region's instability. It was perceived to be a critical area in the global conflict. Both principals in that conflict sought to improve or secure their positions. The accelerating importance of oil in the advanced economies of the world accentuated the external rivalry. Discovery of oil (as in Libya in 1959) trans-formed economic and political possibilities almost monthly. And, in the case of Israel, the United States had a commitment to its continued existence and success which was dictated in large measure by domestic political pressures. Washington could not stay out of the region and, as British commitment weakened, its role expanded. Saudi Arabia became of critical importance. The fact that 'the world' intruded into the Middle East, however, is not the sole explanation for its instability. Was 'the Arab world' only a fantasy—as perhaps 'Europe' was? Were Egyptians really Arabs? If Arabs were all brothers, how to account for the ferocity, on occasion, of the exchanges between Damascus, Baghdad, Amman, Riyadh, and Cairo? And, as change took place in the Maghrib, could an 'Arab world' really extend from Rabat to Muscat, from Khartoum to Beirut? The answer seemed to be 'no', but impossible dreams remained potent. Indeed, part of the undoubted appeal of Nasser's rhetoric lay in the extent to which he was committed to an 'Arab world'. It was not easy, therefore, in the Middle East, or anywhere in the world, to be certain who qualified as 'non-aligned'.

Most importantly, the position of China caused constant debate. China was present at Bandung, but no one could doubt that China was Communist. By the end of the People's Republic's first decade, however, its internal path was no simple reflection of Soviet orthodoxy. Chairman Mao was urging the people, consolidated in communes, to achieve a 'Great Leap Forward' in food and other production. After its optimistic beginning, the drive turned into a disaster. Food shortages led to loss of life on a massive scale. In these same years (1960–1), and thereafter, Sino-Soviet relations deteriorated sharply. The Chinese leadership had never liked Khrushchev's attack on Stalin and his enunciation of 'peaceful coexistence'. In Beijing's eyes, the Soviet Union had become dangerously revisionist. In Moscow's eyes, the Great Leap Forward was an aberrant path. In 1960 all Soviet technical advisers in China were called home, taking their plans with them—with serious consequences for half-completed Chinese plants. The fact that Moscow took a neutral attitude in the Sino-Indian dispute made matters worse. There were border disputes between China and the Soviet Union too, which could also be worked up into a crisis. The way things were going it appeared in the mid-1960s that there could be war.

It was apparent, in other words, that there was ceasing to be the single 'Communist world' which had been supposed to exist a decade earlier. In October 1964, as a further indication of its determination to have an independent status, China exploded an atomic bomb. Thus, whatever its precise alignment, China was necessarily some kind of World Power, though how it would excute that role remained enigmatic.

Japan, too, was represented at Bandung, and it was also an enigmatic kind of World Power. However, it clearly neither possessed nor desired military might. Its 'Self-Defence Force', deliberately so described, remained small. Defence expenditure constituted only around 1 per cent of the country's GNP (British expenditure in this period being around 7 per cent of GNP). Japan's 'Basic Policy for National Defence' (1957) indicated reliance on the United States as the major, if not the sole, shield against external attack. In 1955 the Liberals and Democrats came together to form a single party and from 1958 onwards the Liberal Democrats began a long period of domination in Japanese domestic politics, a domination which was not without a certain murkiness. These were years of extraordinary dynamism in the Japanese economy. Between 1953 and 1965 the country achieved an annual 10 per cent rate of growth in its GNP—though up to 1964 Japan did run a trade deficit with the United States. Such growth mitigated but did not eliminate political dissent. The renewal of the Security Treaty with the United States in 1960 was strongly opposed by Socialists and Communists. In general it can be said that Japan sought world status rather than world power—the successful Olympic Games in Tokyo in 1964 was one such example. Its relations with China and its former colony (South) Korea remained prickly. The traditions of Japanese society remained strong but 'Western' culture and habits also proved attractive. The result was that Japan saw itself increasingly as almost a 'Western' state in East Asia. Neither Americans nor Europeans, however, were sure that this was really the case. Nevertheless, the Japanese–American relationship remained vital to both countries, particularly given the increasing American concern about events in South-East Asia.

In March 1965, following some years in which the Americans had sought to buttress South Vietnam, American marines landed there. President Johnson had been given authority under the Tonkin Resolution in August 1964 to take executive action. The fear was that if South Vietnam fell to the Vietcong insurgents, supported by North Vietnam, the 'domino effect' would ensure that the entire region would succumb to Communism. Another round in the inexorable global struggle was about to begin, whatever the 'non-aligned world' might think.

United Nations?

It became steadily more apparent in the years after 1953, in the light of the events and issues considered in this chapter, that the United Nations Organization had not become the kind of global controlling agency which international idealists had worked for in 1945. The expansion in its membership through this period naturally changed the character of the General Assembly and the flavour of its debates. It became evident that the passing of resolutions did not produce automatic compliance on the part of states affected by them. In addition, new states wanted a new world agenda. The 1960s were declared to be 'Development Decade' by the United Nations. Over the next couple of years, · resolutions affirmed that the promotion of international trade, rather than aid, would open the way to world peace and stability. The 1964 Cairo non-aligned conference declared that the United Nations should be the forum for the promotion of world economic development. Later that year, in Geneva, it sponsored the first UNCTAD (United Nations Conference on Trade and Development). The Great Powers had to work harder to obtain the support they needed, though they normally succeeded. The industrialized world was urged to look again at the prices paid for raw materials and agricultural products from developing countries. The basis of GATT needed to be re-examined in the interests of the 'developing world'. Much of this remained aspiration rather than achievement. Initial examination of particular problems, however, disclosed that there were probably developing *worlds* (and industrial *worlds*) rather than a single coherent developing world.

Taken in the round, therefore, it was generally argued that if the United Nations had not existed it would have been necessary to invent it. While more grandiose visions of its role faded, however, the role of specialized agencies and 'peacekeeping forces' (as in Cyprus in a situation of communal violence in 1964) proved invaluable in containing, if not resolving, otherwise intractable conflicts. Successive Secretary-Generals sought to expand their role.

This was particularly the case with the Swede Dag Hammar-skjöld, who was elected in 1953 and re-elected in 1957. Arguably, the prestige of the United Nations was at its height during his stewardship. His role in the 1956 Suez crisis was important in both assembling a United Nations Expeditionary Force (UNEF) and in persuading Nasser of Egypt to accept it. In the same year, however, his attempt to visit Hungary came to nothing. He maintained that the UN had begun to gain a certain independent position and the Secretary-General was able to engage produc-tively in 'preventive diplomacy'. However, his intervention in the 1960 Congo crisis provoked hostility, particularly from the Soviet Union. A UN force was swiftly dispatched but, in a situation where there was no agreed central authority, it was not clear what precisely it should do. The Soviet Union suspected that Hammarskjöld was trying to get rid of Lumumba (who had just been dismissed as Premier by President Kasavubu). Lumumba was subsequently murdered. The Security Council urged all appropriate measures to prevent the occurrence of civil war. Khrushchev denounced what he called the pro-Western bias of the UN machinery. He proposed the abolition of the post of Secretary-General and its replacement by a 'troika': one West-ern, one Soviet, and one non-aligned. The proposal did not succeed but the concern which lay behind it illustrated how difficult, perhaps how impossible, it was for either an individual or an organization to stand somehow poised above the world in detached fashion. The Soviet Union was anxious to ensure that primary responsibility for peacekeeping operations should rest with the Security Council—a view with which, for its own reasons, the United States came to concur.

On the ground it had looked, for a moment, as though the United Nations was itself going to become a colonial power. Attempts to form a central government foundered on the con-tinuing independence of Tshombe in Katanga province. It was on his way to meet Tshombe (whose forces held Irish UN troops) that Hammarskjöld's plane crashed and he was killed. The problems of government in the Congo (Zaïre) remained intractable, but eventually UN troops left in 1964. Much wran-

gling then followed as to who should pay for the Congo operation. Hammarskjöld's successor, the Burmese U Thant, was
more circumspect but no less determined to maintain an effective
mediating role for the organization. However, he was able to do
little in the opening stages of the Vietnam conflict. Supporters of
intervention argued that the presence of the UN prevented direct
Great Power clashes, but others were more sceptical. It had tried
to do too much; the world was not yet ready for such a world
operation.

Global View

As they looked at the world in which they were living, scholars
grappled with paradoxes. At one level, developments could be
'seen' more clearly. 'Actors' and 'publics', in some countries,
now appeared to be together involved in dangerous decisions
and distant events. In the Cuban missile crisis of 1962 President
Kennedy used the medium of television to speak directly to the
American people. His own assassination a year later flashed
across screens worldwide. President de Gaulle proved an unexpected master of the medium. The funeral of Sir Winston
Churchill, with which this chapter began, was watched by some
350 million people. In these years, techniques of transmission
and presentation were improving all the time. What no one
could tell, however, was the import of these developments for
'world history'. For the first time in human experience, 'the
world' in a sense came daily into the home. Television was in
the process of becoming the source from which most people in
the industrialized nations derived their (incomplete) notions of
world affairs. It would be a hard task, henceforth, for certain
governments to exclude the prying eye of the camera. The images
could of course be distorted. Indeed, academic specialists
doubted whether the medium could ever present an 'objective'
view of international relations. The world, as perceived through
television by 'ordinary people', became an ever more complicated place.

So it also seemed to scholars of international relations. That power, primarily conceived in military terms, determined specific outcomes was obvious and had been demonstrated during the period. The uneasy peace that had generally prevailed, however, notwithstanding particular conflicts, could therefore be explained as the product of a 'balance of power'. Some scholars, however, became increasingly dubious about the term, not least because it proved difficult to agree on its precise meaning. The global setting was likely to make the operation of a balance system more and more difficult (though 'world government' or 'collective security' would be no less fraught as alternative ways of trying to manage world politics). It was, therefore, all the more urgent to think, with the American scholar Morton Kaplan, about *System and Process in International Politics* (1958). Other writers prised open the world as 'grand society' with multiple transactions, some well developed and central and some embryonic and marginal, and sought to move the analysis of global politics away from conceptions simply of power and security. It was hoped that such approaches could give more insight into the dense web of relationships which gave the world the degree of stability and prosperity which appeared to have been achieved by the mid-1960s. And such insights seemed all the more necessary when the optimism which had largely prevailed in the immediate post-war decades began to fade and the world seemed again fragile and in crisis.

4

Devious Decade
c. 1965–1975

The Passage of Time

In August 1975 the 'Final Act' of the Conference on Security and Co-operation in Europe was concluded in Helsinki. The conference had begun in the Finnish capital two years earlier. Whether the 'Final Act', adopted by some thirty European countries, the United States, the Soviet Union, and Canada, would indeed have lasting significance remained to be seen. At the time, the Helsinki Agreement marked an important turning point in East–West relations. The post-war boundaries of Europe were given international, rather than the previous bilateral recognition. 'Confidence-building' measures were set in train, including notification of military exercises close to borders. The Soviet Union accepted, with the other participating states, that it would respect human rights and fundamental freedoms.

The contemporary sense that detente was being achieved in the mid-1970s reflected certain comforting assumptions. It confirmed some observers in the belief that no world relationships could ever be permanent. There were pressures, either internal or external, which would inevitably modify the post-1945 pattern. On this analysis, by 1975, the very passage of time made change possible, though not inevitable. The Second World War could certainly not be 'written out' of the evolving history of the late twentieth century. Its outcome still shaped the fundamental power relationships of 1975. Even so, its significance was necessarily fading. Young people growing up in Europe and America were no longer fed, as their parents had been, on the same diet of war films. While the memories and myths of the war were still referred to, and to some extent still shaped the options before

political leaders, that situation could not last indefinitely. The
Battle of Britain, the Siege of Leningrad, Iwo Jima, the Burma
Road—to take only a few examples—still echoed strongly in
national memories, but they could only do so at a remove for
men and women who were 30-year-olds in the early 1970s.

It was with the passage of time, too, once the immediate
horrors were over, that new and controversial ways of looking
at the war—its causes and consequences—surfaced. In the early
1960s, the English historian A. J. P. Taylor had set off a storm
of controversy with his *The Origins of the Second World War*. In
the formerly occupied countries of continental Europe, awkward
questions about complicity began to be asked afresh and punc-
tured the comforting notions of general 'resistance' during the
period of occupation. At the moment when the 'success' of post-
war reconstruction was being acclaimed, some voices questioned
its very basis. Too much of Europe's recent past had been
banished or sanitized. Too many men with dubious pasts were
to be found in government service—in Federal Germany, for
example, in the case of Hans Globke, who had written the
official commentary on Hitler's Nuremberg laws. A burgeoning
'consumer society' should not be allowed to forget Auschwitz.
'Hiroshima' should continue to haunt a world in which its
leading powers still sought security in the possession of nuclear
weapons. As a totality, therefore, the 'Second World War'
constituted a paradoxical legacy. As collective experience, it
could only continue to slip away but, for individuals, discovery
of their past misdeeds could still destroy careers.

Detente may have been facilitated by the passage of time but
it was not made inevitable. Whatever optimism may have been
felt in 1975, the path even to the Helsinki 'Final Act'—itself
formally only of European significance—was tortuous. Between
1965 and 1975 there had been fits and starts in which 'new
thinking' (particularly on nuclear weapons) coexisted alongside
old assumptions: no one could tell which would predominate. If
there was a route to detente during this period, it was a devious
one. Shortly after his inauguration, US President Johnson met
Soviet Deputy Prime Minister Mikoyan and told him that the

reduction of tension in the world would be a daily occupation. In May 1964 he spoke publicly of 'building bridges' with the Soviet Union. However, as will shortly be seen, Vietnam was to dominate his attention. The British editors of one collection of relevant treaties and documents between 1968 and 1975 took for title *The End of the Post-War Era* (1980). In their view, after 1975, it no longer made sense, except purely literally, to talk about 'post-war'. The wartime Great Powers who had fought against the Axis had finally reached a kind of peace agreement. There was no single dramatic event which made this transition self-evident: the 'end of the Cold War', it was suggested, came about through a series of interlinked developments which were not in themselves spectacular. There were many little 'straws in the wind' which could be used to support this contention. In 1971, for example, President Tito of Yugoslavia became the first Communist Head of State to visit the Pope.

The United States and Vietnam: The Watershed

Lyndon Baines Johnson obtained a landslide victory in the American presidential election of November 1964. During the campaign, he had told the electorate that he was not going to send American boys thousands of miles away from their homes to do what Asian boys should do for themselves. Washington, it appeared, still thought it possible to win the war through a well-supplied South Vietnamese army: the Vietnamese military option could prevail. In March 1965, however, it was announced that two battalions of US marines would be sent to South Vietnam. Behind this fateful action lay months of debate within the administration. The President could not appear to be 'soft' on Communism, but the dispatch of troops would also be unpopular. Negotiations, it seemed, could not even be entertained with the enemy before the military position of Saigon improved. What the United States did possess, however, was the capacity to bomb North Vietnam into submission, or so it was supposed. Such a campaign (which also extended to the South itself), together with the steady increase of US troops (184,000 by the end of 1965) with combat roles, would surely succeed. Johnson reiterated that the United States would not grow tired of its mission. If more men and more bombs were needed, they would be sent.

In the months, and indeed the years, that followed, the formula was relentlessly applied, but without success. There were over 500,000 American ground troops in Vietnam by the end of 1967. 'Bombing pauses' failed to bring the North Vietnamese to the conference table on American terms. From time to time, there were optimistic assessments of 'progress' and hopes were placed in the 'Second Republic of Vietnam' proclaimed by President Nguyen Van Thieu in October 1967. However, the 'Tet' offensive of January 1968, in which Vietcong guerrillas and North Vietnamese troops successfully overran—if temporarily—provincial capitals and Saigon itself, demonstrated that no part of South Vietnam was secure. A Vietcong suicide squad even entered the grounds of the American Embassy. A couple of months later, Johnson announced that he would not seek re-election, would reduce bombing, and would send only token reinforcements of ground troops. Negotiations to end hostilities began in Paris but made little progress as Hanoi awaited the outcome of the American presidential election in November 1968.

There was no doubt that the war in Vietnam had become a 'world event'. Despite the fact that a National Security Council working group had concluded in November 1964 that the primary sources of Communist strength in South Vietnam remained indigenous, the predominant American view was that the outcome had global significance and involved outside players. 'Chinese-type liberation wars', Walt Rostow suggested, would mushroom across the world unless the 'liberation war' in Vietnam was broken. Thailand would certainly 'fall'. It did no harm, from the administration's standpoint, to let it be known that Hawaii or even San Francisco might be next. 'Appeasers' were thought by the President to constitute 'chickenshit'. The United States could afford the cost and, despite occasional anxieties to the contrary, it was probably the case that neither the Soviet

Union nor China would join in. Johnson himself did not want to be blamed for the 'loss of Indo-China' as his predecessors had been blamed for the 'loss of China' in the late 1940s. This was a war that had to be won for the sake of America's standing as a world power, indeed as *the* world power.

Johnson's announcement of March 1968, however, though it did not in fact end the war, was tantamount to an admission that it could not be won. Whether it could *ever* have been won has much exercised commentators. What would have happened if Hanoi itself had been occupied? And so on. Such speculation has been fuelled by this extraordinary outcome. A little 'piss-ant' country, as Senator Fulbright described North Vietnam, had frustrated the greatest power in the world. Some supposed that the men at war had been betrayed by college students on campus back home. Drafts had been dodged. 'Teach-ins' held in colleges across America by dissenting professors, though their scale must not be exaggerated, condemned what their country was doing in South-East Asia. 'Body counts' mounted. What were 50,000 Americans dying in Vietnam for?

The debate widened into a reflection on the whole course of American involvement in world politics since 1945. For some, the Vietnamese quagmire was the grisly apotheosis of a misplaced imperial strategy. The notion that Washington could and should create 'Pax Americana' to replace 'Pax Britannica' had been a fatal delusion of grandeur. Talk of 'the American Century' had got out of hand. 'Containment', while it had seemed in the abstract to be a plausible policy, was now clearly seen to cost lives. The President himself came up against a stark reality: the United States could destroy but it could not control. It was a far cry from the Statue of Liberty to the corrupt politics of crumbling Saigon. The world, and the aspirations of its inhabitants, was a far more complicated place than was perhaps allowed for in the frameworks of American political science. Some commentators suggested that the United States would best serve the world by looking after its own internal affairs.

There was an emerging consensus that the country was in trouble. In August 1964 Johnson had inaugurated a major

Economic Opportunity Policy in support of community action programmes. He held up a vision of a 'Great Society' which would bring Americans of all colours and creeds together—though the expenditure it would require was now threatened by the billions of dollars committed to Vietnam. Johnson was prepared to take inflationary risks by requiring both 'guns and butter'—and the risks turned into realities. The summer of 1965 saw riots in American cities, starting in Watts, Los Angeles. They were followed by demonstrations in Washington against the Vietnam War. The pattern was repeated in subsequent years. In Detroit in July 1967 troops were deployed and there were heavy casualties. The Kerner Report on the 1967 riots warned that the United States was becoming two societies, one black and one white, separate and unequal. President Johnson identified the need for an 'affirmative action' programme which would give African-Americans and other minorities preferential treatment when government contracts were awarded. Another major anti-Vietnam War demonstration occurred in Washington in October. A few days after Johnson's Vietnam announcement in March, Martin Luther King was assassinated in Memphis, Tennessee. His death was followed by widespread rioting across America. In June, Robert Kennedy, who adopted an anti-war platform, was shot in Los Angeles. In August, demonstrations on the subject of Vietnam, and their treatment, provoked ugly scenes at the Democratic Convention in Chicago. No sequence of events could demonstrate more dramatically the interpenetration of 'world politics' and 'American politics'. The United States was in turmoil.

On the other hand, in Johnson, a master of legislative tactics, the United States had a President who responded with great vigour to its problems. The 'War on Poverty' which he declared in 1964 cut the number of Americans who had incomes below the poverty line from 22 per cent in 1960 to 13 per cent in 1970. A flood of housing and urban-renewal measures appeared and federal spending on education, health, and anti-poverty programmes all rose substantially. How much more might have been achieved to advance the 'Great Society' if it had not been for the Vietnam War can only be speculated upon, but the positive legislative programme has to be placed alongside images of doom and despondency. There was, too, another instance where 'world politics' and 'American politics' intersected. The 'Great Society' was under attack from the Republican right. Johnson could not allow it to be thought that he was 'soft' on Communism in Vietnam. To allow such a thought to develop would be to jeopardize the 'Great Society' itself. There is a sense, therefore, in which it was 'progressive' Vietnam which suffered because of Johnson's domestic progressive aspirations. If so, the price was indeed to prove heavy, above all for Vietnam itself.

In the event, however, it was Republican Richard Nixon who defeated Democrat Hubert Humphrey (Johnson's Vice-President) in the November 1968 presidential election. Vietnam overhung the election but neither main candidate nor the third-party candidate, George Wallace, offered opponents of the war (perhaps a third to a half of the American population) an opportunity to vote against its continuance. Nixon was believed to have some kind of secret plan for ending the war, always the best kind of plan to have at election time. He took his time to announce the 'Nixon Doctrine'. The kind of war that Johnson had wanted to win might well be unwinnable but Nixon (like his predecessor) had no wish to be a President to lose a war (and in a strict military sense the United States was never defeated). It was therefore necessary to scale down the troop commitment but not to do so precipitately and not to convey the impression that there was no alternative strategy. The American troop presence peaked at 541,000 in January 1969. Nixon announced the withdrawal of 25,000 troops in June and at intervals thereafter further reductions were implemented. The last US ground combat troops left Vietnam in August 1972, ahead of the upcoming elections in which Nixon would again be a candidate.

This phased withdrawal, however, was not presented as the abandonment of South Vietnam. On the contrary, it was paralleled by the 'Vietnamization' of the conflict. The United States would step up training, supplies, and, if need be, aerial support. All that South Vietnam needed, it seemed, was time. Nixon, without undue regard for constitutional proprieties, extended the war into neighbouring Laos and Cambodia to provide it. Supply routes had to be cut off; it was not to be understood as an invasion. Of course, this strategy prolonged the war and the division in American society, but Nixon reiterated that, if the world's most powerful nation acted like a helpless giant, free nations and institutions would be threatened throughout the world. In May 1970 protesting Kent State university students were shot. In April l971 some half a million anti-war demonstrators marched in Washington.

The President began to appeal to the 'silent majority'—another new expression—who would still patriotically support him. There was, the administration supposed, just a chance that South Vietnam could survive (as South Korea had survived). Indeed, from one perspective the country was prospering—though as an American dependency. However, in March 1972 North Vietnamese forces launched a major offensive across the demilitarized zone. On this occasion, Nixon responded with intensive bombing of the North, including Hanoi and Haiphong. What he really needed, however, to ensure his impending re-election, was the appearance of peace rather than the prospect of escalation. Since August 1969 secret talks had been taking place between Henry Kissinger, Nixon's National Security Adviser, and Le Duc Tho, a Hanoi Politburo member. Over the years, the protracted dialogue led down many alleys. The sticking point, in many sessions, was the future of the South after an American withdrawal (which would include the return by Hanoi of prisoners of war). The United States pressed Hanoi to agree that force would not be used to resolve its future. Thieu had been demanding assurances and Kissinger was in a mood to give them, though not in a position to implement them. Enough was eventually sewn up to allow Nixon to win a great election victory with the promise that 'peace was at hand'. It was to be a peace consummated in January 1973 after a further American pounding of Hanoi. By the end of March, all US military personnel had left Vietnam. The legacy of decades of warfare was all too apparent. Americans thought about their war-dead—some

50,000 killed—but Vietnamese losses were far heavier. Figures are difficult to give exactly but some quarter of a million South Vietnamese forces were killed and 650,000 Communist. Some 300,000 civilians died. Injuries, in addition, were very heavy. The landscape showed only too evidently the effects of heavy bombing.

It was still not a country at peace. All sides manœuvred for position—and Cambodia and Laos remained in ferment. War can be said to have resumed in the South in January 1974. By April 1975, after rapid advances over the previous month, North Vietnamese forces entered Saigon. President Thieu fled to Taiwan. The Khmer Rouge had already taken control in Cambodia.

It was in the early months of 1974 that the Watergate affair, which had rumbled on through 1973, came to a head. Congress had become more assertive on issues of foreign policy. It was not disposed to appropriate additional funds for Thieu's army, despite the pleas of the embattled President. Indo-China had not been 'saved'. A massive pounding of Vietnam from the air—allegedly more bombs had been dropped during the war than on all previous targets in human history—had in the end proved pointless. It left the greatest country in the world demoralized and disorientated. A 'credibility gap'—the expression was new—had opened up between government and governed which could not easily be closed. It was, of course, not only Indo-China that had not been saved. In April 1974 Richard Nixon resigned as President. Some supposed that what had been displayed was not only the wrongdoing of an individual but the sickness of a nation's institutions. There was no integrity left.

These twin events discredited, at least for a time, the mental maps of the world with which American policy-makers had lived since 1945 and the values which they had supposed infused their country's life. A new generation of 'revisionist' historians seized upon the behaviour of 'imperial America' as support for its contention that the United States was as much to blame for the Cold War as the Soviet Union. And there was a determination in Congress, as evidenced by the 1973 War Powers Act, to restrain the capacity of the President to take the country into war by the back door. Yet, if this is evidence of a certain amount of national disorientation, the United States remained capable of extraordinary technical achievements. In December 1968 it was a US rocket which returned from the first manned orbit of the moon, and in July 1969 two Americans, Armstrong and Aldrin, landed on the moon. Such achievements, however, did not eliminate the need to take stock of where America stood on earth.

By 1975, when old French-American Saigon turned into Ho Chi Minh City, steps had already been taken in Washington and elsewhere to delineate the contours of a new international order. It was a task relished by Kissinger, from September 1973 Nixon's (and then Ford's) Secretary of State. Of German-Jewish background, he had made his academic name with *A World Restored* (1957), a study of Metternich, Castlereagh, and the 1814–15 European peace settlement. Compared with the complexities of the early 1970s, the 'world' of 1814–15 was narrowly European. The real twentieth-century world now stood in need of the fresh 'linkages' which his fertile intelligence and ingenious manœuvres could supply. Even supposing that it might be desirable, the simple if frightening confrontations of the early Cold War decades could not be 'restored'. Something at once more flexible, less guided by exhausted ideology, and more sympathetic to the subtle methods of 'old diplomacy' was now required. Kissinger aimed to provide it.

It was indeed the case that the United States had a good deal of ground to make up before 'world opinion'. 'Vietnam' was seized upon by the left in Western Europe as an illustration of the rotten heart of America. American intervention was even worse than the European imperialism which the Americans had once themselves decried. Although direct economic advantage from preserving 'free' Vietnam was difficult to establish, American 'capitalism' was also arraigned. Protest demonstrations became commonplace throughout Western Europe. Prominent European politicians were accused by their angry sons of supine support for the United States.

In fact, European governments were anxious to distance themselves as far as possible from American conduct. The Americans, it would appear, had got themselves into a mess; they could get themselves out of it. Only Australia and New Zealand sent token forces to help them: South-East Asia was part of their world even if it was no longer part of Europe's. This response, however, merits some further commentary. Internally, although the pattern of European immigration to Australia was changing (Asian immigration had still to make its impact), in neither country was there as yet any substantial 'Asian' orientation. In Australia Holt, Menzies' successor, had won a major electoral victory in 1966 as the staunch friend of America. President Johnson attracted large crowds when he visited the country. A few years later, President Nixon was no doubt comforted by the assertion that Australia would go a-waltzing Matilda with him. The Australian force in Vietnam of some 8,000 men was not going to tip the balance. Dissidents in Australia before long shared in the sentiments and language of worldwide protest. A 'new nationalism' was burgeoning, even leading the 'Church of England' in Australia to think that archbishops might be locally recruited. At the same time, the world seemed too dangerous a place for Australia to 'go it alone' or turn its extensive territory into 'fortress Australia'. Gradually, however, the colonial past was being shed, but millions did not want it to be shed completely. Superficially, New Zealand might still seem more British-orientated. It had certainly not had the varied European immigration which Australia had experienced after 1945. Yet, looking to the future, in the aftermath of Vietnam, in 1984 a Labour government came to power in Wellington and declined to permit nuclear-armed ships in New Zealand ports. It was an indication that the relatively uncomplicated relationship between Australia, New Zealand, and the United States had come to an end. Geography was not everything.

Certainly, Vietnam invoked no new 'Commonwealth' initiative. Britain under a Labour government declined to send even a token force to Vietnam. Prime Minister Wilson attempted mediation without success. The French government, still claiming special knowledge of Indo-China, sharply criticized President

Johnson and put forward schemes for neutralization. Administration opinion was not pleased by the reaction of its fair-weather European allies. Secretary of State Rusk told a British journalist that when the Russians invaded Sussex the British government could not expect the United States to come to the rescue. It is not recorded whether that help might have been forthcoming if the Russians reached Oxford, where Rusk was educated. At Oxford itself, a future American President, Bill Clinton, made his student distaste for his country's policies known. Yet, although this disenchantment was serious, it was not fatal to the 'post-war' structures. It did, however, lead the governments of Western Europe to consider their future relationships afresh in a world in which the United States seemed preoccupied with Asia.

Latin America

Further evidence of 'imperial America', in the eyes of its critics, continued to be provided by its policies in Central and South America. In the middle 1960s, Latin America still seemed (in the eyes of both those who welcomed the prospect and those who feared it) to be a likely centre of revolutionary upheaval—with global implications. It would cease to be a marginal continent (as far as its impact on the rest of the world was concerned). Castroists continued to argue that conditions in Latin America were ripe for guerrilla campaigns which, starting in the country-side, could sweep to victory in the cities. Speaking in 1966, the Cuban leader declared that in the immense majority of Latin American countries conditions for making revolution were far superior to those which had existed in Cuba when he had started his own movement. Dependent though he was, to an extent, on the Soviet Union, he was nevertheless critical of the stance its leadership was taking at this time, particularly in relation to the United States. Castro sought to capitalize worldwide on the reputation his revolution had achieved. There might be a new revolutionary axis led by Cuba, Vietnam and North Korea, and such other Latin American countries as could be liberated. It would be a Communist movement but have a revolutionary confidence and conviction which the Soviet Union seemed to be lacking. A Tricontinental Conference of revolutionary organizations from Africa, Asia, and Latin America held in Havana in January 1966 was a sign. It was followed by the formation of a Cuban-sponsored Latin American Solidarity Organization. Tension between orthodox Communist parties in the region and Castro could not be disguised, and the Soviet Union was not pleased. Castro declined to go to Moscow to celebrate the fiftieth anniversary of the Russian Revolution in 1967. Guerrilla warfare was judged most likely to succeed in Colombia, Venezuela, Peru, and Guatemala. Che Guevara had resigned his Cuban posts in 1965 and disappeared into the Bolivian jungle. He hoped to lead impoverished tin-miners and an urban underground movement to victory. The strategy failed disastrously. Bolivian regular troops captured and executed Guevara in 1967. He became, in his death, an icon for radicals throughout the world.

However, the implantation of a guerrilla strategy in Latin America was more difficult to achieve than Castro had supposed. In any case, with the Cuban economy in massive debt to Moscow, he had to be more compliant. He was no friend to the economic ideas which accompanied the 'Prague Spring' of 1968. Internally, though not as successfully as he had hoped, Castro turned his attention to vexing issues of productivity. There was some danger that the revolution was losing its way.

Within a few years, however, Castro had bounced back. The defeat of the United States in Vietnam in particular gave him renewed confidence in Cuba's survival and in the prospects for revolution elsewhere in the world. Castro himself turned increasingly to an international role—in 1972 he was out of the island for two months visiting countries in Africa, Eastern Europe, and the Soviet Union. Cuba joined COMECON in the same year. Technical volunteers were sent abroad, and the end of Portuguese rule in Africa two years later gave him an opportunity to send troops, with considerable success, to Angola to assist the MPLA in the three-cornered fight that developed for control of the country. Cubans had had contact with the MPLA for a decade. Castro took an intense personal interest in this conflict, speaking, so one writer suggests, of Angolan cities, customs, and people as though he had lived there his entire life. This involvement was represented as testimony to the internationalist principles of the Cuban revolution. Castro's homeland was not just Cuba, it was humanity and specifically that of the underdeveloped South in its conflict with the industrialized North. Those not moved by this identification, however, saw in such manœuvres little more than a small and insignificant country acting as surrogate for the Soviet Union in areas where it was too risky for Moscow directly to intervene. The reality, they suggested, was that Castro could not escape his dependence on the Soviet Union—President Brezhnev paid a somewhat puzzled visit to Cuba in 1974—however much his imaginative international strategy gave the illusion of an independent world role. It was important not to be mesmerized by Castro's undoubted charisma into thinking that Cuba could really orchestrate a Third World revolution.

The United States had two central concerns: to maintain pressure, by one means or another, on Cuba itself and to ensure that the Soviet Union should not establish direct influence anywhere from Mexico to Argentina. Yet it became steadily more apparent that co-ordination of an anti-Communist solidarity was not a straightforward matter. 'Latin America' might be conceived from outside as a geographical entity, but each state had its own character. Argentina, Brazil, and Mexico in 1970 had populations in excess of 23 million, 92 million, and 48 million respectively. Brazil in particular trembled on the brink of global status, though it trembled for a long time. The Organization of American States had supported the US blockade during the 1962 Cuban missile crisis and voted in 1964 to impose economic sanctions on Cuba. The United States did still directly intervene militarily—as in the Dominican Republic in 1965. In the circumstances of civil war, that country's nearness to Cuba was held to justify the presence of US marines (subsequently supported by contingents from some other Latin American states). The overseas forces withdrew in 1966 after elections returned a conservative President who was to remain in power for more than a decade. Despite the support which Washington received in this particular operation, there was concern elsewhere in Latin America at the blatant violation of the non-intervention provision enshrined in the charter of the OAS. Compliance might be more difficult for the United States to obtain in the future.

Viewed from Washington, in its relations with its southern (and in some cases somewhat distant) neighbours, there was a difficult balance to be struck. There was indeed a special commercial and financial relationship which remained of great importance, though in fact the proportion of total US foreign investment located in Latin America was beginning to decline appreciably. A new spirit was supposed to be being injected after Kennedy's 1961 'Alliance for Progress'. It was even sometimes referred to as the *Alianza*, as a gesture. The American economist Walt Rostow had discovered *The Stages of Economic Growth*, and application looked straightforward. It was not. Quite apart from whether the rhetoric which accompanied the *Alianza* was naïvely ambitious and culturally blinkered, the Johnson administration grew impatient and detected a more urgent need for alliance funds in the form of counter-insurgency support. The supposed immediacy of the threat of Communist-inspired revolution had priority over measures that might, over a longer term, remove whatever attraction Communism possessed. Military regimes proliferated in country after country with varying degrees of coercion and control. The support given them by the United States seemed to the *Alianza* to be just like old-style US imperialism. And indeed, in some quarters in Washington this policy was an embarrassment. It could only be justified because of the collapse of a 'democratic centre' and the ensuing political polarization.

Events in Chile illustrated the dilemma. Salvador Allende, a long-time presidential candidate, finally won in 1970 in a country beset by chronic inflation, though it was shortly to be beset by even more chronic inflation. Allende was a Marxist, though he had his own Socialist Party which maintained some distance from the Communists. Much was made of his democratic election, though he only had a third of the votes cast—the anti-Socialist vote was split. Allende claimed that he would both carry through a comprehensive programme of nationalization and produce a socialist society, but at the same time maintain parliamentary institutions (which were relatively strong in Chile). On the assumption that he could not in fact do both things, the CIA sought to destabilize the regime by subsidies to its opponents. Inflation mounted. Industrial unrest spread. In effect, the country went bankrupt. In September 1973 President Allende, who had oscillated between approving and containing a 'Far Left' which was indifferent to constitutionalism, was overthrown in a bloody coup and replaced by a military regime under General Pinochet—perhaps an action which most Chileans supported. There was clear CIA involvement, though the extent to which there was complicity from the highest political level in Washington remains contentious. Certainly, Washington's hostility to Allende was very evident. Chile at this juncture was bankrupt and the task of reconstructing the economy was made difficult by the world recession. Nevertheless, Allende was revered in circles well beyond Latin America as a martyr and victim of vicious reaction.

The 'big' countries of Latin America offered no more alluring prospect. In 1964 in Brazil a military coup removed President João Goulart and the army was still firmly in control a decade later. A series of military Presidents ruled by decree. In Argentina, the figure of Juan Perón still loomed in the background in 1965. The following year a junta led by Juan Carlos Ongania deposed President Illia as the army re-entered politics. He lasted for four years before he was removed by a junta dissatisfied by his loss of political control. Free elections later led to the victory of the Peronista party. Perón returned to Argentina after eighteen years of exile and was sworn in as President in 1973 but died the following year. His third wife succeeded him, but economic crises and the activities of left-wing guerrillas (*Montoneros*) made the regime look extremely precarious in 1975.

Economic and political instability also extended, to greater or lesser degree, throughout Central America—in El Salvador and Nicaragua, for example. So long as there was a 'worldwide' Communist movement to be confronted, Washington would support military men whose principles of government hardly matched the ideals of American constitutionalism. Mexico, by contrast, appeared stable. The presidency of Adolfo López Mateos, which came to an end in 1964, had not fundamentally deviated from the strong executive style of his predecessors. Not even the student unrest which accompanied the opening of the 1968 Olympic Games in Mexico City could disturb the lengthy supremacy of the Institutional Revolutionary Party. In 1970 its candidate, Luis Echeverría Álvarez, who had been Interior Minister in 1968, became President and continued, as his predecessors had done, to adhere to 'historic' revolutionary principles which produced right-wing policies and caused its northern neighbour little alarm.

However, beneath the image of a continent plagued by perpetual coups and counter-coups, there were signs in the early 1970s that foundations were being laid which could lead to the emergence of a more assertive collective Latin American voice, differentiated though it would still necessarily be. The economies of the region were growing at a steady rate. There was a determined and partially successful attempt to shift from a reliance on commodity exports to the selling of manufactured goods. Foreign trade as a portion of GNP began to grow and there was a significant manufacturing sector in Argentina, Uruguay, Mexico, and Brazil in particular. The discovery of vast new reserves in Mexico held out the prospect of massive oil revenues in a world crying out for oil. It was a vista which tempted the Mexican government to launch a major programme of public spending—the need in its huge capital city seemed very evident. There was, therefore, despite an established anti-Communism, some disposition to cultivate what may be called a hemispheric strategy. Cuba began gradually to be accommodated into the community of Latin American nations. The military government in Peru, for example, attempting domestically to tackle the country's structural socio-economic problems, renewed diplomatic relations with Cuba in 1972. In 1973 the OAS lifted its sanctions against Cuba—though the island remained firmly outside the organization. In 1975 the Latin American Economic System was established. Cuba was among its twenty-five members, who were to attempt to co-ordinate economic policy, partly with the objective of reducing the influence of the United States. It remained to be seen how far a new pattern of relationships was really emerging in Latin America—and that might hinge as much upon the development of the world economy as upon any indigenous factor.

Western Europe: Friends and Neighbours

Twenty years after the war, Western European governments thought that they had achieved both economic prosperity and social equilibrium. Of course, that equilibrium was neither uniform nor ubiquitous, but it was sufficiently pervasive to breed a sense of maturity. Yet, despite the degree of convergence which was apparent, there remained unresolved uncertainty about the destiny of Europe, as it was sometimes portentously described. The 1963 agreement between France and Germany apparently buried the fractious past for ever as both countries sought mutual understanding and reconciliation at a deeper level than had ever before been attempted. If these states were really locked together in mutual amity, then perhaps Europe did indeed have the basis for a lasting peace.

Yet an era was passing. In that year Adenauer, who had guided the Federal Republic since 1949, stood down as Chancellor; but neither of his successors, Erhard and then Kiesinger, inherited his authority. The Christian Democrats lost ground to the reviving Social Democrats (shorn since 1959 of most of their Marxist baggage) under Willy Brandt. Kiesinger, indeed, was Chancellor in a 'grand coalition' of the two major parties. Brandt became Chancellor in October 1969 and again in November 1972. He remained in office until May 1974, when he resigned following a security scandal. He was replaced by Helmut Schmidt. In France, too, there were changes of personnel, though the Fifth Republic and its new institutions proved unexpectedly resilient. In April 1969 de Gaulle stood down, having failed to gain the vote he required in a referendum on an amendment to the constitution. He was succeeded by Georges Pompidou, who wore the Gaullist mantle, if a little uncomfortably, until his death in April 1974. His successor, Giscard d'Estaing, sought to 'open up' the Gaullist legacy whilst still being dependent upon it for support. In Italy, the turnover of Prime Ministers was such (in the decade 1965–75—Moro, Leone, Rumor, Colombo, Andreotti, Rumor, Moro) that no firm line of national policy can be identified with an individual, but the domination of the Christian Democrats as a party ensured continuity.

Although it is unwise to place excessive stress upon the outlook of particular figures, the above changes were of considerable significance as both France and Federal Germany sought to orientate themselves in the decade after 1965. To 'Anglo-Saxon' ears, de Gaulle became steadily more strident in asserting that France had a distinctive view of the world. France would no more accept American hegemony than Soviet. In 1963, it was apparent that France would not stop the development of its own nuclear weapons, a programme that had been going on for over a decade. In the same year, as has been noted, Paris also vetoed the British application to join the EEC. Two years later, France boycotted the EEC Commission and the Council of Ministers for seven months in a protest against creeping supranationalism. In 1966 France withdrew from the Military Committee of NATO. In 1967 a further British, Irish, Danish, and Norwegian application to join the EEC was blocked. De Gaulle then required the withdrawal of all NATO installations from France by May 1967. Such steps were accompanied by highly publicized foreign excursions between 1966 and 1968—to Moscow, Warsaw, Bucharest, and Quebec. The French President, it appears, thought that he could achieve his own detente with Moscow. His superb showmanship on these occasions served to solidify a national consensus around the notion of *grandeur* and national independence which was neither 'left' nor 'right'. His critics attacked what they saw as a false parallelism in de Gaulle's depiction of the two superpowers, but de Gaulle believed that 'the world' (by which he sometimes meant more than France) could break out of the straitjacket in which it had existed since 1945. By 1969, however, he had not succeeded, perhaps because he was too old and had too little time to exploit the chinks he discerned, and perhaps because, despite his pretensions, France lacked the power to exploit them. Whether the enterprise was foolhardy, misconceived, or merely premature, the voice of France (moderated though it was by Pompidou, who did agree to the entry of Britain, Denmark, and Ireland to the EEC in January 1973) was now significant in world politics.

'Gaullism' constituted a problem for West German governments. Bonn, for obvious security reasons, was not willing to offend Washington by grandiloquent gestures, but also wished to safeguard the relationship with France. The German mark was growing stronger in these years and the dollar weaker: Bonn was no longer so subservient. Even so, despite the substantial and vital military contribution the Federal Republic made to NATO defence, there remained a hesitation about wider foreign policy. The 'German question' seemed as far from solution as ever. Reunification, it seemed, was not in prospect, and the more time passed the more the 'two Germanies' took on an appearance of permanence. Both in the United States and Germany itself, however, there was talk between 1963 and 1965 of a 'policy of movement' towards the countries to the east. Even so, it was only with the Soviet Union that the Federal Republic had established diplomatic relations. Perhaps the way to achieve the peaceful reunification of Germany was through detente rather than through strength. In October 1966 President Johnson told a New York audience that the 'East–West environment' had to be improved in order to achieve the unification of Germany.

What should the Federal Republic itself do? Immediately the complicated politics of the 'Grand Coalition' made a change of approach difficult but the expression *neue Ostpolitik* (new eastern policy) gained currency, though it was not taken to involve any recognition that there was a second German state. Contacts were made with East Berlin 'at party level' between 1966 and 1969 but made scant progress: each side's proposals were unacceptable to the other. However, semi-diplomatic relations were established with several Eastern European states—even though this meant breaking the 'Hallstein Doctrine', which decreed that there should not be relations with any state which recognized the German Democratic Republic. To some extent, therefore, the ground had been laid for the *Ostpolitik* associated with Brandt and his Free Democrat Foreign Minister Scheel after 1969.

A durable detente with Eastern Europe required the agreement of Moscow, and by August 1970 a German–Soviet treaty was signed in the Kremlin. In specific terms it recognized all existing frontiers in Europe including the Oder–Neisse line and the border between the two German states. There was no mention of reunification, but Scheel sent a letter, which the Soviets accepted, reiterating the desire of the Federal Republic to see the German people regain their unity. In December a comparable treaty was signed in Warsaw which confirmed the inviolability of Poland's existing borders. Ratification of these agreements required the Western powers and the Soviet Union to resolve their differences over Berlin. How much or how little integration between the Federal Republic and West Berlin could there be? Eventually, in September 1971, an arrangement was reached on this matter, together with a parallel agreement between the two Germanies a few months later. All the understandings could then come into effect—if the treaties were ratified in the Bundestag. Not unexpectedly, ratification proved contentious and the *Grundvertrag* between the two states was only signed in December 1972 *after* Brandt won the election of November. The precise implication of its language in relation to reunification was subjected to legal review by the Federal Constitutional Supreme Court, which reiterated that Germany was none the less one and indivisible. The treaty, Brandt accepted, did not do away with the Wall and barbed wire, but its various protocols made greater contacts possible. In the circumstances, that was the only way in which the German nation might be preserved. In September

1973 both Germanies were admitted to the United Nations as separate sovereign states. In December, Bonn signed a treaty with Czechoslovakia which annulled the 1938 Munich Agreement.

When in Warsaw, Brandt had knelt during the wreath-laying ceremony for the victims of its ghetto. Such a symbolic act, taken together with the specific treaty arrangements, suggested that between 1969 and 1973 a turning point had been reached. In 1974 the Federal Republic achieved its twenty-fifth anniversary with more optimism about the future than had seemed likely a decade earlier. *Ostpolitik*, though domestically contentious, had not resulted in the Federal Republic slipping from its Adenauer-engineered moorings in the 'Western world'. The strategy clearly met with Washington's approval and formed part of a more general process of detente. The Franco-German axis remained in place, though not without occasional crises. Whether and how German unification could be accomplished still remained a question for the future. A fact of the present was that Germany was becoming, to some extent, less German. By the middle 1970s there were some 2.5 million workers from Turkey and Yugoslavia in the country. They were 'guestworkers', not citizens, but their presence was one further indication that Europe was getting 'all mixed up'.

The above narrative might convey the impression that the two major states of Western Europe, indeed Western Europe as a whole, had achieved a remarkable plateau of political stability. Nevertheless, there were undercurrents of discontent which in 1968, in France at least, challenged and threatened existing institutions. The riots, demonstrations, 'sit-ins', and occupations which took place in Paris, London, Rome, Berlin, and elsewhere have been variously explained. In so far as they were student-led, they reflected the discontents of a new generation—the post-war 'baby boomers'. Students now saw themselves as adults (18-year-olds gained the vote in Britain in 1969 and in Germany in 1970) and in Germany in particular resented 'antiquated' university structures. It was generally held that facilities had not kept pace with the expansion of the student population throughout Western Europe. Student opposition to United States policy in Vietnam contributed to the general atmosphere of discontent and rebellion.

Specific student grievances, however, blended with a quasi-philosophical rejection of the 'routinization' and 'one-dimensionality' deemed to have become characteristic of Western European life. Students claimed to be articulating a critique on behalf of other sections of society. There was an ambivalence towards the material trappings of progress—washing machines and private cars, for example—which now became far more common in Western Europe than ever before. This was 'consumerism without a soul', an analysis which was echoed from a very different quarter, the Vatican, which expressed dismay from its perspective at the attractions of *la dolce vita* and the growing evidence of a decline in churchgoing and the erosion of a Christian view of marriage and family life.

Although the discontent was seized on by Communists—still significant political presences in France and Italy—it was an 'anarchic' mood which expressed itself in hostility as much to the bureaucratic structures of the state and state-owned industries as to private capitalism. Western European man (and even more woman), it was claimed, had become a powerless pawn alienated from the processes of government. In the event, however, while de Gaulle's position in 1968 was temporarily perilous, he succeeded, or perhaps his Prime Minister Pompidou succeeded, in mobilizing powerful support in France as a whole. Within the academic world itself, the 'student movement' brought about some changes in university government, but it did not overthrow 'the system'.

In the longer term, however, '1968' left a legacy of questions. Did Western Europe have a 'world-view' of its own? Did it have its own values? What kind of example, if any, did it offer to the rest of the world? It was argued (prematurely) that 'Christian democracy', which had been so influential in Germany and Italy in particular since 1945, was now exhausted. In Italy 'Christian democracy' was held together, largely if paradoxically, by the continued strength of the Communist Party. The rapid alternation of Centre-Right and Centre-Left governments which had come to seem the norm, together with the elaborate games of musical chairs played by the political élite, hardly corresponded to the hopes expressed in 1945 for a 'new beginning' in Italy.

The questions thrown up in these years came to have a special significance in 1974–5 because it was then that the Iberian peninsula was on the brink of 'rejoining' Western Europe. The Franco regime in Spain had been an embarrassment, though perhaps a necessary embarrassment, since 1945. From a military perspective, Spain was situated at a crucial communications crossroads between Africa and Europe. Spain was initially treated as a 'pariah' among states but from a Western standpoint Franco's anti-Communism was no handicap (though his offer to send troops to Korea in 1950 was not taken up). On the other hand, his regime was clearly not democratic and, whatever trimming he might make, Franco was unlikely to abandon what he considered to be the achievements of the 'National Move-ment'. Spain continued on its own path in a kind of 'arm's length' relationship with Western Europe and the United States. By the 1960s Franco's achievement was being justified as much in terms of his transforming Spain into a modern industrialized society as in upholding Christian civilization. As time passed, however, the question of the succession could not be avoided. As long ago as 1947, it had been decided that a monarchy would be restored. In 1969 it was eventually revealed that Prince Juan Carlos, grandson of King Alfonso XIII, would succeed Franco as head of state. When Franco died in 1975, no one could tell how easy the transition would be.

In Portugal, too, there was change. Dr Salazar had ruled as a virtual dictator since 1928 before handing over to his close associate Marcello Caetano in 1968. Unlike Spain, however, Portugal had been admitted to membership of NATO (from the outset). Lisbon claimed Angola and Mozambique as part of metropolitan Portugal and had resisted decolonization. How-ever, the Portuguese army found itself in increasing difficulties in fighting the liberation movements. In 1974 a military coup was staged 'to save the nation from the government'. General Spínola presided over a coalition Junta of National Salvation. Given the return of Socialist and Communist exiles, it appeared in 1975 that a coup by the extreme left was probable.

The extent to which Britain saw itself as a 'European' player remained enigmatic. Popular discourse in Britain still referred to 'the Europeans' or 'the Continent' as though the British were quite separate. And, indeed, while Britain also experienced 'student troubles' and shared the same broad pattern of social and economic development as most of the other states of Western Europe (though it was often supposed less successfully), Britain still had global linkages which were of greater importance to it than the global linkages of other Western European states (even France) were to them. Wilson, the new Prime Minister in 1964, stressed in Washington in December his attachment to a close relationship with the United States. The two countries, he declared, shared a unity of purpose and objective. Irritated though it was by Britain's refusal to give open support in Vietnam, Washington nevertheless took comfort from the fact that Britain apparently still envisaged a world role. In 1964–5, for example, there was a substantial commitment of troops and ships to support Malaysia in its 'confrontation' with Indonesia. Yet, over the next couple of years, major changes in British policy were being contemplated. There were severe balance of payments problems and accompanying pressures on the pound sterling. Defence expenditure had to be curtailed. The 1966 Defence Review explicitly stated that Britain would not undertake major operations of war except in co-operation with allies. The following year it was announced that British forces in Singapore and Malaysia would be halved in 1970–1 and be withdrawn altogether by the mid-1970s. After a further sterling crisis at the end of 1967, which resulted in the devaluation of the pound, the British Cabinet eventually agreed that commitments as well as capabilities had to be reduced. Except for Hong Kong, Britain would withdraw from 'east of Suez' by the end of 1971. The decision was taken against the wishes of the Gulf states and

Saudi Arabia (which offered financial support). Washington, too, raised the possibility of a joint sterling–dollar area if Britain were to remain, but the offer was not taken up.

Paradoxically, however, during this same period, Britain itself was undergoing significant population change. Emigrants still left its shores in substantial numbers but now Britain was receiving immigrants from its own colonial and former colonial territories. The total 'coloured' population of England and Wales in 1951 was some 75,000. A decade later, the figure had reached 336,000, preponderantly West Indians. By 1966 it had risen to nearly 600,000 or 12.6 per 1,000, with a substantial element from the Indian subcontinent. Four years earlier, the Commonwealth Immigration Act had introduced an entry system based on vouchers. The nature and scale of immigration became a major issue in British politics. Governments introduced further restrictive measures but balanced them by legislation designed to improve race relations. The size of the British immigrant population from the 'new' Commonwealth had grown beyond what would have been imagined in 1945. Its complexity was reflected in, for example, the existence of British communities of Kenyan or Ugandan Asians. Parts of Britain became conspicuously multi-ethnic, multilingual, and multiconfessional. Britain as a whole, therefore, somewhat unexpectedly, became a kind of 'world country', forced to reconsider its own identity. In the event, the 'end of Empire' led to more ethnic mixing than had occurred in the years of its existence. 'Africa', 'Asia', and 'the Caribbean' seemed to have established a permanent place in Britain.

Did this mean that Britain had finally decided to become a European power and draw a line under the global role which it had played for centuries? It was certainly in such a context that the decision was made, without enthusiasm and amidst considerable difference of opinion, to make a further application to join the European Economic Community. In the event that application too was vetoed by de Gaulle. In his opinion, Britain was still not truly European. It was therefore the case that Britain's place in the world became debilitatingly problematic: the European option was not available and the 'special relationship' with the United States could no longer bear the weight that had been placed upon it. Heath, the British Prime Minister after 1970, had the conviction, however, that it was as a central member of the European Community that Britain would henceforth play its role in the world. His 'Atlanticism' was muted and he was willing to accept, without undue concern, the disruptions in established patterns of trade between Britain and the Antipodes which membership would entail. President Pompidou of France did not maintain the old Gaullist veto. After 1973, it could be said that Britain had at last 'come home' to the European continent of which it was an insular part. Perhaps, after all, it would be geography rather than history which would count in a world which seemed increasingly to be organized on regional/ continental lines as the old transcontinental empires disappeared.

Commonwealth Crises

Even so, there might still be a role for a 'Commonwealth of Nations' which transcended the divisions of the world. It was in 1965 that the Commonwealth Secretariat was established, admittedly in London, to take over from the British government responsibility for the organization of the regular meetings of Commonwealth Heads of State. This step symbolized the extent to which the Commonwealth at least aspired to be a distinctive force in world politics. It was no longer to be considered as merely an appendage of Britain, though the British themselves did not find it easy to regard it in this light. A post of Secretary-General was created. The Secretariat also provided assistance to various bodies which continued to promote co-operation on a Commonwealth basis. Yet, during this same period, it was subjected to more acute internal tensions than it had ever previously experienced. Some of its most important member states, not surprisingly, were caught up in the tensions of their own continents. Internal preoccupations and conflicts in practice limited the scope which the Commonwealth might have to play a major role in world politics.

One major locus of friction on the part of many of its members was with Britain itself in relation to the situation in Southern Rhodesia. Its white minority had enjoyed a large measure of internal self-government for decades. In 1965, the Prime Minister, Ian Smith, made a 'unilateral declaration of independence'. Britain deplored the action but would not go beyond the imposition of sanctions against the regime. Its survival—guerrilla war began three years later—became a running sore in Commonwealth exchanges. African members accused Britain of pusillanimity and an excessive concern for 'kith and kin' at the expense of the African majority. Various proposals for an 'internal settlement' came to nothing and, a decade after UDI, Smith was still in power.

It was not only Rhodesia, however, which harmed Commonwealth cohesion. It was a decade of turmoil in Commonwealth Africa. In 1964 British troops had been called in to restore order after army mutinies in Kenya, Tanganyika, and Uganda. In 1966 there was a military coup in Nigeria and the following year its Eastern province broke away and declared itself the independent state of Biafra. A civil war followed which lasted until January 1970, when the remains of the Biafran army surrendered to federal forces. It remained very difficult, however, to devise a structure which would satisfy conflicting regional and religious aspirations. However, whilst 'Biafra' had gained some sympathy outside Nigeria, most African states were frightened that a successful secession might only lead to comparable attempts being made within their own territories. In 1966, President Nkrumah was deposed in a military and police coup in Ghana and in Uganda Milton Obote turned the country into a centralized state. Five years later, Obote was overthrown by a military coup led by General Idi Amin. In 1972 a military coup overthrew the civilian Busia government in Ghana which had been in office since 1969. Sierra Leone had also seen army coups. The significance of these events from an African perspective will be considered subsequently, but from a British perspective they were greeted with a mixture of dismay, apprehension, and cynicism. Hitherto, it had been largely supposed that while the Commonwealth was indubitably multiracial and its member states did not form a bloc in a military sense, it did nevertheless gain a coherence from common broad understandings of the nature of democracy and the rule of law. The British liked to think that this had been their lasting legacy to the Commonwealth. By 1975 it was evident that those understandings were not universal.

It was also in the decade after 1965 that the 1947 independence settlement in the Indian subcontinent was again under intense strain. In 1965, after clashes earlier in the year in Kashmir and elsewhere, serious fighting took place in September between Pakistani and Indian regular forces before a cease-fire was accepted. Relations between the Commonwealth's two senior 'non-British' members remained tense. Kashmir remained in contention. Even more fundamental, however, was the question of the viability of Pakistan, divided as it had been since independence into its two widely separated component parts. Matters came to a head in 1970–1 when the electorally successful Awami League in East Pakistan, led by Sheikh Mujibur Rahman, proclaimed an independent republic under the name Bangladesh. Arrests and fighting followed as the move was resisted. Thousands of refugees fled from East Pakistan into India. In November 1971 the President of Pakistan declared a state of emergency and shortly afterwards Pakistani planes attacked Indian airfields. Indian troops in turn invaded East Pakistan and brought about the surrender of Pakistani forces there. The struggle then ended and what had been East Pakistan became an independent state (Bangladesh) within the Commonwealth. Pakistan, on the other hand, departed in protest at the sequence of events. The entire affair exposed the limitations of the Commonwealth: it could do little effective throughout the crisis. Soon after coming into office, British Prime Minister Wilson had declared, 'our frontiers are in the Himalayas' (he was thinking of the supposed threat to India from China). A decade later it was difficult to conceive that any British Prime Minister could, or would wish to, make such a statement.

It was not even the case that all was peaceful in the 'old' Commonwealth. As far as Canada was concerned, domestic issues were to the fore, specifically concerning the status of Quebec. In 1970 the British Trade Commissioner was kidnapped for several months by Quebec separatists—who were also responsible for the death of the then Minister of Labour, Pierre Laporte. In addition, the time had come to address the significance of the changes in the country's ethnic composition. 'Displaced persons' had come to Canada in substantial numbers in the late 1940s, and in the 1950s a quarter of a million Italians arrived, together with large numbers from Germany, Scandinavia, and the Netherlands. By the mid-1960s a new immigration policy stressed attainment rather than ethnic origin. Native Indian aspirations became more evident. Political leaders therefore increasingly spoke of Canada as being a 'mosaic'. The Maple Leaf emblem was adopted as the national flag in 1964. The 'melting-pot' concept, still dominant in the United States, was not used in Canada, in part because Canada had long operated with two major languages. In 1968, Pierre Trudeau declared 'we'—his Liberal Party—did not want the people of Canada to assimilate. Cultural difference should remain, though everyone should get along in a united country. In October 1971, Canada's official policy in these matters was stated to be multiculturalism in a bicultural framework.

The same processes, though differing in detail and timing, could also be seen in Australia. The year 1966 saw the retirement of Sir Robert Menzies, who had been Prime Minister since 1949. Menzies, a Knight of the Thistle, thought of Britain as 'home', as perhaps still did a majority of Australians. After 1966, however, the pace of cultural adaptation quickened. There was a desire among the new generation to throw off the trappings of dependence: a 'counter-culture' emerged which believed itself to be the authentic expression of Australia's quintessentially democratic ethos. 'White Australia' was abandoned in 1959. Italians (some 250,000 by 1963) and other 'non-traditional' European immigrants arrived in large numbers. Slowly and contentiously, attention was paid to Aboriginal grievances, particularly over land ownership. If queen there was still to be, Elizabeth II (indubitably a 'Pom') should be 'Queen of Australia'. The advent

of a Labor government under Gough Whitlam in 1972 epitomized 'the new nationalism'—and his dismissal by the Governor-
General three years later was held by his supporters to be a sign
of the continuing strength of reactionary influences both within
and beyond the country. It was indisputable, however, that
Australia had changed significantly since 1945. It too was
'multicultural', though without a real consensus as to what the
term implied for Australia's identity and place in the world.

In short, although it was accurately stated that the Commonwealth was a unique voluntary organization of states drawn
from across the world, its member states were not immune from
the problems of the regions in which they existed. The Commonwealth as such could not prevent civil war in Nigeria or Pakistan.
It could not 'settle' disputes between India and Pakistan. Such
impotence was sometimes taken to indicate that it was pointless
and would, quite rapidly, fade into oblivion. Paradoxically,
however, perhaps it was the very fact that it stood out in a world
addicted to alliances and alignments as a conspicuous exception
which gave it a residual if marginal and precarious utility.

Soviet Communist World

In October 1964 Nikita Khrushchev was replaced as First Secretary of the Soviet Communist Party by Leonid Brezhnev and as
Prime Minister by Alexei Kosygin. Many of those colleagues on
whom he had depended for support since 1957 now found him
too erratic. His reorganization of the party and state apparatus
had proved irritating, and some believed that his conduct was
jeopardizing the 'leading role of the party'. Increasing difficulties
in Soviet agriculture were laid at his door, and it was thought
humiliating that the Soviet Union should have to import grain.
The military had their customary reaction to cuts in military
spending. All in all, it was time for Khrushchev to go. He was
to live obscurely on a pension until his death in 1971.

Khrushchev's departure provides a convenient point at which
to assess the continuing significance of the 'socialist camp' or
'Soviet Empire'. The manner of his own going, by vote, was

itself an indication that Soviet politics at the top had become somewhat less brutal. There had been some easing of contacts between the Soviet Union and the Western world and some relaxation of literary control—Solzhenitsyn's novels on Gulag life had recently been allowed to appear. Nevertheless, there could be no pretence that the country was an open society. Great store was still placed upon the party's intimate understanding of the processes of historical development. Soviet technological backwardness in certain spheres led to the establishment of 'joint ventures'—a large contract with the Italian car manufacturer Fiat in 1966, for example. Nevertheless, despite chinks that appeared, it was still correct to think of the Soviet Union as a 'world apart'. Non-Communist outsiders tended to use 'the Soviet Union' and 'Russia' synonymously and to dismiss the extent to which the country was not only a world apart but also a world within itself. To a considerable extent, and partly for political reasons, Soviet industry had indeed been planned on an 'all-Soviet' basis to avoid the emergence of balanced develop- ment in particular locations—whether in the Baltic republics or in Georgia. A sense of self-sufficiency might reawaken political aspirations for independent status. The need for political reassur- ance was also in part the explanation for a growing Russian element in the population of the non-Russian republics. Outside observers, who did not find internal travel easy, tended to the view, at this juncture, that the Soviet Union would remain intact indefinitely. Inside observers, critical of the system, seemed powerless to effect change. In 1974 Alexander Solzhenitsyn was deported from the Soviet Union.

In the wider European 'socialist camp', however, the picture was less clear. A decade after it had occurred, it looked as though the 1956 crisis in the satellite countries had been success- fully surmounted. The men who had then taken control, Gomułka in Poland and Kádár in Hungary, were still in charge. However, even in the late 1950s, Togliatti, the Italian Commun- ist leader, had spoken of the need for some diversity. The Soviet model could not be absolutely obligatory for all Communists. Khrushchev had purported to agree that there could be a multiplicity of forms of socialist development. Indeed, after 1956, the path in Poland was not precisely the same as in Hungary, though in rather different respects from what might have been anticipated. Some had thought Gomułka likely to be 'liberal', given that he had himself been imprisoned in 1949 by the Stalinists. They were to discover that Gomułka's commitment to Communism remained firm and Poland pressed on with industrialization (and a shift to the towns), with the consequence that food shortages appeared. In the 1960s intellectuals continued to complain of the restrictions on their freedom. And, since Poland was overwhelmingly a Catholic country, the church was to hand to constitute a kind of alternative authority. Efforts by the regime to restrict the church's influence had the opposite effect. In 1970 rioting and demonstrations over food prices and economic conditions led to Gomułka's replacement by Gierek, but the underlying problems remained. Even so, from the perspective of Moscow, Poland was not entirely reliable. And, by the early 1970s, with the conclusion of treaties with Bonn, Polish fears of German territorial claims, which made the Soviet Union a necessary ally, had to some extent moderated.

In Hungary, the elevation of Kádár promised a return to rigid Stalinism and the elimination of 'counter-revolutionary forces'. Nagy, whose day of glory had been so brief, was executed, having been tricked out of the Yugoslav Embassy where he was sheltering. Probably some 2,000 Hungarians were shot and ten times that number imprisoned. Kádár pressed ahead rapidly with the collectivization of agriculture, which had not been pushed strongly between 1945 and 1956. By 1960, however, once it believed it had stamped its authority on the country with sufficient vigour, the government began to relax controls on literary and intellectual life. Political prisoners were released and a broad amnesty declared. By the early 1970s more foreign books could be found in the bookshops of Budapest than in any other country in Eastern Europe. Though the party remained firmly in control, it looked as though, twenty years on, Hungary had gained something from the 1956 revolution.

It was from Czechoslovakia that trouble came. The battles

inside its Communist Party in the early 1950s had largely
eliminated more 'liberal' elements. 'De-Stalinization' had largely
passed the party by. Centralized structures oversaw further
industrialization. There was no place for dissent in a country
which had arguably had a more successful pluralist democracy
in the first twenty years of its history between the wars than any
other in Eastern Europe. It was in 1968 that discontent came to
a head and Alexander Dubček replaced Novotný as First Secretary. That Dubček was a Slovak, not a Czech, was significant. It
was claimed in Slovakia that development had been tilted in
favour of the Czech lands. Dubček would put that right—
amongst many other things. This was the 'Prague Spring'. Open
and democratic procedures would come into the organization of
the Communist Party itself and restrictions on freedom of
movement and expression would be lifted. By August, it became
clear that the Soviet Union would not accept Dubček's assurance
that the party remained firmly in control and would not leave
the 'Socialist camp'. Soviet troops and forces from other Warsaw
Pact countries invaded in order to restore the status quo ante.
The Prague Spring, from Moscow's point of view, should never
have happened. Czechoslovakia's Communist neighbours saw
their own positions being threatened if 'the West' obtained a
bridgehead into Central Europe. Dubček was replaced by Husák,
and Soviet troops remained in the country to ensure 'normality',
as indeed appeared outwardly to be the case. In Eastern Europe,
but perhaps only there, the 'Soviet Communist World' seemed
intact. The position in Asia was rather more complicated.

Asian Roads

Before 1965, the Chinese Communist leadership presented an
appearance of unity. Mao's personal standing was weakened by
the failure of the Great Leap Forward, but he remained head of
the party, though he had relinquished his office of state chairman
in 1959. It was in the mid-1960s that this façade of unity was
shattered when Mao felt strong enough to launch the Proletarian
Cultural Revolution, though he did so in confused circum-

stances. A decade of upheaval followed. In the background was disagreement in the hierarchy on how to respond to the war in Vietnam and faction fighting between 'moderates' and 'radicals'. Mao himself felt confident that China could bypass the Soviet Union on the way to Communism. He detected a hardening of bureaucratic arteries, a loss of egalitarian enthusiasm, and a willingness, in practice, to see China take the 'capitalist road'. It was time to fight against these tendencies; selfishness could be rooted out. There was wisdom in the common people, who could, it seemed, carry out any task. In the struggle which he unleashed Mao was determined that true revolution would succeed. Scores of officials were arrested, including Liu Shaoqi, President of the Republic since 1959 and supposedly Mao's heir apparent. Schools were closed and students urged to form units of Red Guards. Teenage gangs smashed monuments and invaded private homes, guided by the thoughts of Chairman Mao collected in the 'Little Red Book'. Millions of young people for a time roamed across China and even caught a glimpse of Chairman Mao in person when they attended mass rallies in Beijing. It was evident, however, that the Chairman felt that there was nothing sacrosanct about the Communist Party as it then existed. During these years the transport system was disrupted and there were strikes in major industrial centres. Full civil war seemed not far away. Different groups of 'rebels' fought against each other even while they were supposedly struggling together against the rightist enemy.

The outside world—both Communist and capitalist—looked on with both amazement and anxiety at the turmoil that was taking place. The country seemed on the brink of forfeiting all the economic gains that had been made over the previous decade. It seemed that China was indeed a world of its own as both the country's own 'feudal' cultural heritage and 'Western' art, music, and literature were denounced. Higher education virtually ceased. Students were sent into the fields and peasants were dragooned into classes; 'half-study, half-work' was apparently the objective for all. Internationally, it appeared that China was withdrawing from 'the world'. The British Embassy in

Beijing was sacked in 1967 and many foreign countries called their ambassadors home.

The fact that China seemed to be turning in on itself only pointed up the contrast with Japan during the same period. There were indeed some demonstrations and riots in 1967–8 in Japanese cities against American policy in Vietnam. The Tokyo University campus was 'occupied' by students. However, the 'Western' orientation of Japan's political élite was not in serious doubt and popular sentiment was assuaged by the return to Japanese sovereignty (1972) of the Ryukyu and other islands which had been used by the Americans during both the Korean and Vietnamese wars.

The Japanese economy continued to grow at an impressive rate until the mid-1970s. Japan seemed to be turning itself into an even more 'advanced' and 'consumer' society, replete with 'white goods', outpacing European countries which had formerly thought of themselves as 'advanced'. In the early 1970s, some 90 per cent of Japanese families possessed refrigerators, washing machines, and television sets. Japan conspicuously succeeded, both in 'old' industries—becoming the world's largest shipbuilders, for example—and in 'new' industries—optics, electronics, and computer technology. The way in which Japan combined governmental 'guidance' with private enterprise was envied across the world. The extent of Japan's success could be seen in its commercial relations with the United States—by 1976 the balance of trade yielded an annual surplus in Japan's favour of $5 billion.

Yet, beneath this 'Western' Japan, there still lurked ambiguity. The exterior marks of a constitutional democracy were clearly in place but political practice still reflected deep-seated cultural notions of consensus and personal loyalty. An aura of scandal and corruption became attached to an entrenched élite. In 1974 Prime Minister Tanaka was forced to resign and subsequently given a prison sentence for accepting a large bribe from the American aircraft firm Lockheed in return for orders. And how far, if at all, Japan should aspire to a world role commensurate with its economic success remained problematic. In one sense, there was scarcely any other country whose prosperity was more bound up with 'the world'. Japan was already the world's largest importer of oil (mainly from the Gulf), and imported about half of its food and a vast array of raw materials for industrial and other use. Japan needed a stable world to which to export, and it was the United States which still made that world possible. It seemed a safe assumption—at least until 1971, as will shortly be seen. In Asia itself, it remained difficult for Japan to strike the right pose. Arguably, Japanese society as a whole had still not come to terms with the war of 1937–45—above all in relation to China. The initial Japanese presidency of the Asia Development Bank (1966) evoked uncomfortable echoes in the independent countries of South-East Asia. Were the Japanese 'Yellow Yankees'?

In 1972 President Nixon visited Beijing. The path had been opened by a secret visit by Kissinger, who had talks with Zhou Enlai. The ensuing wish to 'normalize' relations was a reflection of the difficulties which both countries had been experiencing. The Cultural Revolution put paid to the 'indestructible friendship' with the Soviet Union enshrined in China's 1954 constitution. In 1969 it was reported that clashes occurred between Soviet forces in Xinjiang, in the far west, and also in the northeast. Mao bitterly criticized 'peaceful coexistence' and accused Moscow of succumbing to revisionism. By the early 1970s, the vehemence of the Cultural Revolution was spent. There was clearly a crisis in 1971 which led to the death (perhaps after a failed coup) of Lin Biao, the Defence Minister. The Communist Party apparatus was steadily restored. Trade with capitalist countries expanded, as did diplomatic contacts. Later, in 1973, Deng Xiaoping was rehabilitated and advanced steadily to a pivotal position as both Mao's and Zhou's health deteriorated. Such developments formed the context of the Nixon visit.

It strengthened Washington's hand in dealing with Moscow to seek 'normalization' with China. Nixon's anti-Communism had not weakened but the fissure in the 'Communist world' was very evident. It was time, with Kissinger at his elbow, to come to terms with an acceleratingly 'multi-polar' world. Even during the 'chaos' of the Cultural Revolution it was clear that vital projects had been successfully sealed off from interference. China produced a hydrogen bomb in June 1967. So there were now, perhaps, five significant groupings in the international system— the United States, the Soviet Union, Western Europe, China, and Japan. Their mutual relations were moving beyond 'Communist worlds' and 'non-Communist worlds', though ideology was not yet dead.

Two other significant factors specifically concerning China were also at work. It was evident that Britain and France were releasing themselves from the embargoes on 'sensitive' exports. The lure of a growing Chinese market, in the interests of American exports, could not, therefore, be neglected indefinitely. Secondly, it had become apparent that the People's Republic could not be kept out of the United Nations. The annual resolution before the General Assembly that Beijing should replace Taipei had been gaining support—victory had been in sight in 1965 but then the Cultural Revolution had supervened. In 1971, however, the General Assembly decided that Beijing and not Taipei was 'China', voting to expel the representatives of the latter government by 76 to 35. The Guomindang regime in Taiwan felt itself under threat, a threat reinforced by Nixon's desire for 'normalization' with Beijing. Taiwan had achieved an 'economic miracle' comparable (on a smaller scale) to that of Japan. It sought, and received, some assurances from Washington, but could no longer entirely rely on the formulas that had been used since 1949.

Neither could the Japanese. Tokyo had been surprised and angered by Nixon's announcement in the summer of 1971 of his intention to visit China. However, in 1972, Prime Minister Tanaka visited Beijing and made some apology for previous Japanese actions during the Sino-Japanese war. Full diplomatic relations were established, though it would be an exaggeration to say that the promised 'peace and friendship' immediately ensued. Nor did it between Beijing and Washington. 'Normalization' was never likely to be an instant reality. Nevertheless, the apparently converging roads in Asia were part of the same pattern which produced the Helsinki Agreement in Europe.

These developments in East Asia placed India in a somewhat embarrassed position because, to a large extent, 'non-alignment' was proving a frail reed. The disputes and wars with Pakistan have already been noted and they naturally formed a preoccupation in New Delhi. Nehru, who had been Prime Minister since independence, died in 1964. Succession proved difficult over the next couple of years. In 1966 Nehru's daughter, Indira Gandhi, became Prime Minister and moved India closer to the Soviet Union (as Pakistan maintained connections both with the United States and China). Internally, Indian identity and institutions were both in doubt. The attempt to make Hindi the official language of the country by 1965 failed amidst rioting. English was to remain as an 'associate official language' (though only a small minority used it fluently) so long as non-Hindi-speaking Indians wished. Given these circumstances, it was not difficult to find outside commentators who expressed the view that India would fall apart, for either linguistic or religious reasons. In addition, the Congress which had dominated Indian post-independence politics seemed to be breaking up. Many state governments fell to other groupings and nationally there was a clear fissure between 'old Congress' and 'new Congress' (Mrs Gandhi's wing). In 1971, however, she took her party to a sweeping electoral victory. Thereafter, perhaps boding ill for the future, her rule showed signs of becoming increasingly arbitrary.

Oil, the Middle East, and the World

In 1973 dramatic events took place in the 'Middle East' which emphasized both the region's traditional geopolitical significance and its accelerating importance as the provider of a vital world energy resource—oil. In October, on the day of Yom Kippur, a Jewish religious holiday, Egyptian forces crossed the Suez Canal and overwhelmed Israeli defences in a surprise attack. Syrian forces also attacked in the Golan Heights. However, the tables were soon turned when Israeli forces crossed the Suez Canal themselves and encircled the Egyptian Third Army. A cease-fire followed. In itself this short war simply fitted into the pattern of such encounters between Israel and various Arab neighbours. There had been a 'Six Day' War in June 1967 when Israeli forces struck at Egypt, Jordan, and Syria. Israel had been left in occupation of Jerusalem, the West Bank of the Jordan, and the Golan Heights. The further war of 1973 in the end confirmed Israel's military superiority—the reality which had thus far enabled the state to survive and expand over the quarter-century of its existence. Even so, victory had been achieved at a heavy cost and restored some confidence to Israel's opponents.

The Palestine Liberation Organization (PLO) had been founded by Yasser Arafat in 1964 but it made little progress. Its headquarters moved to Beirut from Jordan in 1970 (King Hussein acted because its presence jeopardized his own authority). The reality was that Israel confronted an 'Arab world' which had little effective substance (though Arab states did agree to fight Israel) and was itself in turmoil. In 1968 Hassan al Bakr seized power in Iraq, the third man to take over in a coup after the overthrow of the Iraqi monarchy in 1958. In 1969 Qaddafi overthrew King Idris in Libya and Nimeiri took over in the Sudan. The monarchies of Jordan and Saudi Arabia appeared to be in danger. In these circumstances, 'Arab unity' could be little more than a phrase. In 1970 Nasser of Egypt died, to be succeeded by Anwar Sadat, a more pragmatic figure, though he deemed it necessary in 1971 to sign a fifteen-year treaty of friendship with the Soviet Union. The following year, however, he dramatically ordered virtually all Soviet advisers out of Egypt. June 1975 saw the reopening of the Suez Canal, which had been closed since the 1967 war. There was little sign of political stability throughout the region, though Sadat edged towards an accommodation with Israel. British withdrawal from the Gulf brought an additional element of uncertainty. The internal instability of the Middle East, made worse by the extent to which the major powers had their own clients, might have been thought to be a regional rather than a global phenomenon.

It was, however, oil which caused the world's spotlight to play on its problems. At this stage, some two-thirds of the then known oil reserves in the world were to be found in the Middle East.

The Organization of Petroleum Exporting Countries (OPEC) was founded in 1960. Pressure began to build upon the major oil companies during years of rapid expansion in the industry as new fields were discovered and exploited. It was only in 1961, for example, that production started in Libya, but by 1969 the country supplied one-quarter of the needs of Western Europe. A struggle ensued between companies and governments which tilted in favour of governments. In Iran, in this decade, oil revenues supported what the Shah described as a 'White Revolution' to transform the living standards of his subjects. That project evidently required vast expenditures on military equipment and a pervasive secret police force, SAVAK! Whatever the impact on living standards, the Shah's policy made his country the strongest military power in the Gulf. In Libya, in 1973 Qaddafi successfully took control of foreign-held oil interests. In state after state, oil companies became more concerned to ensure security of a supply rather than to retain ownership. The United States had long since ceased to be self-sufficient in oil and by the early 1970s was importing a third of its petroleum requirements. In 1973 leading producer countries, with Saudi Arabia in the van, threatened to cut back production and to impose an embargo on certain countries, including the United States. The objective was to compel Washington to reduce its support for Israel—the context was of course the 1973 Yom Kippur War which has just been referred to. As a diplomatic weapon, the embargo was not very successful and was lifted after some months, but a clear signal had been given that oil supply could not be taken for granted. Something of a rift opened up between Washington, which wanted to brazen matters out, and European countries. France in particular sought a 'European–Arab' dialogue. The lasting fact was that oil prices had nearly quadrupled, with consequences to be considered at the end of this chapter. Saudi Arabia, with its huge reserves and small population, was virtually in a position to determine the world's oil price. A new era was dawning in which the meetings of OPEC seemed to hold the key to the economic performance of countries far removed from the Middle East. And indeed, wherever oil was found and exploited in other parts of the world—as in Nigeria, for example—it transformed the political/economic prospects of the country concerned.

United Nations?

The decade had been a bad one for the United Nations. U Thant of Burma was re-elected as Secretary-General in December 1966 but the limitations of his authority were soon exposed. In circumstances which still remain controversial, he appeared to some to acquiesce too readily in 1967 in the withdrawal of the UN forces stationed on Egyptian territory—though it was clear that they could only be stationed there with Egyptian consent. The UN force sent to the Middle East in 1973 did not 'stop' the fighting, though it was of some utility. In 1974, when Waldheim of Austria was Secretary-General, the UN forces in Cyprus were of no consequence when Turkish forces invaded the north of the island. Both of these 'failures' seemed to show that when it came to an actual crisis the much-vaunted 'peacekeeping role' evaporated. More generally, too, there was an increasing gap between the resolutions passed by the General Assembly—now with an Afro-Asian majority—and the capacity of the organization to take action upon them. South Africa and Israel were particularly targeted. In 1971 the General Assembly voted by 79 to 7 with 36 abstentions to require Israel to withdraw from Arab territory which it had acquired by force; Israel declined to do so. In 1974 the credentials of South Africa were not accepted. Such steps, however, were declarations rather than operations.

Questions continued to be asked about the real import of nuclear weapons—now the proud possession of the leading powers and, indeed, perhaps *the* criterion in assessing the balance of power in the world. Academic strategic thinkers and marching anti-nuclear campaigners wrestled in their different ways with a world which grew ever more capable of destroying itself. American strategic doctrine oscillated during the decade between the threat of 'assured destruction' and the promulgation of 'limited strategic options'. Wars, civil or otherwise, and rumours of wars existed—Namibia, Chad, the Philippines, South Yemen, Burundi, Cyprus, Western Sahara can be added to those already discussed—but they had not led to world war. Proponents of nuclear deterrence believed that it had prevented world war, while their opponents held their breath and were sceptical. It could only be a matter of time, some of them thought, before some disastrous 'mistake' occurred. In any event, strategic weaponry was an expensive business. The Soviet Union 'caught up' with the United States in its possession of intercontinental ballistic missiles, submarine-launched ballistic missiles, and long-range bombers between 1963 and 1976, but was there really purpose in continuing competition? Strategic Arms Limitation Talks (SALT) opened in Vienna in 1970 and edged forward over subsequent years. A US–Soviet Threshold Test Ban Treaty was signed in 1975, limiting underground tests. Even as that agreement was concluded, however, India exploded its first atomic device. Even the superpowers, it seemed, could not 'manage' the nuclear world between them.

Population and Resources

There were other anxieties. There had been centuries in the world's history when population had been a fundamental criterion of power, but this was no longer the case. A large population, on the contrary, might indicate national debility. In 1975 the population of the world was estimated at some 4,000 million. Growth had averaged around 2 per cent per annum over the previous decade, and it was not evenly distributed across the globe. The population of China was approaching 950 million in 1975, having grown from 700 million during the decade—though these estimated figures should be treated with caution. India reached some 548 million in 1971. By comparison with Indonesia, Nigeria, or Egypt, for example, the population growth of

European states was considerably slower. If population is taken to be a yardstick, the focus of world development was shifting quite dramatically towards Asia and was little altered by the modest concurrent migration, from the Indian subcontinent in particular, elsewhere. The proportion of the world's population living in towns and cities was constantly growing—around a third in the late 1960s. It was not infrequently concluded that the world could not sustain this demographic explosion without disaster. In China especially, government took draconian steps to try to stem population growth. Birth control measures of one kind or another were encouraged elsewhere. 'Birth control' aroused strong emotions, not only because the Roman Catholic Church mobilized against it, but also because it smacked, in some quarters, of hypocrisy on the part of a 'West' which talked about sustainability but which ravaged the world's resources to satisfy the desires of its affluent if modestly reproductive populations. Meanwhile, efforts were made in developing new plant strains and in increasing agricultural efficiency to keep pace, more or less, with expanding populations.

Argument moved a stage further—to ponder the fate not of human beings in the world but of the world itself. Alliances and alignments, defence treaties and trade pacts were all very well but they would avail little in a world which humans destroyed. In Britain, oil spillage from the tanker *Torrey Canyon* brought home the effects of pollution on the marine environment. A catalogue of analogous disasters began to be reported from across the world. These issues began to be addressed through conferences under the auspices of the United Nations. The 1971 Sea-Bed Treaty, for example, prohibited the emplacement of nuclear weapons on the sea-bed. In the following year, a major UN conference on the Human Environment was held in Stockholm. A world population conference was held in Romania in 1974 and a World Food Conference in Rome in the same year. Campaigning organizations like Friends of the Earth (1971) and Greenpeace (1975) sprang up in Britain, with their counterparts elsewhere. Pollution in the air or at sea did not observe the niceties of national frontiers and boundaries. If the world was to be saved from some cataclysmic catastrophe, environmental writers argued, human beings would have to elevate themselves above their individual or national interests and truly begin to think globally. It was not clear that they intended to do so.

Coming Crisis

A degree of detente between the world's major powers therefore coincided with an economic shock whose consequences were to be experienced in the developed and underdeveloped world alike from 1973 onwards. As has been noted above, it seemed that the era of cheap energy was over. Its availability had underpinned the 'revolution of rising expectations' which had been so prominent an aspect of life in developed countries over the previous decades. In September 1973, after several years of crisis, the United States and European central bank governors ended the Bretton Woods gold agreement of 1944. That agreement had endeavoured to stabilize price levels and avoid competitive devaluations by maintaining a fixed-rate exchange system based on gold. In future the US dollar and European currencies would float against each other as the market dictated. It looked as though the world was dividing into three competing trading blocs based on the Japanese yen, the German mark, and the US dollar. In January 1974 President Nixon, arguing that the energy situation threatened 'to unleash political and economic forces that could cause severe and irreparable damage to the prosperity and stability of the world', tried without great success to orchestrate a response from the 'consuming' countries to the 'producing' countries. In an atmosphere of some panic, states put their own individual interests first. The economies of the member states of the Community began to diverge acutely. Output plummeted. The British government introduced a three-day week. Country after country, to greater or lesser degree, struggled with the problems of meeting external deficits. It is for these reasons that these years, 1973/4, are sometimes referred to as the last of the 'Golden Age': the time when the long post-war boom came to an end. The further working out of these developments will be considered in the next chapter.

The oil price rise, however, was only the most dramatic illustration of world crisis. Famine in the Horn of Africa led to perhaps half a million deaths in the early 1970s. The events of 1968, even though their short-term impact was modest, were seen by some observers as being of world-historical importance. In the Western world, the changing power relations between status groups placed on the political agenda in that year have been described as 'integral to a world in crisis'. It is from 1968, too, that writers in the social sciences, influenced by that agenda, have detected the end of an optimistic certainty which had hitherto prevailed within, for example, the study of human geography. It is problematic, therefore, whether a decade that ends with the apparent confidence of the Helsinki Agreements is a convincing climax. A case could be made with as much plausibility for regarding 1968 or 1973, viewed from different angles, as decisive turning points. Perhaps, however, no single transitional date can possess overwhelming significance in all parts of the world and in all aspects of its affairs.

5

Turbulent Transition
1975–1985

(Short?) Sharp Shock

The years 1973–5, as has just been noted, led many observers to conclude that the world economy was on the brink of fundamental and perhaps frightening change. In addition to the shocks induced by the oil price rise, there was talk of a 'third industrial revolution' resulting from the application of electronic technologies and the 'automation' of industrial processes through the use of robots. The structures and processes which had underpinned the immediate post-war decades were looking obsolescent in the computer age that was dawning. Apple II, launched in 1977, can be described as the first mass-produced personal computer, and in the years that followed improvements in capacity and function multiplied. Everything, and not merely the new French high-speed train (1981), seemed to be moving *à grande vitesse*. Scientific and technological breakthroughs could not be confined, in their applications, to one region of the world. People listened to music everywhere with their 'Walkman'—launched by the Japanese company Sony in 1980. The telephone operator and the bank clerk—to name only two 'safe' occupations—suddenly had bleak employment prospects. Newspapers, on both sides of the Atlantic, trying to inform their readers about such matters, were themselves caught up in industrial disputes as technology transformed production.

European countries, in particular, faced difficulties since it was the United States, and to some extent Japan, which clearly led the way in pioneering major innovations. These changes, still only imperfectly grasped, perhaps raised the possibility of societies in which many long-established jobs and functions simply disappeared. No doubt, as some writers argued at the time, the information revolution would bring great benefit, but in the short term there appeared to be trouble ahead. Heavy industries, with large locally recruited labour forces, copied throughout the world as the engines of economic growth and virility, began to prove an embarrassment in Europe. British coal miners, for example, fought hard against the decline of their industry, ultimately to no avail. French steelworkers in Lorraine struggled similarly. Innovation made middle-aged unskilled men 'redundant' in the widest sense of the term. The future perhaps lay with nimble women and the educable young. The question was whether the latest 'new industry' could generate jobs fast enough to replace those being lost through technological innovation. Pessimists supposed that it could not and that in country after country there would be millions for whom unemployment would be the norm. They would be the casualties of 'progress'. Optimists argued that in every age technical innovation had always produced such fears but that, taken in the round, fears had been exaggerated. Something had always turned up. It would do so again.

Great economists argued on a rather different plane. Some identified 'long cycles' which underlay short-term fluctuations in the economy. 'Take-off' into sustained growth now looked more difficult than it had in the 1960s, but sooner or later there would be a new dynamic upswing. Marxist writers were not impressed. Capitalism was again in crisis. The whole world needed a new system. Perhaps the 'Communisms' in existence were not perfect, but they still pointed the way to the future. From another perspective, however, came a very different message. Neo-liberal economists argued that it was time to return to the free market. The ideal of a 'mixed managed economy' which, to greater or lesser degree, had held sway in the 'advanced' world since 1945 had run its course—into 'stagflation'. 'Monetarist' theories, advanced by Milton Friedman and others, now offered fresh answers in a context where confidence that states could 'manage' economies was crumbling. It was not difficult, in the debates that followed, to discern the extent to which economic doctrine—on all sides—nicely matched political preferences. 'Collectivists' looked for solidarity even if it proved stultifying. 'Free marketeers' looked for enterprise even if it proved divisive.

Commentators sometimes supposed that, at least in the economic sphere, the power of the nation-state was eroding: governments were at the mercy of markets. 'Multinationals' switched their investments across the globe with scant regard for the consequences in any particular national economy. Such indifference was either applauded—'breaking free from the shackles of the nation-state'—or attacked as 'callous exploitation'. Multinational corporations could turn underdeveloped countries into branch-plant countries. What had been for decades an American proclivity (and sometimes fiercely criticized in Europe) was now being adopted by companies and corporations drawn from other industrialized countries. Volkswagen, for example, the German car manufacturer, 'globalized' itself from Brazil to Egypt to Nigeria—to mention only three of its many world locations. The welfare of the corporation, taken as a worldwide whole, might be more important than the interests of its 'home' community or government. Traditional monetary and fiscal instruments of government diminished in effectiveness in open economies. Sometimes observers speculated that before long there would be 'world cars' built in 'world factories', but that proved rather more difficult in reality. The Ford Escort, for example, was successful in Western Europe but not in the United States. Whatever view was taken, the world was certainly populated by more transnational 'actors' than had ever been the case in the past. It was perhaps increasingly a world which could not in fact be 'controlled' by any individual or government.

The same ambiguity existed in the 'media-world'. On the one hand, as television provision exploded across the globe, viewers 'saw' the world in all its diversity with apparently accelerating intimacy. There were reputedly 150 million television sets in the United States in 1979. South Korea, to take another example, soared to virtual television saturation from a very low base in little more than a dozen years. By 1981 there were regular television transmissions in 137 countries. Yet, not unexpectedly, 'the world' as presented in China or Brazil, Australia or Nigeria was not 'the same'. 'News' continued to reflect local perspectives and to be a powerful means of shaping national identities. Chief Awolowo of Nigeria, for example, campaigned for the establishment of a television station in tropical Africa 'to transform Nigeria into a modern and prosperous nation'. In some parts of the world, television and radio stations were more carefully guarded by armoured vehicles than border posts.

In these circumstances, therefore, 'the world' became both easier and more difficult to grasp. The British–French supersonic airliner Concorde began its regular passenger service across the Atlantic in 1976. Almost daily, cultural contours and expectations were undermined as 'world' events took place in unexpected places—as when a Japanese became the first woman to climb Mount Everest, the world chess and world heavyweight boxing championships took place in the Philippines, and Arthur Ashe became the first black American to win the men's singles tennis tournament at Wimbledon—all in 1975. Yet, alongside these sporting triumphs, there still remained the reality of segmented universes, not least between Western and Eastern Europe. Tourism continued to accelerate—but not all destinations were open. 'The West' remained inaccessible to the great majority of Soviet citizens—some 695,000 Soviet citizens visited Western countries in 1985 compared to 589,000 a decade earlier, and such citizens had to gain party approval before being granted exit visas.

To an extent, too, it began to seem that the geographical markers of identity which had for so long done duty in the world's history were losing some of their force. So much of the post-1945 world history covered thus far had been described in terms of 'East–West relations', but the limitations of such a world-picture became increasingly evident. It was thought more important to focus on 'North–South' rather than 'East–West' relationships. It was a tendency which produced *North–South: A Programme for Survival* (1980) by a group under Willy Brandt, the former West German Chancellor. It was the northern hemisphere which was industrialized and rich, and the southern hemisphere which was 'developing' but poor. The extent to which the North prospered precisely because it exploited the South was contentious. The Brandt Report had some public impact in 'the North', though its direct consequences disappointed its authors. The polarization of 'North/South' oversimplified conditions within 'the North' and 'the South'. Nevertheless, the very prominence given to such a categorization of the world was further evidence of its complex alignments. Such underlying ambiguities need to be remembered as we assess global developments over the next decade.

Economic growth, when it resumed, was manifestly not at the rate achieved in the previous decade. Contemporaries, however, could not quite believe that there was a fundamental crisis and reasonably supposed that the world economy would 'pick up' again. In 1978, in Bonn, the first meeting was held of the 'Group of Seven' (G7) largest capitalist economic powers in the world, with the objective of providing a forum for the regular exchange of information and ideas on trends in the world economy. Its membership consisted of the USA, Canada, Japan, West Germany, France, Italy, and Britain. These meetings took place regularly thereafter and formed a part of the global economic policy-making landscape—though without dramatically tangible benefits. In 1985 these countries, with the exception of Canada and Italy (G5), reached an accord designed to stabilize exchange rates—but such agreements, as events were to prove, reckoned without the power of currency speculators to upset governmental intentions. The decade after 1975, in short, was marked by more disorientating turbulence than its predecessor, though contemporaries hoped that such turbulence would be transitional. A more stable order would return.

The United States: World Leader?

Gerald Ford, the unelected President of the United States after Nixon's resignation, had a disconcerting tendency to stumble in public. His haplessness in this respect perhaps stood as a metaphor for his country. Quite suddenly, the 'American Century' had a tired feel about it. It was the United States itself which had fatally undermined the Bretton Woods system when Nixon suspended the dollar's convertibility into gold in August 1971. His action was prompted by a run on US gold reserves. The extent of United States dependence on overseas oil and raw materials could not be disguised. In its rise to globalism the United States had acquired commitments which now seemed difficult to honour if they should all simultaneously be called upon—admittedly an unlikely contingency. In such circumstances, the Ford Presidency lacked distinction, but it was also becoming the conventional wisdom that no one could make a success of the Presidency. The job was impossible.

In 1976 Ford was narrowly defeated by the Democrat Jimmy Carter, a man unblemished by exposure to world politics. Just at the point when a rather sour withdrawal from world affairs might have been anticipated, Carter struck a new note. It was not so much 'the arrogance of power' which now suffused the White House as 'the arrogance of morality'. The new President declared that the United States could never be indifferent to the fate of freedom elsewhere: 'our commitment to human rights must be absolute'. The 1975 Helsinki Agreements, as has been noted in the previous chapter, embodied commitments by the signatories to respect and protect the human rights of their own citizens. Such declarations could be regarded as a late, if overdue, flowering of the universal declaration embodied in the foundation of the United Nations. Carter's declarations on these matters, which stood in contrast to the Realpolitik of Kissinger, were deeply felt though insufficiently considered. The belief in certain inalienable rights had deep roots in American political thought, but its application in the world of the late 1970s was problematic.

Thirty years on from the 1945 declaration (Carter declared that 'human rights' were 'the soul of our foreign policy') it was not self-evident how they should be defined. In some quarters, indeed, what was deemed 'universal' in 1945 now seemed merely an expression of a 'Western' liberalism which happened then to be in apparently unchallengeable ascendancy. Quite apart from the question of whether the states concerned had practised what they preached, and whether internally the United States respected the rights of all its citizens, there were those in the 'non-Western' world who questioned the supposed 'universality' declared in 1945. Philosophical and indeed theological scrutiny could conclude that a single-minded emphasis on 'human rights' was inadequate and partial. Why should one conclude that the uneasy fusion of secular liberalism and Judaeo-Christian teaching to be found in 'human rights' doctrine was universally valid? Paradoxically, therefore, Carter began his crusade for 'human rights' just at the point when it could appear to be another Western bid for hegemony, if one of the mind and spirit.

Internally, however, there were advantages in the new emphasis. It could bring together groups in American society who were often at loggerheads, namely the 'Cold Warriors' whose minds were fixed on the Soviet Union and 'liberals' who worried about South Africa and Chile. A Bureau on Human Rights in the State Department signalled the centrality of the theme for the administration. It was believed that a kind of 'human rights index' could be compiled which would determine the suitability of certain countries to be recipients of American economic, military, or other aid. Countries would no longer be able simply to claim that abuses were contrary to policy and the result of individual actions. Despite this fresh emphasis, it was scarcely conceivable that 'human rights' could simply replace 'national security' as the fundamental underpinning of US foreign policy. Carter prohibited the export of police and military equipment to South Africa, but elsewhere, as policies unfolded, the complications became apparent. The basic difficulty was that Washington's line could only be effective against governments over which it possessed already certain means of leverage—but such governments were allies of a kind. What if regimes were destabilized and replaced not by glowingly liberal structures but by something that was 'worse'? The situation in Latin America was a case in point, and Carter felt it more acutely than his predecessors.

The continued existence of the Castro regime in Cuba was a

reminder (regularly issued by clamorous Cuban exiles in Florida) that Communism remained a threat—of a kind. Castro had continued to bolster 'non-alignment' internationally and to argue that the Soviet Union was the natural friend of non-alignment. However, during the first two years of the Carter administration, some small steps had been taken on both sides to effect an accommodation, though they did not lead to substantial change—US diplomats, for example, took up residence in Cuba for the first time in sixteen years. Washington continued to demand that Cuban troops should leave Africa, while Havana countered by pointing out that there were American troops stationed outside the United States. However, in 1979, the Soviet invasion of Afghanistan (to be discussed shortly) destroyed the detente which had existed, under successive Presidents, for some fifteen years. Castro supported the Soviet-backed Kabul regime as revolutionary—a stance which not only lost him a great deal of non-aligned support, but reinforced Washington's perception of Cuba as an obedient Soviet client.

The problem for the United States, however, in Latin America as a whole, was that in country after country pluralist systems had collapsed. 'Bureaucratic-authoritarian' regimes with a strong military presence entrenched and justified themselves by pointing to the need to defeat various guerrilla insurgencies. The catalogue of such regimes was extensive—Argentina, Brazil, Chile, Uruguay, Bolivia, El Salvador, Guatemala, Haiti, Nicaragua, Paraguay. In Argentina, Isabel Perón was deposed in 1976 by an army coup. The military junta presided over by Generals Videla and then Viola for the next five years led the Carter administration to impose an aid ban because of its human rights violations. Inflation soared. In Brazil, after President Figueiredo took office in March 1979, there was the tantalizing prospect, apparently, of 'a democracy without qualifications', but one could never be sure. In Chile, on the other hand, the Pinochet regime remained firmly in control and held out no immediate prospect of presidential elections.

In the Carter era, Nicaragua was the country where, as one Assistant Secretary in the State Department put it, there would be 'a sharp break from the past'. In mid-1979, the dictator Samoza fled the country alleging that his enemies wanted to make Nicaragua Communist. Arguably, however, it was the withdrawal of support by the Carter administration which was the major factor in his overthrow. The Sandinista regime which succeeded Samoza was not as brutal as its predecessor, but still stopped short of real tolerance. In country after country in the region—it was El Salvador which next attracted most world interest—there was social and economic dislocation and loss of life. Supporters of the Carter strategy saw the United States entering a new era in its relations with its southern neighbours. In 1977, in another gesture, the President signed the Panama Canal Zone Treaty committing the United States to evacuate the zone by the year 2000. Opponents of the new course sought to puncture the pervasive progressivist rhetoric and argued that the policy only served to inaugurate regimes of the left which were as indifferent to human rights as were their predecessors.

There was no lack of comparable paradoxes much further afield. One conspicuous example was the case of Iran. Under Nixon, the Shah had been identified as the regional power whose military and naval forces would keep the Gulf free from Communism and ensure American access to oil. His forces were armed on a vast scale—helping to solve the American balance of payments problem. Carter himself visited Iran in 1977, paid tribute to the 'great leadership' of the Shah, and praised the country for being 'an island of stability in one of the more troubled areas of the world'. For a time, as Iran industrialized and 'modernized' at a rapid rate, the Shah was held to be presiding over a 'success'. However, the excesses of his secret police force SAVAK could not be squared with 'human rights'. As internal opposition grew, spearheaded by Shiite Muslim hostility to the Shah's secular policies and 'Westernization', the ethos of the US administration prevented any attempt to save him. The Human Rights Bureau contributed actively to undermining him.

In January 1979 street demonstrations forced the Shah into exile and power shifted to the Islamic movement led by the

Ayatollah Khomeini. Ruthless steps were immediately taken both to eliminate pro-American elements in Iranian society and to confiscate American economic interests. In November militants, condoned by the Ayatollah, seized American Embassy staff as hostages in an attempt to force the return home from exile of the Shah. In the months that followed, American opinion appeared to be obsessed by their fate. The 'hostage crisis' dominated the headlines for months as Carter ineffectually tried one step after another to secure their release. The ultimate fiasco was the 'rescue mission' of 1980 which had to be aborted because of equipment failure. The Shah himself died in July 1980 in Egypt and, just before the end of his Presidency, Carter agreed a financial deal with the Iranians which gave them far less than they had earlier demanded but which drew a kind of line under two extraordinary years. The two countries had shifted from being 'the best of friends' to 'the worst of enemies'. A perception that the United States had been humiliated played its part in Reagan's massive electoral victory in November.

It is not surprising that in these circumstances leading figures in the Carter administration—among them Cyrus Vance, the Secretary of State, and Brzezinski, the National Security Adviser—were at loggerheads, not only about particulars but also about the extent to which the United States could still play its customary world role. Was it or was it not the case that old categories were losing their force? Men in and around the White House, accustomed to thinking about the world in terms of a Communist/non-Communist dualism, could not easily come to terms with Iran. Prominent Western minds had long ago concluded that religion would be a diminishing factor in the world's affairs. Now they found an Islamic vitality which was by no means confined to Iran. It was pejoratively labelled 'fundamentalism', but its advocates laid claim to human values more profound than the celluloid products of Tinseltown and the antics of Hollywood lovers.

In Rome in October 1978 there was another surprise—a Polish Pope, who took the name John Paul II. Swiftly and dramatically, he covered the globe—the Americas, parts of Europe, Africa, the Middle East, and Asia. His impact was enormous. In the extent of its contacts and congregations the Vatican could lay claim to being more truly global than any other organization. Roman Catholics, according to some calculations, constituted about a fifth of the world's population. In that very fact lay both difficulty and opportunity. It too had its own 'fundamentalism' and challenged the notion that the world should beneficially slip into a comfortable godlessness. A Polish Pope was not likely to look favourably upon Eastern European Communist regimes (nor upon what was called 'liberation theology' as developed in Latin America) but neither could it be assumed that the Church would automatically conform to the prevailing ethos of 'the West'. And indeed there was also vitality within the other great religions of the world, even if that vitality was shown more in inter-religious conflict than in a willingness to seek mutual understanding and tolerance between faiths.

Time alone could tell whether these tendencies would have great significance. What seemed immediately more important was that, despite the assumptions that were sometimes made (at any rate by people who ignored the existence of the Berlin Wall, for example), the Cold War was actually not over and detente was not as deep-seated as many supposed. It was true that in the 1970s there had been deliberate encouragement of 'people-to-people' contacts. In 1975, for example, a joint US/Soviet space mission took place and cultural and educational exchanges expanded. Some 100,000 American tourists per annum visited the Soviet Union by the end of the 1970s. But deep suspicions still accompanied the 'thaw'. The SALT treaty was due to expire in 1977 but negotiation of a successor agreement proved difficult. It was a time when the United States and the Soviet Union (more than normally) suspected each other of stealing a march in the development of new weapons systems. It was also, as will be seen shortly, when the Soviet invasion of Afghanistan substantially changed the international climate. In his inaugural address, Carter had stated that he wanted to rid the world of nuclear weapons; but in practice the American nuclear arsenal continued to be well stocked; cruise missiles, Trident submarines, and neutron bombs added to the variety. The possible damage they could do was as mystifying to ordinary mortals as the code names by which they were known. Eventually, the two sides signed a second SALT agreement in June 1979. Before American ratification, however, a fresh crisis arose with the Soviet deployment of SS-20 land-based mobile missiles which could reach any Western European target. In return, NATO proposed to upgrade the Pershing missiles in West Germany and introduce cruise missiles in a number of Western European countries—a decision which provoked demonstrations in those countries.

Nuclear disarmers were even more alarmed by Reagan's advent to office in January 1981. Certainly the new President and his advisers talked tough. The B-1 bomber, cancelled by Carter, was put into production. Expenditure on both conventional and nuclear forces rose sharply. It was time to restore American pride and prestige. If necessary, the Soviet Union should be confronted head-on. Some officials even appeared to contemplate the possibility of surviving a nuclear war. Ambitious or perhaps fantastic 'star wars' might be envisaged. Yet, although Reagan claimed that SALT II put the United States in an unacceptable position of inferiority, he seemed prepared to abide by the treaty's stipulated limitations if the Soviet Union did likewise. In June 1982 an inconclusive round of Strategic Arms Reduction Talks (START) began in Geneva. Reagan's willingness to continue such talks belied the notion that he was only interested in raising the temperature between East and West.

There was no doubt, however, that the President felt and talked strongly. 'The Soviet Union', he famously declared in March 1983, 'is the focus of evil in the modern world.' At the end of 1983 the United States also detected a perhaps less potent embodiment of that evil in the regime which had taken over in the small Caribbean island of Grenada. US marines were able to put matters to rights, the United States vetoing a UN resolution deploring their invasion. In the eyes of the new Secretary of State, Haig, 'international terrorism' was to take the place of 'human rights' in the foreign policy concerns of the United

States. Moreover, Reagan's great capacity as a communicator massaged a wounded American spirit. It was reassuring to millions of Americans to know that only an 'evil empire' stood in the way of world peace. The Cold War was back. It is not perhaps surprising that 'nuclear politics' heightened suspicions, since error in assessing intentions could have been cataclysmic. It was, however, 'conventional' Soviet activity in different parts of the world, shortly to be explored, which largely contributed to this new deterioration. Reagan scrapped the politics of 'human rights' and largely convinced American opinion that they were in a 'winner takes all' struggle with Soviet power. There seemed every justification for a massive increase in defence expenditure. Detente was dead and the Carter years dismissed as a disastrous period which had given Moscow opportunity after opportunity to expand its global influence.

Closer to home, Reagan and Haig had one particularly awkward problem to deal with. The Galtieri regime in Argentina promised a firm crackdown on the *Montoneros* guerrillas, a prospect which pleased Washington. However, to whip up national support in the face of internal discontent, Galtieri invaded the Falkland Islands (Malvinas) in 1982—to which Britain successfully responded. Here was a nice geopolitical situation. Could Britain be supported in an area which scarcely constituted part of a European 'heartland'? To do so would certainly harm United States relations with Galtieri, though that might in turn lead to his downfall and some prospect of a return to a civilian government. In the event, it was to Britain that Washington gave crucial support.

The only 'success' which Carter was allowed by his critics to retain was his part in promoting peace in the Middle East. In December 1977 President Sadat of Egypt startled the world by going to Israel and speaking in the Knesset (Parliament). He talked of the need for peace but the conditions he attached seemed likely to be unacceptable to the new Israeli Prime Minister, Menachem Begin. Carter summoned both men to intensive conversations with him in the autumn of 1978 at Camp David. They made some progress but could not reach a final agreement on the future of Jerusalem, the West Bank, the Golan Heights, and the PLO. Early in 1979 Carter went to the Middle East himself for further talks which led to Egyptian recognition of Israel and a phased Israeli withdrawal—to be completed in 1982—from the Sinai peninsula—in the context of a general peace treaty signed in March 1979. It was undeniable, however, that the really thorny issues which affected non-Egyptians had not been resolved. Sadat was frequently denounced in the Arab press as a traitor to the cause and he was assassinated in October 1981. Egypt (which had a Coptic Christian minority and internal problems of its own) sometimes held itself aloof from Arab concerns. Sadat's successor, Hosni Mubarak, adhered to Sadat's approach where Israel was concerned but, by offering some support to Iraq in its war with Iran, brought his country back into the 'Arab world'.

There was indeed much unfinished business in the Middle East, as will emerge later in this chapter, but Carter's mediation had achieved more than most observers had thought likely. Carter had to tread carefully because of the support for Israel in the United States, but he appreciated the importance of good relations with Arab rulers in a region of seemingly endemic turbulence, as in turn did Reagan.

Soviet Resurgence?

During the 1980 election campaign, a poll found that some 84 per cent of Americans agreed with the proposition that their country was in 'deep and serious trouble'. They feared 'loss of control'. By contrast, the Soviet Union seemed both domestically stable and eager to operate in parts of the world where it had not hitherto directly intervened. Stability stemmed from the dominant position of Leonid Brezhnev, now (1977) the head of state as well as General Secretary of the party (which since 1964 had been the real locus of his power). And not only was he also a Marshal of the Soviet Union but the literary merits of his memoirs gained him the Lenin Prize for literature. This was leadership in the round! This stability was not to be shaken by the 'distorted' view of 'human rights' subscribed to by those tiresome Helsinki 'monitoring groups' which sprang up from Moscow to Armenia. The *nomenklatura* (the ruling Soviet élite which controlled the means of production) did not envisage 'loss of control', and continuing dissent was equated with treason. The most famous of Soviet dissidents, Andrei Sakharov, was placed under house arrest and sent into internal exile. Perhaps only his reputation beyond the Soviet Union saved him from 'psychiatric' treatment meted out to lesser-known figures. Carter's concern for human rights within the Soviet Union irritated and was one of the factors which made progress on nuclear issues difficult during 1977–9.

The stability of the Soviet Union was therefore maintained by force and repression. Other observers, however, wondered whether the Soviet Union was not so much a stable society as a stagnating one: the evil emperors, after all, were themselves elderly. Brezhnev had been born before the First World War and when he did die, in 1982, his successor, Andropov, was 69 and sick. He lasted little more than a year in office. Chernenko, his successor, was also suitably elderly. Continuity in these circumstances was maintained by the ever-present Andrei Gromyko, the most durable foreign minister in the world. Andropov, in his brief tenure, brought to his office more enthusiasm for economic reform than might be naturally inferred from his past as the longest-serving head of the KGB. There were changes in ministerial and party appointments, in part designed to root out corruption, but he did not bring on a new generation. There was no denying that Soviet society was presided over by an elderly oligarchy. When it finally disappeared, would it be followed by a deluge? In March 1985, the 54-year-old Mikhail Gorbachev became General Secretary. It was now Ronald Reagan who was the old man of the world.

The notion that the Soviet leadership was both despotic and arthritic appeared to be contradicted by the vigour with which it challenged the existing world naval balance. Admiral Gorshkov oversaw a fleet accumulation which comfortably exceeded the American by the mid-1970s and was replete with nuclear submarines and carriers. A presence in the Eastern Mediterranean had become permanent. The Soviet navy was ready to move into the Indian Ocean (port facilities had been arranged on the Gulf of Aden by an agreement with Somalia) and perhaps the South Atlantic. Its expansion was interpreted in the United States as a challenge for which there was no rational justification. There had to be a sinister explanation—that the Soviet Union was bent on 'taking over' Africa.

The continent in 1975 was hardly in a condition to resist continuing external involvement in its affairs. The Organization of African Unity had little substance. When its 1976 conference was held on the island of Mauritius only seven of the forty-eight-nation membership were represented by heads of state. The Soviet foothold in Somalia was quickly complicated by the revolution in neighbouring Ethiopia, where Emperor Haile Selassie had been overthrown in 1974 and replaced by a revolutionary regime within which, a few years later, Colonel Mengistu emerged supreme. It was unfortunate for the Soviet Union that Somalia and Ethiopia went to war over possession of the Ogaden region. The Somali leader turned to Washington—relations with Cuba were broken off—and revoked the use of port facilities. Moscow in turn sent vital supplies to aid Mengistu. By 1978 Ethiopia won the war and the Soviet Union was rewarded by facilities at the port of Massawa. What had happened in this instance might be repeated elsewhere in Africa.

The struggle in Angola, in the opposite corner of Africa, was a case in point. Portugal had in the end conceded Angolan independence in 1975 but it did so in the context of a three-way struggle for the succession between competing movements, each of which had external backers—the Soviet Union/Cuba, the United States, and South Africa. The most dramatic external intervention came from Cuban forces arriving under Soviet naval escort (later, Cuban forces moved up to Ethiopia and elsewhere). South African forces moved up from the south. In the event, however, outside intervention did not prove quickly decisive in support of any faction. Angola found itself trapped into what proved to be the longest-running civil war in Africa. Naturally, it was the Cuban involvement, as has been noted, perceived as the activity of a Soviet surrogate, which attracted most attention in the United States, giving rise to calls upon the Carter administration to find some effective means of countering what seemed to be a steady Soviet advance. However, other voices advised caution. The more directly it intervened, the more the Soviet Union made itself vulnerable to charges that it too was 'imperialist' and even had self-interested motives which extended beyond comforting 'Marxist-Leninist' regimes. And indeed Africa as a whole did not succumb to Soviet blandishments (nor to American), though the sense after 1975 that there was a new 'scramble for Africa' was a defining dimension in the 'new' Cold War.

It is possible that without the crisis in Afghanistan the Soviet Union would have stirred the African pot with even more vigour than it did. The zeal with which the peoples of Afghanistan fought against foreigners, as the Soviet troops were to find to their cost, was only matched by their antecedent and subsequent zeal in fighting each other. The Afghan monarchy had been abolished in 1973 but the ensuing republican regime was itself overthrown in April 1978 by an 'Armed Forces Revolutionary Council' in which, for the moment, a pro-Soviet faction was in the ascendancy. Replacement of the Islamic green flag by the red flag was symbolic of the social transformation that was to be attempted and which provoked considerable popular hostility. Sensing that the regime in Kabul was in danger, Moscow sent in 100,000 troops. Its chosen man, Babrak Karmal, was purportedly moderate. In the early 1980s Soviet forces found themselves fighting skilled mujahedin with the aid, if that is the word, of an Afghan army of dubious allegiance. It was a war analogous to the American experience in Vietnam. Soviet forces could not be defeated and driven out, but neither could they subdue the countryside beyond the towns and roads they controlled. The guerrillas, supported from Pakistan (whither a large Afghan population had fled), sapped the morale of Soviet soldiers and increasingly left generals with the sense that they were fighting a war that they could not win. It was a situation of stalemate: Afghanistan itself was devastated.

Internationally, the imbroglio was a propaganda disaster. It was the first time that the Soviet Union had directly intervened in the internal affairs of a country outside the *de facto* post-war division of spheres between the major blocs. The Islamic world reacted with indignation. President Carter urged that the Olympic Games, scheduled for Moscow in May 1980, should be abandoned, postponed, or boycotted. The United States led a band of countries which declined to attend. Afghanistan, it was claimed, showed the Soviet Union in its true light as an imperialist power. It must be doubtful whether even Brezhnev was altogether comfortable with this application of his 'doctrine' (that no 'socialist' state should be allowed to revert to non-socialism).

Poland had been part of the 'Soviet sphere' since 1945 but with the passage of time had grown no more contented in this fact. In the mid-1970s there was again unrest. As before, it was the level of subsidy which the government was prepared to pay to prevent high food prices in the towns which triggered dissent. Gierek, the party leader, was forced to withdraw proposed increases. Opponents of the regime gained confidence. The significance of the election of Cardinal Wojtyła of Cracow as pope is not to be underestimated. He returned to his homeland in June 1979 and emphasized the Catholicism of the Polish nation. Spiritually, it belonged to the West not to the East. Strikes in 1980 witnessed the emergence of Solidarity, an independent trade union led by Lech Wałęsa which gained millions of members. The state had to make concessions. International attention was focused on the Lenin shipyard at Gdańsk. The demands of the protesters ceased to be purely economic. Unrest continued through the winter of 1980/1 and raised the spectre of Soviet intervention to quell it. In December 1981, General Jaruzelski, appointed Prime Minister and then party leader some months earlier, proclaimed martial law and arrested and interned Solidarity leaders. He claimed in defence of his action that the country was on the brink of civil war. Some easement of restrictions followed over the next few years but there was neither an economic nor a political solution. These events were naturally pondered over throughout Eastern and South-Eastern Europe.

Taken together, however, Poland and Afghanistan revealed the vulnerability (though not yet the untenability) of the 'Soviet sphere' and the difficulty of deciding how it should be defined and how it could be best safeguarded. The Soviet state, in a simple military sense, appeared more powerful than it had ever been, but the more it encountered problems in contiguous countries the more it found it difficult to deploy that power effectively. Of course, in Poland, unlike in Afghanistan, the Soviet Union had not intervened directly and the analogy is therefore not complete. Nevertheless, in the winter of 1980/1, foreign observers suspected that there might be armed intervention in Poland by Soviet forces. The fact that such an intervention did not occur illustrates the dilemma in which Moscow found itself.

Superpower Struggle

In many respects, therefore, despite their renewed antagonism towards each other and the significant differences in their internal institutions and values, the 'superpowers' had analogous experiences and to some extent comparable difficulties. The nuclear and conventional resources at their command were enormous and gave them, at first glance, a capacity to impose solutions as they wished. They were both indubitably 'World Powers' in their global outreach but even so, in Vietnam and Afghanistan respectively, they had failed adequately to take the true measure of their local opponents. In this sense, their respective failures reflected a perhaps inescapable ethnocentricity in both Washington and Moscow. However, it would be wrong to dwell unduly on the similarities in their experiences in third countries. What was very clear, for the moment at least, was that deep hostility had returned in their own direct relationship.

'If detente unravels in America,' Nixon warned Brezhnev in 1974, 'the hawks will take over'. That moment had now arrived.

European Opportunity?

The problems that beset the 'Great Powers' might be thought to have given the European Community an opportunity to consolidate its function and purpose—and to seek, through a 'common foreign policy', a distinctive international role. The reality, however, was that the leading members of the Community remained acutely aware of the importance of NATO and American military support. The United States had not been hostile to European integration, indeed had urged it. It was perhaps only in France, which sat within NATO in a kind of semi-detached position, that the notion of a European world-role had some attraction. Nevertheless in attempting, on a part-continental basis, to create new structures in Western Europe, some member states, or at least some individuals within governments, urged 'ever closer union'. Success might incidentally (somewhat optimistically) demonstrate that something comparable in economic/political union might be attempted in other continents. On the other hand, sceptics doubted whether 'one Europe' (in reality still only a portion of the continent) could be achieved during a period of rapid change. The nation-state remained fundamental. A glance at some central aspects of the history of the major states illustrates this last point.

The accession of Britain, Denmark, and Ireland in January 1973 had constituted an important turning point since, in the case of Britain in particular, its post-war reluctance to 'join Europe' has been evident in previous chapters. British membership, although ratified in a referendum held in June 1975 by a majority of two to one, was most problematic. Heath, a British Prime Minister who allowed himself some enthusiasm for the European experiment, was defeated in the February 1974 election. Neither Wilson nor Callaghan, his Labour successors, showed comparable commitment. Even if they had done, the times were not propitious for adventures into the unknown.

Governments seemed compelled, under the impact of the oil crisis, to look after their own citizens. Attempts to establish a 'common energy policy', advocated by the European Commission, made little progress. Member states struggled to find their individual way out of the crisis. The Community lost its direction, both economically and politically. It seemed apparent that in shipbuilding, steel, consumer electronics, and car manufacture the pace was being set by the Asian periphery—no longer just Japan but also South Korea, Taiwan, Singapore, and Hong Kong.

Member states attempted different solutions to their common problems, steering an uncertain course between deflation and inflation in the process. Inflation in Britain reached 23 per cent in 1976 and the Labour government wrestled with a series of industrial and banking crises. An attempt was made to govern by means of a 'Social Contract' with the trade unions, but it was under increasing strain. In 1976 the Cabinet agreed that Britain had no alternative but to accept an IMF loan, with consequential cuts in expenditure. It was widely taken as a humiliating recognition that Britain could not 'pay its way' in the world, perhaps was even becoming 'ungovernable'. A more hopeful assessment was that time had been bought to enable Britain to rebuild its economy with the aid of the North Sea oil production that was now accelerating. There were, indeed, signs that this was happening, but the winter of 1978/9, nicknamed the 'Winter of Discontent', saw a series of public-sector disputes which deepened gloom and despondency. In March 1979 the Labour government lost a vote of confidence. It was the first time in over half a century that a British administration had actually been voted out of office.

The Conservative government headed by Margaret Thatcher was determined to reverse or at least halt national decline. The ingredients of what came to be called 'Thatcherism' began to emerge through a series of industrial confrontations and policy shifts. Neo-Keynesian macroeconomics went out of fashion, as did a tripartite management of the economy—industry, trade unions, and government. A second oil crisis, caused by the collapse of oil production in Iran and Iraq (countries at war with each other) in these years complicated the picture further. The Prime Minister was vigorous in defence of 'our money' in the EC. The Common Agricultural Policy was considered an expensive disaster. Even so, the British Treasury could not ignore the fact that in 1979 42 per cent of Britain's export trade went to, and 44 per cent came from, the EC. In practice, however, all the major institutions in British life found it difficult to be *communautaire* and some did not try very hard. Suspicion of the EC was also strong in Labour ranks and hardened into an election pledge under Foot that, if successful, Labour would take Britain out of the EC altogether.

The direct style of the Thatcher government and its economic policy, though contentious and often unpopular, proved no obstacle to its re-election in 1983 with a strong majority. The successful campaign to recapture the Falkland Islands in the previous year played a part in this victory. Inflation hit a fifteen-year low. In the following year a major and protracted dispute in the coal industry began. When it ended, in 1985, it was on the government's terms. The Prime Minister was now in a position to press further ahead with a programme of 'privatization' which had begun with British Telecom in 1984. The British political agenda changed in a way that would have been scarcely conceivable a decade earlier. It was also apparent that the British left was divided and in some disarray. Prominent defectors from the Labour Party had formed the Social Democratic Party which, in alliance with a periodically reviving Liberal Party, made a strong (though not decisive) showing in the early 1980s. In the event, the Labour Party survived but its ideology looked obsolete as class alignments lost their potency.

Naturally, there were features of the British experience in this decade that were peculiar and related to the state's long history—the return of the 'Irish question', the issue of devolution in Scotland and Wales (not sufficiently supported in 1979)—but the structural adjustments, with their political ramifications, reflected a common European pattern. The trade union movements of Western Europe as a whole all suffered heavy losses of membership in this decade. The shift from employment in the industrial sector to the tertiary or service sector produced a crumbling of old allegiances and loyalties. The working agricultural population continued to decline (it fell to under 10 per cent in France for the first time in 1975).

In these circumstances, to move across the Channel, President Giscard d'Estaing in France attempted after 1974 to deliver 'change without risk', having narrowly defeated the Socialist Mitterrand, who had the support of the Communists. Although the relationship between President and Prime Minister was never easy in the system of the Fifth Republic, that system survived. Giscard's success (personal rather than party) posed particular problems for the left. Socialists and Communists were engaged in a struggle for supremacy against each other as much as against the centre/right. In 1981, third time lucky, Mitterrand succeeded in his bid for the presidency and set about achieving the decisive 'break with capitalism'. He was, of course, the first Socialist President of France during the Fifth Republic. It was hoped that nationalization would modernize French industry (and devaluations of the franc would also help). Reflation was better than deflation. In the event, growth was insufficient and inflation took off. Unemployment rose, contrary to promises. In response, Mitterrand about-turned in March 1983—the month of a major currency crisis—and began thereafter to cut public expenditure and take some cautious steps in the direction of privatization.

His critics interpreted this U-turn as a betrayal of the Socialist heritage. Other commentators drew different conclusions. As in Britain, it appeared that the Socialist agenda, as attempted since 1945—high taxation, high public expenditure, nationalized industry—was played out. Even in Sweden, the Social Democratic Party was defeated in 1976—for the first time in forty-four years. Additionally, it was evident that even a country such as France, with its strong tradition of *étatisme*, could not 'go it alone' but was at the mercy of currency fluctuation and 'the international market'. Taken in the round, therefore, despite differences in personalities and in policy detail, it did appear in the case of both Britain and France, to take but these two examples, that 'the world' dictated the parameters of state action in Western Europe.

There remained no doubt that the Federal Republic of Germany was the economic powerhouse of the EC. However, it was not immunized against the underlying tendencies which have been noted elsewhere, although it prospered regardless. Schmidt, the Social Democrat Chancellor from 1974 to 1982 (when his coalition with the Free Democrats collapsed), came to epitomize successful pragmatism. It was not a difficulty, on most issues, to work in close tandem with the non-Socialist Giscard. Commentators outside Germany looked admiringly at German industrial relations and thought, for example, that Schmidt's legislation giving workers a 50 per cent representation on the board of big companies and a guaranteed share of their profits went a long way to explaining the success of 'Germany Limited'. Yet the picture became more complicated in Germany too. Even the 'wonder state' shared in the inflation and unemployment to be found elsewhere in Europe, though not to the same degree. Was it best tackled by work programmes sponsored by the state and paid for out of taxation or by lower taxation and less public expenditure? Stated thus crudely, it was the common problem in advanced societies. Schmidt's Free Democratic partners, in some danger of political extinction, opted for the latter, broke up the government, and paved the way for the Christian Democrat victory of 1983 under Helmut Kohl. Yet it would be misleading to see any substantial similarity between British Conservative policies at this time and those of other European parties of the right. The ethos of Christian Democracy was not 'Thatcherite'. In short, therefore, although Federal Germany had moved to the 'right' by 1985, and thus could be said to conform to a trend at least in the northern half of Western Europe, though not a ubiquitous one, in particulars its politics still reflected its own history and constitutional culture.

The sense that the new European internal order was moving away from the egalitarian impulses which had been strongly expressed after 1945 provoked differing responses. It was time, some Communists argued, to make their party more attractive; otherwise, driven by the refusal of most Western European opinion to find in the Soviet Union a satisfying exemplar and by the social changes just referred to, it would become a rudderless rump. From 1975, when the word first appeared in a newspaper, there was much talk of 'Eurocommunism' (although the turn away from the notion that Moscow was always right can be traced back to the revulsion felt by a significant number of Western European Communists at the Soviet intervention in Hungary). At one level, the term merely referred to the common situation of Communist parties in parliamentary systems—in France, Italy, and now Spain. More ambitiously, however, it was supposed to denote a new maturity and reflected the fact that there was now no single world centre which gave directives and imposed discipline on Communist parties, or so it was said. Western Europe in the late 1970s was not what it had been before 1945. Sympathizers with this 'mature' Communism suggested that there was no need to overthrow existing governments by force. They put it about that Communists could be reliable coalition partners who would play by the rules of the parliamentary game—Mitterrand in fact appointed four Communists to his Cabinet (in carefully selected positions) in 1981. The Communists withdrew support from Mitterrand in July 1984. What 'Eurocommunism' would mean in practice, therefore, would necessarily vary from country to country. Sceptical opponents supposed that this 'conversion' was only tactical, but enthusiasts on the left felt that this was not only a strategy for survival in Western Europe but one which offered, in Italy at least, and perhaps in Spain, a real chance of genuine political power.

Another alternative, attractive to a small minority, was not to seek some accommodation with what had been achieved in Western Europe since 1945 but to seek to undermine it by terror and violence. The Baader-Meinhof Gang or 'Red Army Faction', active in the early 1970s, was followed by the 'Movement of June 2' which undertook a number of violent acts against judges and businessmen. In 1977 German terrorists killed Hans-Martin Schleyer, head of the Federal Republic's Employers'

Federation. Such actions, however, did not elicit the desired public sympathy, nor provoke repressive state reaction, which might also then have evoked that sympathy. The threat in Germany receded, though it did not totally disappear. It was in Italy, however, that terrorism was most conspicuous. The 'Red Brigade', formed in 1971, justified its existence by claiming that the Italian state was threatened by a coup from the right. It had supporters and sympathizers in unexpected places and carried out acts of violence seemingly with impunity. In 1978 Aldo Moro, former Christian Democrat Prime Minister, was kidnapped in Rome and then found dead. In 1980 a terrorist bomb exploded at Bologna railway station, killing seventy-six people. Although the police made some progress thereafter, the brigade still constituted some kind of threat to public safety. Perhaps even more insidious, corruption and political warfare extended deep into Italian public life. Pope John Paul II was shot and injured by a Turkish terrorist in 1981. These incidents, in so far as Communists/anarchists were involved in them, together with the use of bombs by the IRA in Britain (a bomb at the Grand Hotel, Brighton, narrowly missed killing Mrs Thatcher in October 1984), refuted notions, even those of bland Eurocommunists, that political change in Europe would only henceforth be sought without resort to violence.

It would be an exaggeration, therefore, to paint all of Western Europe as a part-continent of peaceful progress. Yet a process of broad political convergence was discernible and, both compared with its own past and with other parts of the world, Western Europe was indeed politically stable. Suppositions, for example, that newly democratic Spain after 1975 would experience a period of protracted political instability proved unfounded. One attempted military coup in February 1981 failed miserably, and in 1982, after the general election, office passed calmly from the Suárez government which had been in power since 1976 to the Socialists under Felipe González. In 1982 Spain joined NATO and the passage of both Iberian countries to membership of the EC (January 1986) went relatively smoothly. In Greece, too, after the military regime stepped down in 1974, democratic institutions seemed more firmly embedded. Socialists won a general election for the first time in 1981 and in that same year Greece joined the EC. In the background, however, lay unresolved tension between Greece and Turkey—the independent island of Cyprus remained divided, as it had been since 1974 when Turkish forces moved into Northern Cyprus following a coup attempt by Greek Cypriot officers favouring union with Greece. United Nations forces remained on the island, where they had been since 1964.

If there was a common acceptance of 'parliamentary democracy' as the necessary basis for convergence, the ultimate goal of the EC was unclear. At one level, the politics of the Community seemed to be little more than self-interested national bargaining in difficult economic circumstances. Protectionist impulses were almost inevitable during a recession. Yet there were other developments which suggested that the 'European idea' had not been altogether submerged. The European Parliament was to be elected by direct suffrage (1975) and the European Regional Development Fund (also 1975) represented at least an attempt on the part of the European Commission to address issues of regional disparity.

Monetary issues continued to receive much attention. The Werner Committee (1970) had advocated monetary union by 1980, but as time passed that seemed unrealistic. However, after much debate, a European Monetary System (EMS) came into existence in 1979. It created a common European Currency Unit (ECU) which linked the exchange rates of member countries. Britain joined the EMS but refused at this time, with Greece, Spain, and Portugal, to join the Exchange Rate Mechanism (ERM) which would lead, it was anticipated, to a European Monetary Fund with pooled reserves. It would be misleading, however, to convey an impression that such steps easily or more than temporarily provided economic stability. There were many months when the institutions and procedures of the Community seemed to become bogged down in irritating but necessary detail as issues of 'harmonization' were tackled. Below the formal level of government, it was apparent that pan-Community networks were growing ever stronger, formed by large firms but also mirrored by lobbying groups of one kind and another. In these circumstances, it was difficult to find the right political language to define the Community and its constituent states.

Such integration did not obliterate continuing national priorities and still made even the approximation to a 'common foreign policy' difficult. Particular issues could still reveal fundamental disagreement between member states. In 1982 when the British government went to war to recover the Falkland Islands in the South Atlantic the support it received was less than full-hearted—Dublin was not enthusiastic about this outpost of the defunct British Empire, and Rome and Bonn were reminded of the Italian- and German-descended populations of Argentina. Europe's complicated past still got in the way of the present. The British expedition only succeeded because of the co-operation not of European 'partners' but of Washington. Yet, in relation to the United States and Japan in particular, on trade matters, it seemed necessary for Western Europe as an entity at least to flex if not to use its rather flabby muscle. Western European countries, to give another example, did not readily fall into line with the American response to the Soviet invasion of Afghanistan. A pipeline treaty had been signed with the Soviet Union in 1978 which would bring natural gas from northern Siberia to southern Germany. Europeans could not ignore its supposed economic benefits and were prepared to face American wrath to retain them. The extent to which the Community functioned as an entity was therefore problematic. And, despite the use of the word 'European', it could not be forgotten that the institutions which used that label only operated in half of the continent. Furthermore, prominent member states were still bequeathed particular agendas by the Europe that emerged after 1945. The Schmidt government broadly continued the *Ostpolitik* initiated by Brandt but did not put its 'allegiance' to the West in doubt. It was inescapable, however, that Bonn had concerns which other member states did not share.

Over its long past, some historians had explained the extraordinary impact of the continent of Europe on the world by referring to its multi-ethnic polycentrism. Its very competitive diversity, within a flimsy unity, had produced a dynamism which had impacted on other continents—for good or ill—to a degree unmatched by any other continent in its external dealings. The question for 'Europe' in the mid-1980s was whether it could or should organize itself, on a consensual basis, to a degree never previously achieved. To that question there remained no clear answer. 'One Europe' was certainly nearer in its political, economic, and social integration than 'One World', but that was not saying very much.

Organizing Africa?

The Western European picture presented a sharp contrast with an African continent over which West Europeans had exercised such direct influence until the previous decade. And indeed it was only in 1977, when Djibouti in the north-east became an independent state, that France completed its formal withdrawal from continental African territory. Even so, 'Eur-Africa', as some kind of entity, still had a powerful appeal, particularly for French minds. There could be a 'special relationship'. The European Commission had from an early stage taken a particular interest in African matters. The Treaty of Rome had allowed for the 'association' of non-European countries. European member states had a duty to promote 'the economic and social development of the Overseas countries and territories associated with them by letting these countries and territories share in the prosperity, the rise in the standard of living, and the increase in production to be expected in the Community'. The Yaoundé agreements (and the Arusha Convention of 1968 which extended arrangements to Kenya, Tanzania, and Uganda) from the mid-1960s had worked out basic principles. Associated members (most ex-colonial African territories) enjoyed a preferential status because they were included in the free trade area inside the common external tariff. A European Development Fund was also established; most of the appropriations went to sub-Saharan states with close ties to France. In turn, EEC countries were privileged exporters to the associated countries. However, the preferences established under the Yaoundé agreements attracted criticism from countries in Africa, Asia, and Latin America which were not associated. George Ball gave a US State Department view that the system constituted 'a poor use of world resources'. It was evident, indeed, that France in particular was not thinking globally but rather of the consolidation of a particular axis, largely Euro-African.

By the mid-1970s, changes had become necessary, partly because of British membership of the EC. In addition, since the first Yaoundé conference UNCTAD (the United Nations Conference on Trade and Development) had condemned what it regarded as nationally orientated economic systems. Yaoundé smacked of 'neo-colonialism'. Industrial countries, UNCTAD declared, had to accept a preferential system for importing industrial goods from developing countries. In 1974 the United Nations discussed the Charter of the Economic Rights and Obligations of States which would establish the framework for a New International Economic Order. In February 1975 in Lomé, capital of Togo, a new convention was reached between the EC and forty-six developing countries—not only African but also small Caribbean and Pacific countries. Technical aid could be used to promote industrial development and EC countries gave up their privileged entry into the associated markets. In practice, however, the nexus remained one of commodities (African) for manufactures (European). Four years later, a second Lomé Convention (now extended to sixty-seven countries) removed various non-tariff barriers which had restricted the exports of associated countries to the EC. The period up to 1985 was supposed to see a considerable expansion of financial aid but in the event the financial problems of France in the early 1980s limited its extent. Critics of the 'Lomé regime' deplored the way in which Africa still seemed locked into Western Europe.

This Euro-African economic sketch illustrates the tension between the pursuit of world trade liberalization and the pursuit of bloc integration. The tension occurred in other parts of the world also. The aims and objectives of the respective players fluctuated. Within the EC there tended to be a difference between 'world/free trade' perspectives (northern countries) and 'protectionist/bloc' perspectives (southern countries). And the 'Group of Seventy-Seven' non-industrialized countries organized in Algiers in 1967 was in some disarray a decade later. The oil crisis in particular had dramatically improved the trade balances of some members but had accentuated the problems of others. By the time of the fifth UNCTAD conference in Manila in 1980 these differences were transparent. The 'developing world' itself contained three 'worlds': oil-rich countries rapidly developing and broadening their economic base; industrializing countries, but without oil; countries which had no oil and which were scarcely industrializing at all. Examples from all of these categories could be found in Africa, though in the case of its oil-rich countries (Nigeria, Algeria, and Libya) the broadening of their economic base still had a long way to go.

In the decade after 1975, the rhetoric of African unity and self-sufficiency, expressed so strongly a decade earlier, exhausted itself. Optimism was replaced by pessimism. The collapse of commodity prices as a consequence of the drop in demand from the recession-stricken industrial world in the early 1970s had catastrophic consequences. Most African states had to seek loans from the International Monetary Fund or from Western commercial banks. Africa's foreign debt more than tripled in the decade after 1976. The ratio of total debt to GNP of all the countries on the continent doubled. And how could debt on this scale ever be repaid? A spiral of decline set in. Populations were growing rapidly but the drift to towns in search of work adversely impacted on food production. Drought accentuated the problem. In some cases the infrastructure of transport and communications could no longer cope. An image of Africa as a continent of famine, disease, and disaster began to establish itself in the rest of the world. Africa conspicuously lacked, for the most part, durable functioning states with political systems which allowed the orderly transmission of power. The regime of Idi Amin in Uganda, which Tanzanian forces brought to an end in 1979, was abhorred. Military leaders, quite widely—sometimes without malign motives—moved in to fill the vacuum, sort things out, and then restore civilian government, but others did not invariably have such intentions. The extent to which leaders could rely on support, sometimes even direct military support, from outside the continent has already been noted early in this chapter.

There were periodic efforts to restore a sense of continental identity. In 1976, for example, there was an attempt to establish an African Economic Community on the analogy of the EEC but it came to nothing. 'Africa' in this sense did not, perhaps could not, exist. Regional associations within the continent offered more possibility of meaningful co-operation but they too were fraught with difficulties. The Economic Community for West African States (1975) made some progress and in 1980 African states in the Lagos Plan of Action backed the strengthening of regional associations in other areas of the continent. Yet real co-operation was vitiated in part by diverse colonial heritages (anglophone versus francophone) and in part by the disparity of resources between potential partners and the volatility of prices obtainable for the region's resources. In West Africa, for example, oil/petrol-rich Nigeria, whose population approximated to that of the combined population of its francophone West African neighbours, sought a hegemonic role, in part as a means of strengthening its own precarious internal unity after the end of the civil war. By the middle 1980s, as oil prices declined, the limitations of the Nigerian strategy became apparent.

And, quite apart from the allegedly ideological alignments which blossomed and divided, Africa was too huge and frail to constitute a 'world'. The Sahara remained a great cultural as well as natural divide—and 'Christian' and 'Islamic' worlds interacted and sometimes clashed (Chad) at its extremity. The North African states of the Mediterranean littoral had their own agendas and relationships which were only partially 'African'. The fate of the western Sahara proved particularly contentious, involving fierce battles between Moroccan forces and Polisario guerrillas—a struggle which also drew in neighbouring states in opposition to Morocco. The war dragged on through the late 1970s. The Boumédienne presidency which had lasted in Algeria since 1965 was followed (without violence) by that of Benjedid Chadli, which began in 1979 (Chadli was to survive in office until 1992). Algeria's oil and natural gas reserves enabled an optimistic picture to be painted. Yet the country's identity was still problematic. Relations with France improved somewhat but the extent to which Algeria should retain any aspects of its 'French' inheritance became increasingly contentious. In 1974–6 there were clashes, for example, in the eastern city of Constantine between students who had been primarily educated in Arabic and those educated in French as to whether the civil law should or should not be based upon Islam. Algeria seemed perpetually poised between Mecca and Paris; perhaps only internal violence would resolve the issue. At the same time, an ambitious foreign policy was attempted. Algeria saw itself as a valuable international mediator—it played a crucial role, for example, in securing the release of the American hostages in Iran in 1981. The world of Algiers was very different from that of Nairobi. What was true of Algeria obtained elsewhere in ex-French North Africa. PLO fighters, exiled from Beirut in 1982 to Tunisia, noted that the culture of their hosts remained French—books, newspapers, films. Allegedly, they spoke Arabic but thought in French and then translated.

At the opposite end of the continent, South Africa remained defiantly and deliberately a world apart, ostracized and condemned not only by African states but also, formally at least, by the 'world community'. The massacre of unarmed black demonstrators at Sharpeville in 1960 was regularly referred to by the country's critics. The exclusion of the black majority from political rights became increasingly anomalous and intolerable. The African National Congress (ANC) began to see no alternative but armed struggle. In 1976 there was an uprising in Soweto, a black township outside Johannesburg, which left perhaps as many as 700 people dead. International calls for sanctions, boycotts, and other punitive measures strengthened. However, in 1977, the National Party gained its largest ever majority in the general election. It had increased its support amongst English-speaking white South Africans in addition to the Afrikaner population on which it could rely.

A new Prime Minister, P. W. Botha, who took office in 1978, tentatively tried a twin-track approach to his country's difficulties. Independence for Zimbabwe in 1980 and the ending of Portuguese colonial rule had removed the 'buffer' against the Black African 'Frontline States' which South Africa had hitherto enjoyed. Botha, however, was able to put pressure on Mozambique and other neighbours to prevent them giving sanctuary to ANC guerrillas and thus display the toughness which many of his electors required. He was also under strong international pressure to effect a transfer of sovereignty in South-West Africa (Namibia), where an insurrection was proving increasingly successful, but negotiations stalled. On the other hand, a new South African constitution, approved by referendum in November 1983, established a tricameral parliament (whites, coloureds, and Asians). It represented a significant constitutional change but still did nothing for the African majority; even so it gave impetus to white political forces which thought that the National Party was losing its way. Although some African leaders (Banda of Malawi and Houphouët-Boigny of the Ivory Coast) believed that something could be achieved by dialogue, most African leaders continued to urge economic sanctions, boycott, and support for the ANC as the only course which would end white rule in South Africa. Britain under Mrs Thatcher, with its strong historical and continuing economic ties with South Africa, resisted the imposition of sanctions. Botha's declaration of a state of emergency in July 1985 suggested a deepening of the crisis.

Both in North America and in Western Europe the South African question had come to evoke ambivalent feelings. Looked at in a global context, South Africa was undoubtedly a bulwark against Communism at a time when Communist influence or control was evident in the guerrilla movements of neighbouring countries. Of course apartheid was abhorrent, but, despite governmental scandals and military/police repression, South Africa did still possess a functioning parliamentary system and sophisticated sectors of its economy. The outside world could not ignore the importance of South Africa's gold. Could its achievements be preserved when its fundamental flaws were removed? It appeared that at least the southern half of Africa needed a 'cleansed' South Africa to act as a motor and inspiration for the entire region. In 1985, however, it was most often bloody revolution on a scale not seen anywhere else even in Africa which was most frequently forecast. South Africa and its problems received more attention in the northern hemisphere than was the case with any other part of the continent. However, there were occasions when its geographical distance, viewed from a European or North American perspective, brought some relief from anxiety for its white rulers.

Middle Eastern Turmoil

The Middle East is never easy to define exactly (what is 'west' and what is 'east' is never as obvious as what is 'north' and 'south'). It merges into an 'Islamic world' which can be said to embrace peripheral Afghanistan or the Sudan. President Carter's security adviser, Zbigniew Brzezinski, termed Afghanistan, Iran, South Yemen, and Ethiopia the 'Arc of Crisis' in these years. The involvement of the Soviet Union (Afghanistan) and the United States (the Camp David Accords), as has already been noted, testified to the extent to which, in different ways, the superpowers both saw themselves with a direct role in a generously defined Middle East. One sign of a changed situation, however, was the dissolution in 1979 of the Central Treaty Organization with the withdrawal of Iran, Pakistan, and Turkey. That organization clearly belonged to a rather different era in the northern Middle East, before the Iranian Revolution, though it had never been very effective.

Arab intellectuals often argued that it was the direct or indirect involvement of outside powers which made the Middle East unstable. They resented the apparently patronizing attitude to be found amongst outsiders. It was a sentiment later to be elaborated as *Orientalism* and given a historical pedigree by the

Palestinian writer Edward Said (1978), who himself lived in the United States. If 'the world' would only leave it alone, the countries of the region would sort out their own affairs more peaceably. It was only oil which prevented this prospect. Oil was indeed still of great world importance but, ironically, the Iran–Iraq war in the Gulf did not prove as catastrophic for the world's supplies as had been feared. Alternative sources of oil were being found and fuel economies developed after the first 'oil crisis' had begun to be effective in the developed world.

Malign influences may be attributed to outsiders, but what was characteristic of the decade after 1975 was the extent to which internal disputes proliferated. As in Africa, territorial claims and state frailty were close to the heart of the matter. Democratic/constitutional governments, as understood contemporaneously in Europe, were scarcely to be seen anywhere, though their absence does not necessarily imply instability. To make that assumption would be to misunderstand the centrality of Islam in their life. Particularly in the smaller states of the Gulf, the standard of living, of health care, and of education rose dramatically.

The state of Israel, within the borders to which it had expanded—the Golan Heights were annexed in 1981—was offered by some as an explanation for instability. In contrast to its neighbours, Israel was distinctively a 'world state', albeit situated in the Middle East, in the sense that it had drawn into its population Jews from very different parts of the world who had experienced different cultural milieux. Its admirers pointed to its urban cultural sophistication and progressive democratic system—which they contrasted with the fragile and fractious systems in surrounding countries. Yet there were also tensions within Israeli society. By the later 1970s, Ashkenazi (originally Eastern European) Jews, who had played so critical a part in the foundation of the state, were outnumbered by Sephardic Jews who came from North Africa and Arab countries. How was the essence of Jewishness to be defined? Orthodox Jews, though undoubtedly a minority, became steadily more hostile towards the 'secular' tone which pervaded much of Israeli life. Questions of national security naturally continued to dominate public life, but for some the issue of where Israelis 'belonged' became steadily more important. Was it not vital to be seen as a quintessentially Middle Eastern state if lasting peace was to be achieved? But how could that be done without sacrificing equally vital links with world Jewry? The future of the city of Jerusalem, the eastern part of which Israel annexed in 1980, hung over every political discussion. The Arab population of Israel grew rapidly and constituted about 15 per cent of the population. That too complicated the question of identity.

Israel's Arab population was part-Christian and part-Muslim. A similar religious divide threatened the viability of its northern neighbour, Lebanon. There had been one civil war in 1958, which had produced an American intervention. Broadly, Lebanon's Maronite Christians thought of themselves as 'Western'—religiously linked to Rome and culturally still, in many respects, linked to France—while its Muslims saw themselves as authentically part of the Muslim Middle East. The presence of Palestinian refugees, expelled from Jordan in 1971, complicated the position still further. Lebanon was torn between two worlds, and its doom was frequently pronounced. Fresh internal fighting began in 1975 and a year later Syrian forces intervened. Subsequent cease-fires did not hold for long. Palestinian raids into Israel produced an Israeli incursion into Lebanon in 1978 and it was followed, four years later, by a full-scale Israeli invasion.

It was hoped to destroy the PLO and perhaps to install a pro-Israel regime in Lebanon. Vibrant Beirut was reduced to rubble and there were massacres in refugee camps. The PLO was driven out, but Israel failed to establish a compliant regime in Lebanon. US marines were briefly deployed but withdrew after a bombing incident in which they suffered heavy casualties. The drive north had given rise to some opposition in Israel and there was anxiety about possible economic collapse. A new government of National Unity, produced after elections in 1984, announced a phased withdrawal, to be completed in 1985. Israeli clients, however, would maintain a buffer zone in South Lebanon. Whether some kind of 'Lebanon' would survive or be swallowed up in a Greater Syria remained uncertain. For the moment, at any rate, it looked as though the checks and balances designed in the past to ensure that Lebanon straddled two worlds could no longer function. The internal landscape of its communities had been drastically altered and some kind of Syrian hegemony looked most likely.

The broad international impact of the fall of the Shah of Iran in 1979 has already been noted. It is the consequence for the Middle East of the triumph of the Ayatollah Khomeini that now requires attention. The fact that it was from France that he returned should not mislead. Most of his previous exile had been spent in Iraq. He had not returned to give Iran a 'genuine' Western constitution, though its preamble stated that the affairs of the country should be administered by relying upon public opinion expressed through elections. The Shiite tradition, represented by Khomeini, looked forward to the coming of a Twelfth Imam who would inaugurate a 'world government of God'. The new Iranian Constitution expressed the hope that the twentieth century would be the century of a world rule by the hitherto 'oppressed peoples'. Here was a concept both revolutionary and dynamic but quite unlike the notions of world government which existed in Western countries.

In 1975 the Iraqi government had concluded an agreement with the Shah concerning the Shatt al-Arab waterway which emptied into the Gulf. Joint control was theoretically to operate, though neither country was really satisfied with this solution. In 1979, Saddam Hussein, previously Vice-President to Hassan al-Bakr and the regime's 'strong man', became President. He had made a name for himself in handling the most recent phase of Kurdish rebellion. Saddam Hussein proceeded to deal ruthlessly with both Communists and Shiite leaders in the south of the country (where Khomeini had been exiled). The Iraqis, hoping to exploit the instability in Iran, launched a full-scale war against the Ayatollah's regime in September 1980. Khorramshahr was captured in the following month but the Iranian forces then stood their ground—Khorramshahr was recaptured by the Iranians in 1982. Both sides were well equipped, and heavy casualties

ensued. The oil installations of both countries were badly damaged and shipping in the Gulf was interfered with. It appeared in
1985 that, having withstood the initial onslaught, Iran was poised
to launch a counter-offensive. Indeed, with superior resources
and manpower, it ought in theory to have been able to win the
war by this date. It was a bloody conflict which consumed the
resources of both sides, though it was only the Iraqis who
borrowed heavily abroad. It was impossible to say when it would
end. The outside powers with major interests in the region—the
United States, the Soviet Union, France, and Britain—did not
intervene directly but, for the moment at least, Iran seemed the
greatest danger to their respective interests. It was Iraq which
received significant intelligence and military aid, by one means or
another. The 'tilt' in the direction of Iraq was subsequently to be
criticized when it appeared that it was Saddam Hussein who
posed the graver threat to Western interests.

No country in the Middle East could ignore what was going
on. The conflict gave impetus to the formation in 1981 of the
Gulf Co-operation Council which brought together Bahrain,
Kuwait, Saudi Arabia, Qatar, Oman, and the United Arab
Emirates. Hussein could make some appeal to Arab solidarity
against the Iranians but it had limited effect. Hussein's regime,
which inherited a Ba'athist secularism, had no attraction for the
conservative states of the Gulf and Saudi Arabia. However, the
subversive potential of the Ayatollah's message was also recognized, particularly in the Gulf states and the Eastern Province of
Saudi Arabia. In late 1981, it was Crown Prince Fahd of Saudi
Arabia who tried to organize a summit in Fez which would look
at the problems of the region in the round (including the
question of how Israel might be accommodated); but President
Assad of Syria, in particular, distrusted what he saw as Saudi
subservience to the United States. The summit made little
progress. It was evident that 'the Arab world' was still a con-
stellation of worlds and no one was more adept than the
British-educated King Hussein of Jordan in steering a way
through them. In Libya, the regime continued on its own
idiosyncratic course. Colonel Qaddafi was at loggerheads with

Egypt and interfered, directly or by proxy, in the internal affairs of Tunisia, Chad, and Morocco. His agents pursued expatriate Libyans in European capitals and his support, or at least his alleged support, for terrorism led to a steady build-up of tension with the United States. United States and Libyan planes engaged in a dog-fight over the Gulf of Sirte in August 1981, and there were further incidents to come. Qaddafi himself, however, proved a great survivor.

Observers saw another conflict gathering momentum throughout the region—between movements seeking a social and political order which was thoroughly Islamic and those who doubted whether the sharia, sacred Islamic law as traditionally understood and interpreted, could be a sufficient basis in societies which were becoming more complex and sophisticated. Islam could not seal itself off from the rest of the world. The resurgence of Islamic fundamentalism proved to be universal in the Islamic world. And could or should the sharia be applied in countries where there were different religious communities? In 1983, in the Sudan, where General Nimeiri had been in power since 1969, it was announced that the sharia would be the law of the land. Alcohol was forbidden and somewhat severe Koranic punishments instituted. It was stated that the law would not be applied to non-Muslims but there was great scepticism about such a promise in the Christian and pagan south of the country. Protracted internal war and strife began and did not end with Nimeiry's downfall in 1985.

The pervasive nature of this problem could even be found in Turkey. The Kemalist constitutional 'secular' inheritance remained powerful—the Republic had been declared in 1923—but in the post-war decades Turkish government had oscillated between civilian and military rule. In 1978–80 the country seemed on the brink of collapsing into civil war as the discontents of national minorities—Kurds and Armenians—were added to the feuds between left and right in circumstances of accelerating inflation. Four or five thousand people died in political violence. Islamic factions poured open contempt on the Kemalist legacy and proclaimed that secularism was atheism.

The Koran should be the constitution. In September 1980 the Turkish army took over and imposed martial law, which succeeded in bringing back a degree of peace and order. A further constitution followed and fresh steps to restore a kind of political life. The religious issue, however, was by no means resolved. At the same time, however, Turkey remained firmly in NATO and sought to strengthen its 'European' credentials. Turkey was exceptional in certain respects but in seemingly 'facing both ways' its dilemma in the mid-1980s was shared, to greater or lesser degree, throughout the Middle East as a whole.

Asia Ascendant?

In 1975, Emperor Hirohito of Japan visited the United States—many Americans were apparently amazed to learn that he was still alive—and received a Mickey Mouse wristwatch on a visit to Disneyland. Thirty years earlier a Gallup poll had recorded that 70 per cent of Americans favoured either his execution or some harsh punishment. A visit from the only emperor left in the world (Hirohito was to be joined by Marshal Bokassa of the Central African Republic who proclaimed himself Emperor Bokassa I in 1976—but perhaps, even so, was not altogether an imperial figure) was certainly something exceptional. American reporters, however, naturally asked this frail figure how he believed Japanese values to have changed in three decades. His enigmatic reply stated that in the broadest perspective there had not been any change between the pre-war and post-war periods. It was a comment which caused consternation amongst American old soldiers. True, in his own person, Hirohito represented continuity (though it was difficult, seeing him visiting Disneyland, to recognize the erstwhile god-emperor) but there was a deep difference between the militarism of the early Showa period and the values Japan had espoused since 1945. Perhaps, however, the emperor was being honest: deep down, Japanese values had not changed, or at least for men of his generation they had not.

A decade later, Japanese relations with the United States (and also with the European Community) were clearly under strain and gave rise to speculation that a fundamental shift in world power was taking place. Statistic after statistic was produced to illustrate Japan's amazing economic progress. By 1984 Japan manufactured nearly a quarter of the world's cars—in 1960 it had made a mere 1 per cent. World markets were being 'saturchated', to use the common expression in the press, by high-quality technology-intensive products—computers, precision instruments, electrical machinery. Kyushu, the southernmost island, once celebrated for its oranges, now became famous for its integrated circuits. Japan generated enormous annual trade surpluses around the world—in 1985 its large surplus with the European Community was nearly double what it had been a decade earlier. According to the normal economic indicators, Japan had already become the world's second industrial power. Moreover, during the first half of the 1980s, Japan was generally taken to have replaced the United States as the world's leading banker.

This transformation naturally had repercussions. European Community governments came under pressure from their own industries to erect selective barriers against Japanese imports. They in turn sought to persuade the Japanese government to remove the devices and constraints which made it difficult, they claimed, to export their goods into the Japanese market. However, formulating a Community policy was not easy. Britain, for example, made representations but also sought a 'special relationship' with Japan. The two countries, after all, had been allies for twenty years and, despite the memories of the Second World War, the notion of two island countries similarly ambiguous about their relationship with their mainland neighbours was not without its appeal. France had no such framework and exulted in complex customs procedures which it used against Japanese penetration of its markets. American manufacturers exerted similar pressure on their governments to act to restrict Japanese access. What was required from the Japanese was 'voluntary export restraint'. The Japanese government took some measures designed to head off the rampant protectionism which threatened but at the same time observed that in previous decades the United States had not shown a disposition to exercise 'voluntary export restraint'.

The economic success also raised deeper issues about Japanese identity and place in the world which had been shelved, as it were, in the immediate post-war decades. In part, racial stereotypes and old anxieties revived abroad. 'You never know when the Japanese will go ape' had been an expression used by George Ball in 1972 in the *New York Times*. A decade later there were fears that Japan might attempt to break away from the post-war world order. In 1982 Japan announced plans to increase military spending by 60 per cent over the next four years. It was a decision which evoked a mixed response from military commentators in the United States, some of whom thought it appropriate that Japan should increase its capability, having been a 'free-rider' for too long, while others thought it an unwelcome sign that Japan might again in due course become a significant military power. There was some suggestion in the United States that a nuclear-armed Japan, should it emerge, would have suicidal tendencies. It has been noted that in 1980s America the double entendre possibilities in the word 'yen' were a gift to certain mass media titles—'Yen for Power' was one of them. The Japanese, in short, were being presented in such works as a 'little people' peculiarly devoted to economic masochism and social regimentation with little true creative capacity: wealth without joy was apparently the Japanese fate. Examples of such attitudes can be found at various levels of American society at this time. Discussing such stereotypes, the American historian of Japanese–American relations, John Dower, regards it as a grave mistake to dismiss them as casual rhetoric or vulgarism on the part of ignorant and parochial people in the United States. They reflected 'upper-class white supremacism' in the United States as a whole, though that may be too sweeping an assessment on his part.

Japanese business corporations, however, were apparently untroubled by external criticism. There was no need to apologize for singing the company song: Japan was unique. Some Japanese business spokesmen were prepared to argue that Japanese commercial success reflected the racial purity of Japan when compared with a 'mongrelized' America. In turn, some American commentators drew parallels between US–Japan relations in 1937–41 and the position in the early 1980s. The element of hysteria in some American observations in part stemmed from the unexpected gravity of the position in which the United States found itself. Foreign historians suggested that Japanese historiography had as yet not adequately come to terms with Japan's role between 1931 and 1945. The Australian historian Richard Bosworth has noted that, unlike the position in Germany, Italy, and other erstwhile belligerent countries, 'revisionist' historians have been peripheral figures in the Japanese historicization of the 'long Second World War'. It was, however, sometimes admitted externally that critical comments made about Japan had their origin in a certain jealousy. It was also a fact that a new generation of Japanese was eager to travel the world—and had the money to do so. In the decade after 1975 probably more Japanese visited other parts of the world, particularly North America and Europe, than had ever travelled abroad in previous Japanese history. It has also been noted that English terms were being introduced into the daily use of Japanese without provoking official attempts (as in France or Iceland) to keep them out. In the war of words, it was also sometimes forgotten at the time that Japan was still a functioning democracy, though one in which its Prime Ministers seemed to come and go somewhat mysteriously.

It was not only in relation to the United States, however, that difficulty caused by Japanese success appeared. 'Asia' also caused Japan problems. The earlier Asian war would still not go away. Perhaps as many as 15 million Chinese had died at Japanese hands, and China was disinclined to forget it. The scale of Chinese suffering after the Japanese sack of Nanjing in December 1937, however, was still disputed in Japan. In 1982 both the People's Republic and South Korea reacted strongly to suggestions that officially sanctioned Japanese textbooks should have a more 'patriotic' tone. The Nakasone government

(1982–7) did not indulge in excessive humility about the past, though in 1986 an Education Minister who publicly defended Japanese imperialism in Korea was dropped. To some extent, the emotions aroused on these matters undid the tactful diplomacy followed by Prime Minister Fukuda a few years earlier. On the other hand, as had been true forty or so years earlier, Japan's achievement was also a kind of inspiration in East Asia. It was perhaps Japan, and not the West, which offered the model for Asian 'take-off'.

Indeed, by 1985, it was readily apparent that Japan itself was coming under pressure from Asian competitors—a fact which explains the paradox that Japanese business and government was beginning to worry about 'decline' just at the point when the rest of the industrialized world was complaining about Japanese success. The 'Newly Industrializing Countries' (NICs)—initially thought of as South Korea, Taiwan, Singapore, and Hong Kong—watched Japan very carefully and often moved into markets which the Japanese had initially developed, with products of comparable quality but which undercut the Japanese for price. All had ample labour, initiative, and enterprise. Their economies developed in a remarkable way, though the structures within which they operated were by no means uniform. The paradox that the existence or survival of these entities had depended, and perhaps still depended, upon American military power in East Asia was not lost on Washington.

Then, in turn, the NICs were being challenged by other East Asian countries which, unlike them, did possess indigenous raw materials. It was apparent by the late 1970s that the ASEAN countries—Indonesia, Malaysia, Thailand, the Philippines, Brunei—were not content to envisage a future in which their economies were complementary to those of the NICs and Japan, that is to say a situation in which they were junior commodity partners. They too wished to industrialize and thus, they believed, get the best of both worlds—though tiny Brunei, with its oil wealth, had no need of a broader strategy. Inevitably, industrialization would take time (though time had a habit of being foreshortened) and would inevitably be socially disruptive, but it would be achieved. There were tensions within ASEAN but its success, notwithstanding cultural/religious differences between the nations, prompted fresh thought in Canberra. Perhaps Australia ought increasingly to think of itself as primarily belonging to the community of South-East Asian states. It should see its future not as a 'branch office of empire', as Prime Minister Keating was subsequently to put it, subsisting on an obsolete British diet. Geography (and the fact of a rapid expansion of Australian trade with Asia) should be uppermost in determining policy. It was an issue which was to become even more contentious in Australia in the next decade.

From South Korea to Indonesia and the Philippines to Malaysia, however, there remained an unresolved question: the relationship between economies which were expanding and diversifying, often at a rapid rate, and 'democracy'. Sukarno of Indonesia had died in 1970, having lost effective power to General Suharto a few years earlier. The new leader's conception of democracy was no less 'guided' than his predecessor's, and he seemed set for a no less lengthy rule. In the Philippines, Marcos, who had been in power since 1965, had consolidated his position in a new constitution which had been proclaimed by presidential decree under martial law. In 1975 his rule still had another decade to run before he was overthrown. In 1983 Benigno Aquino, who opposed the regime, was assassinated on his return to Manila from the United States. South Korea, too, witnessed authoritarian government punctuated by elections.

In short, it could not be claimed that 'Western' understandings of democracy were firmly established. Those external commentators who believed that 'Western democracy' was the goal which lay in the 'logic of history' or, more prosaically, was simply desirable, viewed these countries—and, as will subsequently be seen, China itself—with some puzzlement. Some argued that 'the people' accepted authoritarian regimes during a process of modernization/industrialization but, as greater economic prosperity and education spread, they became more critical and wanted more democracy. Others remained unconvinced that there was any such simple link. If, as in the case of

Singapore under Lee Kuan Yew, a system could develop which brought conspicuous prosperity, it would be accepted, though it was semi-authoritarian. There was no reason to suppose that 'the people' would hanker after a purer democracy, a democracy which might not be able to bring comparable economic success. Viewed in this light, authoritarian aspects of government in Malaysia or Thailand, to take two further examples, were understandable.

In any case, some restrictions on freedom in economically advancing countries could seem acceptable if that enabled them to maintain internal stability. The grim fate of Cambodia offered a warning of what could happen in a civil war. After years of bloody fighting, effective control was exercised by the vicious regime of Prime Minister Pol Pot. Open warfare began between Cambodia (Kampuchea) and Vietnam in December 1978, and over the next couple of years there was savage fighting between rival Cambodian forces and their external backers, both near and far. These were indeed 'killing fields' with half the estimated population of the country meeting their deaths. In the early 1980s, with outside support, some recovery was made, but the situation remained precarious.

All the countries referred to above—Brunei excepted—had shown major population growth through this period; but even the most populous, Japan and Indonesia (some 117 million and 150 million respectively in 1980), were dwarfed by China, which topped the billion mark in the same year. In 1981 the Indian census reported a population of 683 million. Despite the dynamism of the 'tiny tigers', therefore, what the ascendancy of Asia in the world might really entail depended ultimately on Sino-Indian relations. The population of Asia as a whole continued to outstrip that of all other continents.

In China, 1976 was a year of significant transition. Zhou Enlai, long-time Prime Minister, died in January, and in the months that followed factions manœuvred for position. Immediately, however, he was succeeded by his deputy, Hua Guofeng—who also became both party chairman and military affairs commission chairman. Deng Xiaoping was dismissed from all his posts in April, being blamed for disorders in Tiananmen Square when there had been demonstrations in honour of Zhou's memory. Deng had been circulating documents which identified him, in the eyes of opponents, as the 'number two capitalist roader'. The 'Gang of Four', which included Mao's wife Jiang Qing, still enjoyed Mao's support, and Jiang Qing wanted Deng out of the way. Mao died in September 1976. The 'Gang of Four' were under arrest within a month. It is not altogether clear whether a coup was actually planned, but Hua gave that possibility as justification for the arrests. It was not until the winter of 1980–1, however, that they were put on trial. Jiang Qing claimed that everything she had done had been on the orders of Mao. She was given a suspended death sentence, as was Zhang Chunqiao. The two others who had confessed and expressed repentance were given long prison terms. Deng Xiaoping bided his time in South China as Hua Guofeng failed to consolidate his position—despite the plenitude of his formal offices. 'Rightist' supporters of Deng made progress, though we must remember that simple terminology right/left, conservative/radical to define individuals is inadequate to describe a volatile and complex situation. Zhao Ziyang replaced Hua Guofeng as Premier in September 1980, and Hu Yaobang as party chairman in June 1981. In the same month Deng himself became chairman of the military affairs committee. Past 'excesses', formerly laid at the door of Lin Biao or the Gang of Four, were now openly attributed to Mao himself, though his merits were still supposed to be primary and his errors secondary.

Deng, nevertheless, was clear that a new start had to be made, and that included the rehabilitation of millions of people who had been purged over the previous couple of decades. China had to come fully into the world. The country's diplomatic isolation had already ended, as noted in the previous chapter, but Deng wanted to take matters much further, though the scale of what needed to be attempted can only be hinted at here. In 1979 he became the first top-ranking Chinese Communist leader to visit Washington. There was irony in the promotion of an 'Open Door' policy which had for so long been denounced as simply a means by which Western imperialists had sought control of China. A coastal development strategy had already begun in 1979 with the creation of four 'special economic zones' which encouraged joint ventures with foreign companies. The result here, and in other subsequently designated zones, was striking. Of course, the experiment was limited, deliberately so, to extend to an area in which only some 200 million of the Chinese population lived—but there was a strong hope that there would be a 'trickle-down' effect which would benefit backward regions in the interior. In effect, at least for a time, this meant that there would be 'two Chinas'. Shanghai resumed its place as China exported onto the world market. Sino-Japanese trade expanded rapidly, despite the political uncertainties which have been alluded to, to mutual benefit. Sino-American trade likewise built up with great speed. China's offshore oil reserves offered enormous possibilities. Factory directors ordered new foreign plant with neophytic enthusiasm. The long-term aim was to give China its own technological base—and to help towards this objective tens of thousands of Chinese students were sent abroad to foreign universities to study. It was announced that China now accepted 'all the common practices known to world trade'. In 1980 China obtained membership in the World Bank and billions of dollars of loans followed over the next few years. Given an almost frenetic pace of change, it was almost inevitable that disaster sometimes threatened, as in 1984–5 when China's foreign exchange reserves fell sharply. Might everything simply get out of control? The Five Year Plan of 1985 tried to slow down the pace. Fewer cities were to be open to foreign investment.

It had sometimes been supposed that China would be 'the country of the future' and that it possessed 'enormous potential', a potential sometimes as much feared as welcomed (the 'Yellow Peril')—but China had suffered a series of humiliations at the hands of the Western powers. China had remained 'a sleeping giant', to use Napoleon's phrase. Now the transformation did appear to be happening, but it remained difficult to penetrate to the heart of China. Perhaps, indeed, there were many Chinas, all coexisting alongside each other in an unstable relationship: the

China whose armed forces attempted to give the Vietnamese a military lesson in 1979 but received heavy casualties in the process; the China which was testing inter-continental ballistic missiles (ICBMs); the China still of rural poverty and some urban squalor—though it was a country in 1985 which produced 100 million more tons of grain than it had done a decade earlier. It was the largest Communist country in the world. The party was still in control but it was difficult to determine, after the ditching of so much hallowed dogma, just what its ruling ideology now was.

And there lay another problem, perhaps the central problem. Could China now join the world at such breakneck speed and yet still preserve itself inviolate? Foreign tourists came in increasing millions and restrictions on their travel were to a considerable extent lifted, though the impact of outsiders should not be exaggerated. Chinese people were keen to talk to them—but they were usually only to be encountered on the well-beaten paths. Rural China was scarcely disturbed by their arrival. A generation whose lives had been disrupted by the Cultural Revolution began to breathe again—and learning English opened a wider vista. But were there no limits? Was the corollary of the 'Open Door' that China should be an 'Open Society'? Some writers argued that there was no need to be defensive. Opening the country to the outside world was not a temporary expedient but a fundamental principle: 'open the doors and windows wide to the world'. Others were not so sure: 'the world' was not entirely admirable and one had to be careful. John Gittings tells us of a book written by an Englishman, D. H. Lawrence, bewilderingly referred to as *Lady Thatcher's Lover* in a public discussion (erroneously!), which was thought likely to corrupt youthful morals and, in addition, make relations with Britain difficult.

Returning Chinese students from the United States and elsewhere (and substantial numbers found a 'need' to extend their stays abroad) challenged the environment culturally, socially, and even politically—though there is always the danger of exaggerating the influence and importance of an articulate but still very small minority of the population. Civil liberties had been supposedly guaranteed in China by the 1982 constitution, but those who now appealed to it did not find their interpretation altogether to accord with the still prevailing party and governmental ethos. Manœuvring China in the way that Deng was attempting inevitably entailed risks. Apparently, firm authority was still necessary to prevent the country falling apart as disparities of wealth, health, and opportunity became evident, as between both individuals and provinces. 'New world democrats' were not convinced, arguing, rather, that authoritarian structures and a one-party system impeded economic change. The debate continued.

In a more formal sense, too, new China had to define itself in the world. Here, again, a radical jettisoning of past policy occurred. Mao had frightened Moscow (and not only Moscow) by arguing that world war was inevitable and that socialism would survive it. He seemed to be taking excessive comfort from the size of China's population. It was in 1980 that Hu Yaobang stated publicly that imperialist war could be postponed or even prevented. Indeed, what was uppermost in the mind of Beijing was not 'imperialist war' so much as Soviet activity in Afghanistan. China's 1950 friendship treaty with the Soviet Union was allowed to expire—thus formally ending a relationship which, as noted earlier, had collapsed after 1960. Beijing collaborated with Washington in supplying the anti-Soviet resistance through Pakistan. It was the same fear of Soviet intentions, as allegedly expressed through the vehicle of a victorious Vietnam which was making difficulties for ethnic Chinese, which precipitated the not very successful attempt to 'teach the Vietnamese a lesson'. Relations with the United States steadily improved. In December 1978 President Carter announced the imminent inauguration of full diplomatic relations with the People's Republic. The United States–Taiwan Defence Treaty would expire in January 1980. President Reagan took a somewhat different view on the Taiwan issue, which complicated matters but did not fundamentally upset the Sino-American relationship in the early 1980s. Reagan visited China in 1984 and signed economic and technological agreements with Deng Xiaoping. In the following year, a

US–China nuclear co-operation agreement was signed in Washington. Such developments, however, did not altogether close the door to Moscow. In 1984 China and the Soviet Union signed four new co-operation agreements which indicated some thaw in Sino-Soviet relations.

In September 1984 Beijing reached an agreement with Britain for the reversion of Hong Kong to China in 1997. It was anticipated that there would be 'one country, two systems'. Hong Kong, already China's largest trading partner, would have substantial autonomy and the capitalist system could survive for at least fifty years. Perhaps there was a model here for another thriving island with which, through Hong Kong, China now enjoyed substantial trade—Taiwan itself. An offer of a 'comprehensive peace proposal' to Taiwan came to nothing in 1981, but the matter would probably be returned to in the future.

Such specific steps fitted within a broader framework. It was clearly the case that China was abandoning its role as 'backer of the Third World'—if the Third World still existed. It was no longer seeking self-sufficiency and self-reliance outside the world 'capitalist' system. The notion of a New International Economic Order, entailing a global transfer of wealth from north to south, no longer had appeal. China was carving for itself a niche, a substantial niche, it was hoped, in the international division of labour and production. It would still take time for that integration to be fully accomplished—perhaps it would be the middle of the twenty-first century before China was on a par with the world's most developed nations, but that was the goal. Globally, perhaps there was a trilateral relationship—China, the Soviet Union, and the United States—but that might be a premature description. It might be more realistic to think of China, the United States, the Soviet Union, and Japan as an 'Asian quadrilateral' and China, the United States, the Soviet Union, and the European Community as a kind of 'European quadrilateral': the 'Pacific Rim' versus the 'Atlantic Rim'. China, in any event, now seemed determined to belong to 'the world'.

Comparisons between China and India had not infrequently been made over the nearly thirty-year span of their revolutionary/independent existence. The proclaimed Indian attachment to non-alignment caused irritation in the West but that stance was compensated for in Western eyes by India's steadfast adherence to democratic and constitutional government. It was noted in the previous chapter, however, that in the early 1970s Mrs Gandhi's government showed signs of behaving increasingly arbitrarily. In 1975, when a state court pronounced her guilty of electoral campaign irregularities, she did not resign but instead ordered the arrest of her political opponents. The President of India was induced to proclaim a 'state of emergency', which in turn led to censorship, suspension of civil liberties, and continuing arrests and detentions. It seemed that the foremost 'showpiece' of democracy in Asia was crumbling. The freedom with which she had allowed her son Sanjay to promote draconian birth-control schemes and clear slum dwellings in Delhi provoked widespread opposition, at least to the manner of their implementation. In 1977, in the expectation of a victory which would allow her to 'legitimate' procedures which had been introduced under the state of emergency, Mrs Gandhi went to the country. To her chagrin, she lost the election to Morarji Desai, who headed the new Janata Alliance (a motley coalition of parties). The significance of the result was that for the first time the Congress had lost power. Desai had himself long been active in the Congress—he was 81—but had broken with it in 1969. He restored many of the democratic institutions suspended during the state of emergency (he had himself been imprisoned), but the coalition was ineffective and chaos threatened. Moreover, it was not immune from the corruption which it had itself criticized in Mrs Gandhi. The former Prime Minister, who had lost her seat in the election, returned to parliament in a by-election and contrived to present herself as an injured victim. When another general election was held in January 1980, Mrs Gandhi swept back to power in a landslide victory. Was India to be perpetually faced with a choice between tyranny and chaos?

In what were to prove the last four years of her power, the focus of the problems with which she had been previously concerned shifted. Her son Sanjay was killed in a plane crash in

1980. While his mother grieved for him, his death none the less meant that he could be made to take the blame for previous actions under the State of Emergency. What came more to the fore were issues of religious and communal identity. They were not, of course, new but yet one more manifestation of the ethnic, linguistic, and religious complexity of India—which contrasted so sharply with the largely homogeneous China (though China's national minorities are often overlooked). Matters were indeed so complex that the outside world largely ignored them. It was only when tension exploded into open conflict that foreign media took an interest. In February 1983, for example, local elections in Assam were reported as leading to some 1,500 deaths in violent clashes. Here, as elsewhere, there were doubts about the impartiality and probity of the police and the army, and their subjection to effective civilian control.

The most serious problem, however, was the position of the Sikhs. The protection of their faith from the Hinduism into which it could conceivably be absorbed had been fundamental for centuries, as had been resistance to conversion to Islam. In the new circumstance of post-independence India, however, the question of their status had gained fresh urgency. Sikhs had long been identified and identified themselves as a 'martial race' (and had been disproportionately prominent in the Indian army under the British Raj). To this communal self-image was added in the 1960s an accretion of wealth amongst Sikhs in the Punjab which stemmed from the agricultural revolution. Something like 60 per cent of Indian grain came from the area by the early 1980s. But prosperity revived old fears about identity in so far as there was a considerable Hindu migration into the Punjab. Sikhs calculated that they constituted a bare majority in their own state. In the Indian army, civil service, and police, the proportion of Sikhs comfortably exceeded their proportion of the total Indian population, but for militants that was no guarantee of survival. That could only come from an independent 'Khalistan'. Tension and extremism grew throughout the Punjab, little alleviated by the Delhi government's decision to amend the Punjabi state constitution to acknowledge Sikhism as a religion distinct from

Hinduism. Central policy wavered between conciliation and coercion (proximity to Pakistan in what was after all a partitioned province was in Delhi's mind—and in this respect the Sikh question must be seen in the context of Indo-Pakistani relations as a whole). In June 1984, 250 Sikh extremists were killed when Indian troops stormed the Sikh Golden Temple at Amritsar. Mrs Gandhi dismissed the governor and police chief in the Punjab later in the month. In October she was killed—assassinated by the Sikh bodyguards on whose loyalty she had mistakenly thought she could still rely. Communal violence followed, not only involving attacks by Hindus on Sikhs. They brought to the surface other animosities in other parts of the country. India's 'secular state' looked more ragged than at any time since it was proclaimed. Contemporaries opined that 1984 was turning into the most dangerous year in the life of India. In a situation of apparently incipient fragmentation continuity was sought in a political succession that was almost dynastic—Mrs Gandhi's son Rajiv.

His problems were indeed formidable, the more so since India had conspicuously failed to generate the dynamic if problematic growth being achieved contemporaneously in China. To the ethnic/religious problems which were endemic were added the difficulties of a planning and control structure whose rigidity had perhaps generated the corruption which had widely penetrated it. It had been a mould established under the first Nehru, attracted as he was by creating in India some kind of synthesis between Soviet planning and the best the British Labour Party could offer. Of course, there had been growth and notable achievements over the ensuing decades but, by the early 1980s, India seemed sluggish by comparison with what was going on elsewhere in Asia. Was it time to break out of the cocoon of protection?

The combination of political and economic problems referred to above had combined to diminish India's capacity to play a role in the world commensurate with its size. Bandung and non-alignment and Third World leadership seemed increasingly remote. By the mid-1980s, it was an Indian writer, Shiva Naipaul, who had no hesitation in saying that the term 'Third World' exuded 'bloodless universality' which robbed individuals and societies of their particularity. To subsume, say, Ethiopia, India, and Brazil under the banner of Third Worldhood was absurd and denigrating.

And, too often it appeared, the obsession with Pakistan blocked a broader vision. It was almost impossible to separate 'domestic' and 'foreign' issues, particularly in the case of Kashmir. Of course, that worked both ways. Pakistan too fashioned its foreign policy with a constant eye on New Delhi. Until 1977, it had been shaped by a civilian government under the flamboyant Zulfikar Ali Bhutto—like Mrs Gandhi, Oxford-educated. In that year, however, he was deposed in a military coup by Zia ul-Haq. Within two years, Bhutto had been sentenced to death and hanged. Zia ul-Haq had been sworn in as President in 1978. He banned all political parties and embarked upon a programme of Islamicization which steered his country more in the direction of the Middle East (where employment was to be found in the Gulf and loans might be obtained). The Afghanistan crisis put Pakistan in the front line and the country's problems were compounded by the refugee influx. As with India, it was increasingly asked whether Pakistan could survive. Zia ul-Haq was re-elected President in a 1984 referendum and enhanced his powers in the following year, though he also announced plans for the introduction of a modified form of constitutional government which would replace the martial law that he administered. In a curious way, however, while the protracted tension between the two countries was debilitating, its continued centrality also had the effect of shoring up fragile unity. In 1984, when both countries were in serious trouble, the Pakistanis launched an attack to try to dislodge Indian troops who had moved onto the disputed Sianchin glacier in Kashmir. In 1985 both countries engaged in aerial combat over the same area.

Fragile unity was also the picture in the two outliers to former British India, Burma (Myanmar) and Ceylon (which became Sri Lanka in 1972). Since its independence in 1948 Burma had been plagued by rebellion amongst minority groups, notably the Karens, sometimes supported by Communist China. The army had been in control since 1962 and military expenditure was endemically high. There seemed no prospect of a return to a parliamentary form of government, and the country seemed to outsiders to retreat ever more into itself. Sri Lanka, on the other hand, had initially seemed a stable island after its independence. Yet the balance between the Sinhalese majority and the Tamil minority (largely in the north-east of the island) was always delicate. A determined attempt to supplant the English language by Sinhalese in the 1960s led to rioting. In 1977, after his election, which had been accompanied by rioting in Tamil areas, Junius Jayawardene strengthened the powers of the President. Four years later, a state of emergency was declared because of attacks by the Tamil Liberation Tigers. Thereafter, serious violence between the two communities regularly occurred.

Balance Sheet

What gives the decade which has just been considered its particular flavour is the extent of the interaction between the two superpowers and Third World states. The post-war division of the globe into a hierarchical bipolar arrangement of spheres of influence remained, but previously hard edges became blurred. Rivalries became more multidimensional and alignments less rigid. The superpowers had to work harder to gain endorsement or bring clients into line. Established relationships could collapse completely; like the Russians earlier in Egypt, the Americans found this in Iran. Western European states refused to comply with the embargo placed on European suppliers to the Siberian gas pipeline by the Reagan administration in 1982. Immanuel Wallerstein, whose multi-volume *The Modern World-System* had provided an influential Marxist analysis a decade earlier, speculated in 1984 on the possibility of Western Europe (without Britain) and Eastern Europe forming a bloc which confronted a Pacific Alliance of the United States, Japan, and China. That such speculation could be made was an indication of a perceived new volatility in the international scene. It will become clear in the next chapter, however, that what actually happened at the end of the 1980s was rather different.

6

Brave New World?
1985–

All Change

It was in the second half of the 1980s that the structures and
assumptions which had still largely prevailed in the world since
1945 were dramatically reshaped. The 'Cold War', which had
subsisted for decades, though with fluctuating intensity, was
finally over. Its tentacles, as we have noted in previous chapters,
had spread beyond Europe and complicated other conflicts
elsewhere which had deeper and indigenous ethnic or religious
causes. There had been moments of detente in previous decades,
but they had turned out to be 'false dawns'. Indeed, some
scholars speak of a 'Second Cold War' in the early 1980s when
the optimism engendered by the Helsinki Agreements gave way
to the renewed and potentially explosive rivalry discussed in the
previous chapter. The later 1980s, however, cannot yet be explained definitively. And, when change did come, both its scope
and timing were rarely predicted—a fact that makes one cautious
about academic claims to understand both the international
'system' and the dynamics of domestic change.

The decade after 1985 presents special problems. World history has been littered since 1945 with real wars which began
(whether formally 'declared' or not) at a certain point and were
concluded by some more or less formal peace treaty. Such
treaties normally reflected an identifiable 'victory'. The shape of
the world after 1945 was determined by the outcome of the
1939–45 war just as the years between 1919 and 1939 had been
shaped by the previous 'world war'. In the case of what happened after 1985, however, 'victories' cannot formally be identified. Indeed, what characterizes the world after 1985, to a quite

remarkable degree, is that it has seen change on a scale which has in the past only resulted from the conclusion of a cataclysmic conflict.

Such a fact, however, has its complications. At its various heights, the Cold War was a source of profound anxiety. The world's survival seemed unlikely. Nuclear weapons, in particular, gave rise to *dicta* from wise men who believed that the year 2000 would not be reached. Hans J. Morgenthau, the American scholar who had devoted a lifetime to studying international relations, had been very gloomy in 1979. The world, in his opinion, was moving 'ineluctably' towards a third war, which would be a strategic nuclear war. Nothing could be done to prevent it. 'The international system', he wrote, 'is simply too unstable to survive for long.' Such pessimism, before the second half of the 1980s, could be illustrated from the works of leading thinkers across the globe.

The demise of the Cold War, however, has not yet produced an uncomplicated sense of relief. Indeed, the way in which the superpowers once enrolled their clients and established their own hegemonies has come to be seen in some quarters as providing a necessary kind of stability. It has thus far been impossible to be certain what kind of world order actually exists in the 1990s. For decades, although a 'Third World' had tenuously established a kind of independence and identity, it remained the case that the central axis of potential conflict revolved around the United States and its clients/allies and the Soviet Union and its clients. There was an all-embracing argument between 'Capitalism' and 'Communism' and competing conceptions of freedom and democracy. Alliances and alignments in one part of the globe could precipitate conflict elsewhere, but they could also contain them. Great Powers, if they were so minded, could prevent local difficulties getting out of hand. In the 1990s, however, there was no longer such assurance. It was unlikely, at least to judge by the past, that conflict would completely disappear from the world, but its main source had been removed. However, the diffusion of power might make international behaviour more erratic. The problems posed by the possession of nuclear weapons had still not been solved. There might well be flashpoints when the economic or other interests of individual states clashed.

The 'End of Ideology' had been predicted for more than thirty years by both American and European writers, but ideology had proved obstinately enduring. Now, however, perhaps the moment had come. There were suggestions that the 'End of History' had been reached—that is to say that after the upheavals of the century ideological systems had exhausted themselves. The American Francis Fukuyama was only one of a number of writers, at the end of the 1980s and into the 1990s, to elaborate theses along these lines. Liberal democracy, largely in its American form, would be the world's norm because history had sensibly demonstrated that this should be the case. The mould of the world was set. Other commentators, however, expressed scepticism about any such 'end' of history. The world was a much more complicated place than envisaged in Fukuyama's philosophy. They suggested that a closer look, continent by continent, offered little ground for such complacent and indeed arrogant assumptions. It is necessary, therefore, to look more closely at what actually happened in the later 1980s before succumbing to simplistic assumptions, one way or another, about what the future holds.

Soviet Crisis

In December 1991 the Union of Soviet Socialist Republics was formally disbanded. Presidents Yeltsin (Russia), Kravchuk (Ukraine), and Shushkevich (Belarus) declared that the state no longer existed either as a subject of international law or as a geopolitical reality. The Soviet Union was to be replaced by a 'Commonwealth of Independent States'. It was an untidy end. It affronted some other constituent republics in so far as they had not even been consulted about the demise of the state to which they belonged. At the time, however, there was a lot that was untidy about the Soviet Union.

The election of Mikhail Gorbachev in March 1985 at the age of 54 to the General Secretaryship of the Communist Party seemed to indicate an awareness that the Soviet Union needed to change. That does not mean, however, that a consensus existed on the direction it should take in other than very general terms. Indeed, what remains disputed is the extent to which, from the very beginning, Gorbachev himself had a deep appreciation of the risks he was taking—and whether he would have behaved very differently if he had known to what his reforms would ultimately lead. He was relatively young and undoubtedly anxious to make his mark. He did not, however, set out to dissolve the Soviet Union or even to dislodge the party from its leading position. It was necessary, however, to wage internal war on corruption, lethargy, and drunkenness. Two terms came to be associated with his vision—*perestroika* (restructuring) and *glasnost* (openness). It was vital, Gorbachev believed, that the Soviet Union should break out from stagnation. However, there is at least a case for arguing that there was a fundamental incompatibility between these two slogans. *Glasnost* even gave encouragement to writers who had been previously banned or exiled to join in the fight against managerial privileges. Such steps alarmed those who thought that *perestroika* should be an 'inside job'. 'Restructuring' was of course an extremely difficult task in itself and one for which there was no effective precedent. The objective seemed to be some kind of modified market economy which could actually respond to the aspirations of Soviet consumers. Alongside it went a determination to try to establish the rule of law in Soviet society in a quite new way. There were also to be secret ballots for the election of party officials. In 1988, as a further sign of openness, leading churchmen from around the world came to Moscow to celebrate one thousand years of Christianity in Russia.

Additionally, in the initial years, Gorbachev was still waging the war in Afghanistan which he had inherited. It could not be sustained. By 1988–9 he had initiated a phased withdrawal of Soviet forces. A few years earlier, at the 1986 Party Congress, Gorbachev had made public his abandonment of the idea of inevitable world conflict. It was acknowledged that there were thriving capitalist economies in the world. The great rival system was not on the point of collapse. There was a need to build a new understanding with the West based on fresh assumptions. It was no longer necessary to assume a perpetual military confrontation and global competition. He made it clear that he was prepared to ban all nuclear weapons. In October 1986 Gorbachev and Reagan met at Reykjavik and, to the subsequent dismay of their respective allies, the two men came close to abolishing all ballistic missiles. They even contemplated total nuclear disarmament. In December 1987 what was signed between the two superpowers was an agreement on intermediate-range nuclear forces (INF) in Europe. The Soviet insistence on the termination of the Strategic Defense Initiative was dropped—the United States only formally abandoned it in May 1993. Moscow also agreed to destroy far more launchers and missiles than the United States and, moreover, to accept an intrusive inspection regime. The significance of the treaty was that it eliminated an entire category of nuclear weapons, though of course there remained many others in existence. Strategic Arms Reduction Talks, as they were now called, resumed. In December 1988, at the United Nations, Gorbachev announced a major reduction in Soviet conventional forces. A new negotiating forum—the Conventional Armed Forces in Europe (CFE) talks—produced a treaty in November 1990 under which the Soviet Union agreed to remove a substantial proportion of its military hardware from the region west of the Urals. The objective was to establish a balance of conventional forces between the two sides in Europe.

In so far as Gorbachev took the risks and the initiative in these matters, up to this juncture, both internally and internationally, he paved the way for ending the Cold War. He was a new man, someone with whom, as the British Prime Minister Margaret Thatcher famously declared, it was possible to do business. What is difficult to decide, however, is the relative importance of 'push' and 'pull' in this process of change. Certainly there was an openness on the part of Gorbachev, but was it caused by the weakness of the Soviet economy and system, which could no longer be disguised and which left him with little option?

The question can be put another way by asking about the motives and objectives of the military build-up undertaken by the Reagan administration in the first half of the 1980s. The flavour of Reagan's sentiments about the Soviet Union has been given in the previous chapter. The administration pushed ahead with deployments and technical developments across a broad front. The allies of the United States in Europe had to face down the opposition, sometimes quite strong, to the positioning of cruise missiles. In the end, however, some contend, the build-up worked. Reagan so raised the technological stakes that the Soviet Union could not compete. It was the American President who 'won' the Cold War. Things are rarely so simple, however. In so far as there was a 'Reagan Doctrine', it only led to the ending of the Cold War because in Gorbachev there was a Russian who was prepared to respond in a new way to the pressures put upon him. Another man might not have been so adventurous. In any case, as the scale of the US budget deficit became apparent, even the United States could not continue its military efforts indefinitely. The two leaders, at a particular juncture, needed each other and each was able to rationalize his achievement to his own satisfaction.

The Soviet Union, however, was still in place. Indeed, both inside and outside the country there remained considerable scepticism as to what Gorbachev was really seeking to achieve. He was certainly a reformer, it was admitted, but he did not tamper with the fundamentals of Soviet society. Historians could point to previous periods in Russian history when energetic bouts of reform had been followed by reaction. And some commentators still suspected that what Gorbachev was really after was a breathing-space. After an interval of consolidation, an anti-Western campaign would resume. Despite clever manipulation of the Western media, nothing had really changed. Gorbachev remained a Leninist who was determined to keep the Soviet Union intact; if it seemed necessary to 'sacrifice' Eastern

Europe to preserve the Soviet Union, he would do so. Perhaps it was an *ex post facto* rationalization, but statements were made in 1990 around the Soviet leadership which claimed that the Soviet Union's financial and defence position had improved by 'shedding' Eastern Europe. On this analysis, Gorbachev's reaction to the unfolding events of 1989 was prudential rather than particularly 'enlightened'. It became clear, with remarkable speed, that he was being faced with the collapse of Soviet authority, though it is not easy to say categorically which set of circumstances in which country triggered the process. Some suggest, with a degree of plausibility, that it was Soviet 'meddling' which actually destabilized the position elsewhere—they have the divergence between Moscow and East Berlin primarily in mind—by holding out the example of 'reform' in circumstances which would undermine what was the most 'Stalinist' Communist regime.

In any case, the Soviet Union was not in fact in a position to 'call the tune' throughout Eastern Europe. In each country there were particular indigenous circumstances which applied. In Hungary, by the mid-1980s, there appeared a growing contradiction between the amount of private enterprise which the Kádár regime had permitted for many years and the still rigid political system. In 1988, the long-serving Kádár was replaced by Imre Pozsgay. In January 1989 the Hungarian parliament passed a law allowing the formation of political parties. Pozsgay hoped that his reformed Communists would triumph in free elections. It was accepted that the 1956 rising had not been a 'counter-revolution'. In May, the Hungarian army started to take down the security fence along the border with neighbouring Austria. In June, Nagy and other heroes of 1956 were reburied—an event witnessed by perhaps a quarter of a million people. It was at this point that the Communist Party lost its grip. In September, the Hungarian government allowed citizens of the German Democratic Republic to cross freely to the West. In October, a new republic was declared with a constitution which permitted multi-party democracy. Elections in December—the first genuine multi-party elections in the Soviet bloc—produced success not for the Communists but for the Hungarian Democratic Forum led by József Antall. The renamed Communists came fourth. This sequence discloses a transition which was peaceful, though not without precarious moments. The contrast with 1956 was in this respect complete.

In Poland, further strikes began in May 1988 involving ship-yard workers—there was a certain irony in the fact that they were visited in December by Margaret Thatcher, the epitome of 'capitalism' and not renowned in her own country for her partiality for strikers. The stature of the British Prime Minister in dissident circles in Central Europe was particularly high at this juncture. The Polish government had resumed talks with the Solidarity union in August—it had been banned since 1981. The Jaruzelski regime reluctantly and gradually moved towards re-legalizing Solidarity. Its leader, Lech Wałęsa, reached agreement on various political and economic reforms in April 1989. In the following month the Roman Catholic Church was granted many privileges, including the right to run schools and to have confis-cated property restored. In June Solidarity triumphed in elec-tions leading to the appointment, after protracted talks, of a non-Communist government under Mazowiecki. Jaruzelski, the only candidate, was elected, though without public enthusiasm, to the post of President. In October Poland opened its border with the German Democratic Republic and announced a willing-ness to accept refugees. Poland, it seemed, was firmly on a path to democracy and market economics.

These events in Hungary and Poland, which interacted, were also being watched, and to some extent imitated, elsewhere. In Czechoslovakia, there were major changes in the government and in the Communist Party in October 1988. The twentieth anniversary of the suicide of Jan Palach was marked in January 1989 by a demonstration which was broken up by police. In the following month, Václav Havel, the Czech playwright, was imprisoned. However, in April the first multi-party elections were held in Czechoslovakia since 1946. Strikes and demonstra-tions began in November culminating in demands for the end of Communist rule, which were successful. In December Havel became the first non-Communist President of Czechoslovakia for forty-one years. Twenty years after the 'Prague Spring' had been crushed, its spirit was reborn. An assurance was given to the Czechoslovaks, as it was to the Hungarians, that Soviet troops would be withdrawn by the summer of 1991.

In Bulgaria, although there was change—Zhivkov, who had been General Secretary of the Communist Party for thirty-five years, stood down—it was neither smooth nor complete in 1989–90. Neither was it in Romania, where Ceauşescu ruled as a personal dictator, buttressed by a formidable security apparatus. He was determined to hold on to power. Fighting and disturbances took place in Bucharest and elsewhere. Ceauşescu and his wife were captured and executed. In these two countries, therefore, although the dominant personalities had been removed, it was far from clear to what extent the fundamentals of the system over which they had presided had in fact been changed.

The opening of the Berlin Wall on 9 November 1989 was the most dramatic expression of the changes sweeping through Communist East-Central Europe. The momentum for change in the German Democratic Republic (celebrating its fortieth birthday in 1989) had very evidently become irresistible. Even so, it was not an outcome which had been universally predicted. Earlier, the party leadership, under the ailing Honecker, seemed prepared to meet demonstrations with violence. The Protestant Church had given a home to protesters and a 'New Forum' looked for some change in the direction of political pluralism. Honecker made way for Krenz as party leader and a new Prime Minister was brought in, but to no avail. The demonstrations grew in numbers and it was in this context that the decision was taken to open the border. Even so, it was initially hoped by the party leadership, and by some citizens, that the state could survive, albeit with some changes, as a socialist alternative to the Federal Republic. Revelations of corruption and mounting economic problems made that increasingly unlikely. In elections in March 1990 an 'Alliance for Germany', closely linked to the Christian Democrats in the Federal Republic, won nearly half the vote. It advocated rapid monetary union and subsequent accession to the Federal Republic. The parties of the Federal Republic had taken a major role in the election—as had the Federal Chancellor, Helmut Kohl.

Change in the German Democratic Republic (and its demise) raised issues of a different order. The partition of Germany had been on the agenda since 1945 and a reunited country had major implications for 'Europe' and for East–West relations in Europe. Kohl's commitment to unification reflected not only personal conviction but also knowledge that East Germans would flood westwards as the German Democratic Republic collapsed. Suddenly, all the major powers who had dabbled with 'solutions' to the German question for decades now had to face reality. It was going to happen. London and Paris had grown accustomed to thinking that since unification was not going to happen they could safely regret partition. Now, with some (though differing) reluctance, both Thatcher and Mitterrand came to accept that there was no alternative to unification. Perhaps, even so, it would be Moscow which would impose a veto. Kohl and Gorbachev met in February 1990 in Moscow and, over subsequent months, a deal was struck. Reunification took effect on 3 October 1990. After some hesitation and delay, Kohl had agreed formally to recognize the Oder–Neisse line as the new Germany's eastern frontier. He successfully resisted Gorbachev's initial demand that the new Germany should leave NATO. The details of the deal also included arrangements for a phased withdrawal of Soviet troops, renunciation of nuclear, chemical, or biological weapons, and German economic aid to the Soviet Union. Naturally, it was the new Poland which was most anxious about the Oder–Neisse border.

A formal line under the dissolution of the satellite system was drawn with the end of the military and political structures of the Warsaw Pact on 1 April and 1 July 1991 respectively. Comecon was abolished on 28 June 1991.

It was obvious, however, that the Soviet Union could not be insulated. It was itself vulnerable to fissiparous tendencies. In not infrequently speaking of the Soviet Union as 'Russia', the outside world had for decades taken insufficient note of its multinational character. The Baltic republics, Estonia, Latvia, and Lithuania, had been independent for some twenty years—previously they had been within the Tsarist Empire—before being incorporated into the Soviet Union in 1940. Through 1987–8, movements for a restoration of national rights, perhaps even the regaining of independence, gathered momentum. 'Popular Fronts' emerged and won strong support at all-Soviet elections in 1989. The position of the Russian populations of Estonia and Latvia in particular complicated the picture. Gorbachev tried an economic blockade of Lithuania (which had declared independence in March 1990) but then scrapped it and instead sought a new Union Treaty which would allow the republics 'home rule' but leave defence, foreign policy, and economic co-ordination to Moscow. Soviet Interior troops stormed the television station in Vilnius, Lithuania, in January 1991 but that proved to be the last throw. Referendums in Lithuania (February) and Latvia and Estonia (March) produced majorities for independence, and Gorbachev accepted the outcome with great reluctance. It was not until after his resignation that the formal grant of independence was made by Moscow.

The situation in the Baltic states had been watched with some concern in the West. It was sometimes felt that to give them support might encourage Gorbachev's 'conservative' opponents, lead to his overthrow, and thus jeopardize continuing East–West detente. It was actually desirable, from some Western standpoints, that the Soviet Union should survive; if this required its retention of the Baltic republics, so be it. Others, however, found such Realpolitik intolerable. Of course the republics had the right to be free. Gorbachev should only be supported when and where he accepted the fundamental principle of democratic consent. In the event, as has been noted, the Soviet Union did lose the Baltic states.

It was not even the case, however, that the Baltic states could be regarded as totally exceptional. It was suddenly necessary to research the circumstances in which the Soviet Union had been formed in 1922 and to pay attention to such entities as Moldova (Moldavia), Armenia, Azerbaijan, Georgia, Kazakhstan, Belarus

(Bielorussia), Ukraine, to name only some of the republics where old and new issues came to the fore. Did they desire independence and the complete breakup of the Union or some confederal solution? The conflicts that broke out most violently, however, revolved around, or at least embraced, ethnic and religious issues that long anteceded the Soviet state. To whom, for example, did Nagorny Karabakh belong? This mountainous region was mainly Armenian in population but had been incorporated into the Azerbaijan Republic in 1921. Bitter fighting ensued between the two national groups, with the Soviet Army oscillating between spasmodic brutality and total indifference. In Georgia 'national revival' was proclaimed and elections in May 1991 brought to power Zviad Gamsakhurdia, who declared himself unwilling to compromise with Soviet institutions—and within a few years there was rebellion in the region of Abkhazia. In Belarus and Ukraine an emphasis on 'nationalism' raised awkward questions about its content. Time and again in the late 1980s and early 1990s, the revival of both long-cherished but also long-forgotten aspirations threatened conflict and crisis. National enthusiasm could not altogether stifle doubts about the economic viability of independent states—particularly since economic planning in the Soviet Union had been deliberately designed to promote interdependence (and thus buttress unity) and to ensure that few republics were self-supporting.

In all this ferment, Russians themselves were in a most uncomfortable position, scattered through the Soviet Union as they were. Whilst 'Popular Fronts' emerged in many Soviet nations, a 'Popular Front' was problematic for them. The Russians were the 'imperial nation'. What about the rights of Russia itself? A Russian declaration of sovereignty was made in June 1990 and Boris Yeltsin (who had earlier been sacked by Gorbachev) became the first directly elected President of the Russian Federation a year later. Over the next few years, as it became evident that the old global role had gone, the Russian leadership had to face up to a quite new position. In addition, there were some 25 million Russians beyond the borders of the new Russian state, though it was also the case, as events were shortly to demonstrate, that the Russian Federation itself contained restless non-Russian peoples.

The Central Asian Republics similarly looked as though they were in the middle of a process of cultural and geographical realignment as Islam revived and they returned (somewhat ambivalently) to old contacts to the south which had grown rusty through the Soviet years. Turkey and Iran looked north, in turn, with fresh interest and (perhaps) competing aspirations.

The reverberations of these momentous changes continue and it would indeed have been surprising if an instant era of democratic vitality, economic prosperity, and national harmony had supervened. The heady euphoria of freedom gave way in the 1990s in instance after instance to more sober reflection on future prospects and, in some cases, considerable internal dissension. A new course might be being set, but the journey was likely to prove problematic. In governmental and constitutional terms, the development of multi-party politics proved anything but straightforward. It was not as though the previous inter-war experience of Poland or Hungary, to take two examples, had been one of democratic success. The opening up of government files left old scores to be settled. There remained an enduring suspicion that, whatever their current professions and labels, the former Communist parties had not really accepted the rules of pluralist democracy. Whether or not such suspicions were justified, by May 1994 elections in Hungary, for example, gave a clear majority to the former communist Socialist Party, as had happened in Poland in September 1993. The concept of a civil service at the disposal of governments of different political colours was not easy to implant. What was to be done with armies? Even though the states of Eastern Europe were more ethnically homogeneous than their inter-war predecessors, there remained minority issues—Hungarians in Romania or Slovakia, for example—which could prove explosive. Even in Czechoslovakia where, in the past, democracy had proved relatively successful, tension between Czechs and Slovaks proved so great that the newly free country split in two, though without violence—the Czech Republic and Slovakia (1993). Moreover, institutions which had acted in effect as islands of opposition under Communist rule soon found that they no longer enjoyed unquestioning allegiance. This was most conspicuously the case where the Roman Catholic Church in Poland was concerned. Perhaps pluralist democracy did not require Catholic hegemony? And heroes—such as Lech Wałęsa in Poland—were to find within a few years that, although the past catapulted them into office, government was different from opposition. By 1997 a post-Solidarity government 'successfully' closed the Gdańsk shipyards where the Solidarity movement had been born.

In addition, the transition from a Communist planned economy to (more or less) a market economy was inescapably painful. Exposed to competition, antiquated industries with large labour forces could not survive. No doubt, the phase was only transitional and, by means of joint ventures and the application of Western know-how and investment, economies would improve, but that might not be soon enough to prevent the emergence of social discontent. The Communist system might come to seem not so bad after all. In this situation, outside advice varied and with it the policies adopted. Some believed that there was no alternative to root-and-branch restructuring, others that drastic privatization would produce unacceptable social dislocation; change was therefore better introduced gradually. In short, while there might be a goal and a strategy, tactics varied according to circumstances. It was unlikely that each Eastern European economy would move forward at the same pace and with the same degree of success. The Czech Republic, Hungary, and to some extent Poland began to emerge as 'winners' in this process, whereas in Bulgaria or Romania, where in any case the extent of political change still remained uncertain, the economies seemed to be moving backwards. The Soviet 'satellites' had never been absolutely uniform, but in the years after 1989 it was becoming steadily more difficult to think of a 'bloc'. As the common experience of Soviet hegemony began to fade, diversity became more evident.

There also existed throughout Eastern Europe a certain nervousness about the disintegrating Soviet Union. It seemed self-evident that after nearly three-quarters of a century of Communism and, before that, a Tsarist system only lightly touched by 'Western' democratic notions, Russia would be unlikely to grow a fully-fledged and functioning system of pluralist democracy overnight. The attempted coup in August 1991 seemed to justify such anxiety. Its leaders talked of the need to maintain unity, law and order, and the world status of the Soviet state. President Gorbachev was placed under house arrest in the Crimea. Yeltsin resisted the coup and in the end successfully appealed for loyalty to him as elected President of Russia. In the wake of the coup's failure, Yeltsin suspended the Communist Party and asserted his supremacy over Gorbachev. The latter, protesting, resigned as General Secretary of the CPSU and told its Central Committee that it should disband. The coup, far from preserving the Soviet Union, accelerated its demise. In December 1991 Gorbachev announced his resignation as its President and the Russian tricolour flew over the Kremlin.

Naturally, the Russian Federation did not live happily ever after. Its problems of industrial regeneration were as acute as any elsewhere. The creation of a genuine 'civil society' was arguably more difficult. There were clear signs, albeit in rather different form, of that old cleavage in Russian history between 'Westernizers' and 'Slavophiles', and indeed between the cultural orientations of different parts of Russia. Leningrad became St Petersburg once more in 1991, perhaps with a renewed sense of its historic significance. The influx of foreigners seeking to convert souls or premises (and sometimes both) was sometimes too overwhelming, yet it was also matched by a determination, particularly on the part of the younger generation, that Russia should not be introverted. Russia could not afford to pine over its fate or immerse itself in the uncovering of its layers of suffering and deprivation. Russia had to join the world. Alongside such enthusiastic idealism, however, went signs of deteriorating morale, of crime and social disorientation. Stability was not to be easily found as new parties and new political stars shone fitfully and then disappeared. The strategy of Yeltsin lurched one way and then another as, on occasion, he himself did. Old Communists sensed that there was a possibility of a comeback. Some nationalists, exuding xenophobia, preached that Russia was being ravaged by American wolves. The success of Zhirinovsky in the parliamentary elections of December 1993 was taken to demonstrate a paradox of 'democratization': extreme nationalism had a popular appeal. However, two years later, Zhirinovsky's party received only half the votes it had attracted in 1993. It became evident that Yeltsin was adept at stealing the clothes of his opponents as he asserted a more 'nationalist' tone in 1996, ahead of the presidential elections.

The possible eastward expansion of NATO membership by the inclusion of at least Poland, the Czech Republic, and Hungary became contentious in the middle 1990s. Moscow made it plain that such expansion would not be welcome and could be perceived as unfriendly. The states which wished to join thought that to allow a Russian veto on such a step was to imply that they were, after everything that had happened, still not really able to make their own decisions. They were adamant that there was no longer a kind of 'Russian world' in East-Central Europe. Washington sought to ease Russian fears. That such strong feelings could exist in 1997 on both sides reveals, not surprisingly, that the past has not been totally forgotten. In the event, in 1997, it was agreed that Poland, the Czech Republic, and Hungary should be admitted to NATO (though not Romania and Slovenia). Certain assurances were given to a still unhappy Russia.

The integrity of the Russian Federation was itself threatened as minorities it contained—most notably the Chechens—sought to break away in the mid-1990s to form republics of their own. Fearful that his own position would be threatened unless he showed vigour in defending the Federation, Yeltsin permitted Russian forces to launch an offensive against Grozny, the capital of rebellious Chechnya, in December 1994. The conflict that ensued there soon showed every sign of being as protracted and bloody as the Soviet campaign in Afghanistan had been—and as futile. It severely tarnished Yeltsin's image in liberal eyes. More discreetly, however, from 1993 onwards, Russian military, economic, and political pressure was placed with some success on Georgia, Azerbaijan, and Ukraine in a way which suggested that old Moscow habits died hard. The Commonwealth of Independent States was not allowed to fade away.

During these years, when it was very difficult to guess how Russian internal politics would develop, Yeltsin's career was thought to be in jeopardy and his ill-health increased. Yet it proved premature to write him off. In 1997, having won another presidential election, he remained in charge and, given time, it still seemed plausible to envisage the evolution of a democratically stable Russia: plausible, but not certain. Much would depend on whether a fundamental transformation of the Russian economy could be achieved: possible, but not likely.

Community Relaunch

In 1984, when France held its presidency, President Mitterrand toured Community capitals and talked of relaunching the European Community. Few disputed that it lacked direction, having been wounded by oil crises and budget conflicts. For several years, however, Commission officials had been looking at ways in which momentum could be recovered. Four options seemed to be available: monetary union, foreign and defence policy co-operation, institutional reform, and an internal market. It was only the last option which seemed likely to command sufficient political support. Arthur Cockfield, a British Commissioner, drew up a White Paper which could provide the basis for such a scheme. It would tackle frontier, technical, and fiscal issues. The way forward could only involve complex negotiations. There was Continental distrust of what seemed to be a British 'supermarket mentality' under the Thatcher government. There was matching British mistrust of attempts to build in too much political solidarity and cohesion, not to mention monetary union. Between these two broad approaches lay a host of individual concerns and objectives which had to be addressed. In addition, Spain and Portugal were due to come into the Community in 1986 and this further complicated the picture.

Their adhesion reinforced fears in Ireland and Greece in particular that a single market would have serious consequences for
their economies. 'Structural Funds' were devised to moderate
the impact of the Single European Act which was agreed at the
Luxembourg summit in December 1985—to come into operation
in July 1987. By the end of 1992 the twelve member states, it
was anticipated, would have achieved full economic integration.
All non-tariff barriers to the free movement of goods, services,
people, and capital within the Community would be removed.
The European show was apparently back on the road.

There was irony, therefore, in the contrary paths being taken
in Europe as a whole after 1985: in the West integration, and in
the East disintegration. In reality, however, there was still considerable debate both within and between member states on the
precise path to be followed. In agreeing to some extension of
qualified majority voting and to additional powers of initiative
on the part of the Commission, the Luxembourg Council opened
the way to economic and monetary union. However, there
remained both national and ideological differences as to what
that should entail. The British emphasis remained upon the
single market conceived as essentially an economic enterprise.
Elsewhere, to greater or lesser degree, there were assertions that
a 'social market' was needed, that is to say where social considerations balanced the free play of economic forces. There was
also some feeling abroad that only an 'organized' Community
could really meet the challenge posed by the United States and
Japan.

The re-election of Margaret Thatcher as British Prime Minister in June 1987 ensured that the debate about the future of
Europe would continue. In September 1988 she delivered a
celebrated speech in Belgium in which she rejected the notion of
an 'identikit European personality'. The British people did not
want a bureaucratized and centralized 'Eurostate'. She rejected
what she perceived as socialism by the back door. The British
Labour Party was beginning to sound a little more sympathetic
to the Community but it had fought the 1983 General Election
on a promise to remove Britain from it within the lifetime of a

Labour government. It was apparent that so long as there was agreement between France and Germany—in effect between Mitterrand and Kohl—a direction would be maintained with which Britain would not be happy. Much time had therefore to be spent on working out the detailed implications of further integration in taxation, law, transport, and manufacturing and environmental standards, amongst other matters. Plans were unveiled in 1989 for European Monetary Union (EMU) which would involve the creation of a European Central Bank and a common currency. Jacques Delors, the President of the Commission, in a speech in January 1989 to the European Parliament made it clear that he heard the voice of history calling. It would not be enough to create a vast economic area. The Community had to have a little more soul.

In the same year, after resisting stoutly, Thatcher did allow Britain to join the Exchange Rate Mechanism (ERM) of the European Monetary System. The European Monetary System had been in existence since 1979, linking the exchange rates of individual countries. Currencies were to be kept fixed in relation to each other, subject to permissible variation. It represented an attempt to steer a path between flexibility and predictability in currency management. Britain, with several other countries, initially stayed outside the ERM which operated the system. By the end of 1990, however, Thatcher had been compelled to resign office. Her hostility to European integration was a factor in losing the support of many of her own MPs. However, in September 1992, under her successor John Major, market pressure forced the British government to withdraw from the ERM.

At Maastricht in December 1991, the member governments agreed on a Treaty on European Union which would come into force a year later. A complex set of interlinked matters had been settled after long debate. Qualified majority voting in the Council of Ministers was extended, as were the powers and competences of the European Parliament and Court. The project of EMU was firmly endorsed with the objective of setting up a central bank and common currency by 1999 at the latest. Plans were also set in hand for further conferences and discussion which would address both general and particular issues: democracy and legitimacy, 'transparency' and 'subsidiarity', effectiveness and consistency, common foreign and security policy. Britain, however, obtained 'opt-outs'. The 'Social Chapter', which attempted to establish uniform provisions across a raft of social and industrial issues, would not be implemented. The government also made it clear that Britain reserved its position in relation to a single currency and central bank. 'Subsidiarity' was supposedly enshrined by agreement that the European Union (as it became) would only act where 'the proposed action cannot be achieved by member states'—a baffling statement. 'Transparency' was supposed to entail that funding methodologies and outcomes were 'public' rather than the product of private inscrutable deals. The word 'federal' was excised, but a commitment to 'ever closer union' seemed to mean much the same.

Ratification of Maastricht, however, proved much more difficult than had been anticipated by the governments concerned. There was strong opposition from sections of the British Conservative Party. The Danish people initially rejected it in a referendum, while in September 1992 it was only by a narrow margin that the French people voted for it. Eventually, ratification was achieved—a further summit was held in Edinburgh in December 1992—but a severe jolt had been administered to the process of integration. Over the years immediately following, a great deal of attention was devoted to the specifics—exchange rate convergence, public debt ratios, inflation—without which no scheme could work. There was much uncertainty both about whether monetary union would indeed begin in 1999 and about the identity of the countries which would join at the beginning.

It was evident that the British were most out of sympathy with the direction in which Europe was moving. In the British General Election of 1997 much hostility was expressed, particularly within the Conservative Party, towards the idea of any further European integration and to British participation in monetary union. British unease, however, could not be entirely discounted as mere insularity. In France, in particular, there was a tendency in some rather strident quarters to see a federalist

Europe as a vehicle for German hegemony. On the other hand, it was also argued that it seemed sensible that Germany should be 'tied in' and remain Western-orientated. At the same time, it had to be accepted that the new Germany would straddle Central Europe in a way that the old Federal Republic had not done. The decision that Berlin would resume its place as the national capital did not in the short term indicate any shift in the unified country's commitment to European integration. Nevertheless, over time, there were those who thought that a capital in Berlin rather than Bonn would make Germany less 'Western European' in outlook.

For Germany itself, there was an even more fundamental question. Clinton, the first US President to give a speech on the eastern side of the Brandenburg Gate in Berlin, demanded that Germany—'a special partner'—should take a more extended role in world affairs. Germany had now grown up. However, it was not until July 1994 that the German Federal Court decided, contrary to a widespread assumption, that the constitution did not prevent Germany using force in any circumstance other than in defence of German territory. In the 1990s there no longer existed any direct threat to German territory. Did that mean a role for Germany in global politics? That remained an open question, with German opinion divided. Some 'neo-conservatives' argued that it was time to contribute actively to 'policing' the world. Their critics argued that Germany had enough to do at home as things stood. It had indeed become clear by the middle 1990s that the costs of 'restructuring' in the former GDR exceeded expectations. No doubt, the benefits would show through, both for its inhabitants and for the German economy as a whole, but for a moment it began to falter and unemployment rose. There were some neo-Nazi attacks on immigrants. The sheet-anchor of European integration for decades looked somewhat more vulnerable, though the European vision of Chancellor Kohl did not waver.

Even those who remained committed to the European ideal expressed doubts about the manageability of the Union (joined further by Sweden, Finland, and Austria in 1995—Norway's referendum rejected membership). And, above all, it was recognized that a decade after the 'relaunch' of Europe in 1985 the continent had changed in a way not conceivable at the earlier date. There would have to be a place, at some date, for countries in East-Central Europe who were now free to join and wished to do so. The establishment in 1989 of the European Reconstruction Development Bank to provide assistance to Eastern Europe was a recognition, perhaps an inadequate one, of a common continental mutual interest.

Once again, however, the question had to be asked: what kind of world was 'Europe' and where, in global terms, did it now belong? The more closely the position was examined in the mid-1990s the more a simple contrast between an 'integrating' Western Europe and a 'disintegrating' Eastern Europe seemed inadequate. The events of the decade did disclose that a 'Common European Home'—a phrase used by Gorbachev in a somewhat optimistic moment—which stretched from the Atlantic to the Urals, could be a possibility. They also disclosed, however, that, notwithstanding the 'supranationality' which had been emphasized or imposed (militarily or ideologically) since 1945, national sentiment remained strong, and classical questions of balance of power in Europe had not been buried. There had indeed been a 'Europeanization' of Europe, as the continent achieved a degree of institutional and ideological commonality, from Riga to Lisbon, from Stockholm to Athens, which could not have been envisaged in 1945. Yet this new world was still fragile.

The disintegration of Yugoslavia, the country for so long poised between East and West, made the point. Arguably, the country had been in slow-motion dissolution for some years. Marshal Tito had died in 1980 and commentators had sometimes expressed the view that the state-structure which he had created would die with him. This author, however, visiting the country on several occasions in the late 1980s and in 1990, recalls firm assurances given him in conversation by 'knowledgeable' Slovenes, Serbs, and Croats that Yugoslavia would survive. Thus, the eventual crisis came as something of a surprise, as did the depth of animosity. In June 1991, Croatia and Slovenia, the

most 'Western' and economically advanced republics of Yugoslavia, seceded from the federation, a step recognized by the EC
in January 1992. Independence was not something which the
Serb-dominated federal forces were prepared to tolerate. In
Serbia itself, Slobodan Milosević had routed his rivals in the
Communist Party in 1987 and proceeded to secure the backing
of the nationalist Serb constituency. Fighting flared up quickly
(Macedonia and Bosnia-Herzegovina also declared their independence). There were some fears that the entire Balkans would
be drawn into the conflict. The position of Albania was particularly precarious. The outside world quickly became aware of
the complex ethnic and religious composition of Yugoslavia.
Inconvenient enclaves were identified on maps and shown on
television screens. Mediators from the European Union and US
ex-President Carter came and went, as did arms embargoes,
cease-fires, and patched-up settlements. The Secretary-General
of the United Nations had a special envoy in place, though not
to great effect. At times, disputes outside Yugoslavia on how
intervention might bring about a solution threatened to reopen
East–West tension. The Russian Duma passed resolutions urging
the government to be more assertive. A gruesome catalogue of
bombardments and massacres ensued, and the city of Sarajevo
came under siege from Serb forces. For a time, images of these
events dominated television screens across the world.

As the conflict extended over years, and as it became apparent
that the European Union could not sort out this particularly
European conflict, 'peace' was in the end—if end it be—engineered by the United States and made practically possible by the
presence of British and other foreign troops during the crucial
monitoring period. It stood out that despite endless Brussels
discussion of 'co-ordinating foreign policy' amongst member
states of the EU, no effective policy had been hammered out
and implemented.

The Yugoslav conflict was a savage story, made all the more
disturbing because it demonstrated how unsound was the
assumption that such things would never again happen in
Europe after the 1939–45 war. And, in so far as conflict had a

Christian/Muslim edge to it, as in Bosnia-Herzegovina, there was a reminder of a very long past and some realization that Europe might not be as detached from ethnic/religious conflicts in the rest of the world as had often been supposed since 1945.

Lone Star and Rising Sun

There was a paradoxical aspect to these major changes in 'Great Europe' including the demise of the Soviet Union. In the middle 1980s it was the fate of the United States, rather than the collapse of Communism, which remained an engrossing topic in the United States, even an election issue. An Englishman at Yale University, Paul Kennedy, produced a bestseller, *The Rise and Fall of the Great Powers* (1987), which stimulated debate and discussion far beyond academic circles. Suggesting that the dynamic of the Great Power system was caused by uneven economic growth, he argued that it created an imbalance between military capacity and inherited military commitments. The strongest power in the system became overstretched and was likely to lose economic energy in maintaining a position it had won for itself in easier times. Professor Joseph Nye, however, argued in *Bound to Lead* (1990) that the United States still could and should show confidence and exercise leadership in international relations. Even so, an important section of American opinion wondered whether it could continue to do so. Kennedy's critics suggested that if there was 'imperial overstretch' (which some also denied) it was caused not by defence as a percentage of US GNP but by the expanding welfare-state entitlement menu. Nye argued that the US defence burden was lighter in 1990 than it had been in the 1950s and, as a percentage of GNP, did not compare with that of other powers in the past with which the United States was being compared. The only answer, however, which Professor Kennedy himself felt able to give to the question whether the United States could maintain its existing position in the world was 'no'. No society could *permanently* remain ahead of all the others.

In terms of geographical extent, population, and natural

resources, the United States ought to possess perhaps 16 or 18 per cent of the world's wealth and power. In fact, in 1945, Kennedy suggested that it possessed around 40 per cent. What was therefore being witnessed was the early stage of the ebbing away of a percentage that was extraordinarily and unnaturally high. That decline was being masked by the enormous military strength of the United States and the extent to which it had 'internationalized' American capitalism and culture. He did not believe that the United States would ever shrink into the relative obscurity of erstwhile 'world leaders' in earlier centuries such as Spain or the Netherlands, but the task before American states-men was undoubtedly the management of relative decline. The task might be easier because he suspected that the Soviet Union might be even more affected by the changing dynamics of world power. That point, however, was not strongly stressed because even in 1987 it did not seem likely that the world would turn out to be what it was to become a decade later.

In October 1987 there occurred 'Black Monday', when the Dow–Jones Average fell 23 per cent—triggering large falls in share prices across the world. Two American journalists writing at the time claimed to have detected 'one of those rare days in history when the shift in power from one empire to another can be marked, precisely and indelibly'. What they had in mind was the rise of Japan. They further argued, in a continuation of a theme noted in the previous chapter, that no nation was better shaped by its own history and nationalistic necessities than Japan to 'exercise control' over the United States. It was sug-gested that Japan always thought long-term and was patient. The groundwork had been laid for the economic domination of the United States. Industrial policy aimed at achieving 'economic security' had become Japan's national security strategy, other writers argued. It was noted in June 1990 that Japan was determined to go ahead with its loan package for China (the Tiananmen Square crisis will be shortly considered). It was evident that Japan wanted to make large-scale investments in Chinese industry and was not much moved by the notion that China had first to mend its ways.

When President Bush visited Japan in January 1992 (the first visit by a president since that of President Reagan in November 1983) a prominent Washington research institution called for government intervention to save the dying American automobile industry. It was a year after the Gulf War (shortly to be considered) when there was still an American feeling that Japan had not contributed enough to its costs (not having participated in the war but having benefited from its outcome). The Bush visit had something of the appearance of a glorified trade negotiation mission. Great satisfaction was derived from a 'concession' that Japanese auto companies would substantially increase their purchases from American auto parts suppliers.

Sometimes, too, there was a conviction in the United States (echoed on occasion in Europe) that it was time to 'Japanize' the American economy. It was a startling reversal of the post-1945 'Americanization' of Japan. The 'Japanization' of the United States required, apparently, a kind of corporatist fusion of labour, capital, and the state. There was something specially admirable about Japanese company loyalty and family discipline. The United States had to learn before it was too late.

It was a moot point, however, whether the 'American way of life' could be redesigned—or whether it should. There continued to be questions asked about the extent to which Japan had 'really changed'. In January 1989 Emperor Hirohito, whose reign had begun in December 1926, died. It was a passing which forced Japanese people to reflect on their identity and place in the world. Commentators noted that the most potent expressions of Japanese separateness (and superiority?) were inseparable from emperor worship. Emperor Akihito was enthroned in November 1990. His personality and conduct did much to reassure outside opinion which had feared renewed internal expressions of imperial veneration and even of deification. Nevertheless, the ceremonial did remind the outside world that Japan was 'different'.

In any event, as Japan's economy faltered somewhat in the middle 1990s, the more strident expressions of American anxiety moderated. It became apparent from some Japanese press comment that Japan was as apprehensive about the continuing growth of competing Asian 'tiger' economies as American comment was apprehensive about Japan. It was indeed the case that the smaller NICs—Taiwan, South Korea, Thailand, Malaysia—continued to make their mark in a manner identified in the previous chapter, though as will shortly be noted they in turn ran into economic difficulties. It was also the case that domestic Japanese political factors prevented Japanese governments from being as 'liberal' in trade policy as they might have liked. This was illustrated by the 1993 GATT negotiations, the 'Uruguay Round'. It is arguable that the long-serving ruling party, the Liberal Democratic Party, was defeated in elections because rural communities dependent on rice production voted against it in protest against the GATT agreement which required Japan to permit the import of cheaper American rice.

Even so (and not only in relation to Japan), official and public opinion in the United States remained in a somewhat bemused condition about that country's place in the world. Although in a different fashion, the end of the Cold War was as disorientating for the United States as it was for the disintegrating Soviet Union. The reality was that now the United States was the only world superpower, whether or not it was also a declining superstar. No other country equalled its might. Having assumed the habit of power for so long, it would in practice continue to exercise it. Others pointed out, however, that the term had become virtually meaningless. There was only sense in trying to be a superpower if some other state also had aspirations to such a status. All that for decades had been involved in being a superpower had quite suddenly become redundant. The erstwhile allies and dependencies of the United States would increasingly become its rivals. The end of the Cold War meant *not* that the United States would be able to determine the course of events but that it would experience a rapid decline in its ability to do so. Commentators had little doubt that the United States would have to live henceforth in a multi-polar world but, beyond this portentous revelation, there was little agreement about what that actually entailed. Much academic writing in this vein in the early

1990s was necessarily speculative but it was symptomatic of a sense of unease and insecurity. This is scarcely surprising. *Any* change of the magnitude that was taking place in the international system could bring quite unpredictable consequences. There were even some who thought that nuclear war would be more likely in the 1990s than it had been during the Cold War. Nightmare scenarios were conjured up in which nuclear weapons got into the hands of international blackmailers, as the Soviet Union dissolved.

Hemispheric Home?

Of course, these analyses were not confined to academics. In September 1990 President Bush, who had taken office in 1989, talked of a 'New World Order' which would replace the Cold War. It was an arresting if somewhat opaque expression—in Europe a 'new order' of any kind had somewhat fascist associations. He envisaged a world 'quite different from the one we have known' in which the 'rule of law' supplanted the 'rule of the jungle'. Initially, in practice, Washington's responses to particular problems seemed to conform to an old order: Latin America remained its own backyard or jungle. In December 1989 US forces intervened in Panama to overthrow and capture its dictator General Noriega, who faced drug-trafficking charges in the United States. He had also annulled elections won by his opponents. In short, it seemed, Noriega was an 'outlaw' who was being arrested by the internationally acknowledged chief of police. In some other Latin American countries, however, 'Operation Just Cause' looked like a sign that the United States would now be willing and able to impose its wishes on the hemisphere with remarkable freedom.

In fact, this was not the beginning of a series of direct interventions, partly because, slowly and unevenly, in these years Latin American countries began to emerge from the military and bureaucratic-authoritarian regimes which had been characteristic. In Brazil, for example, although in 1987 there was an economic crisis which led to the suspension of interest payments on foreign debt, civilian government was uneasily restored. In Argentina, military insurrections against the government of Raúl Alfonsín failed. In 1989 Carlos Menem, the candidate of the Peronists, won the presidential election. In 1989 Patricio Aylwin (Christian Democrat) won an overwhelming victory in presidential elections in Chile—the Pinochet regime was at an end. In Paraguay in 1989 General Stroessner's lengthy dictatorship came to an end by military coup. Its leader subsequently won an electoral victory, if somewhat dubiously.

It would be wrong to paint a picture of a universal and complete transformation by the early 1990s, and the rise of the drug barons in Colombia and elsewhere added fresh problems. Brazil, Mexico, and Argentina still had very large international debts. Yet the changes elsewhere in the world impacted on this region also. Castro told Gorbachev on his visit to Cuba in April 1989 that he did not see any sign that the imperialists had adopted the 'new international thinking'. However, he was shortly to find both that the Soviet Union in its final years saw no role for Cuban military missions abroad and that it weakened its support for the Cuban economy. It was announced in September 1991 that Soviet troops would be leaving Cuba. 'Communism/anti-Communism' began to lose its value as a litmus-test for regimes throughout the region.

Slowly, too, against this background some stability returned to Central America as the Soviet Union and the United States moderated or withdrew the support they offered to proxies. A peace plan in 1987, drawn up by the Costa Rican President and endorsed by five other Central American presidents, urged just such a withdrawal, called for a cease-fire, and urged the holding of free elections in Nicaragua. The government of Sandinista President Daniel Ortega, burdened by military expenditure together with rampant inflation and expecting to win, organized such elections in 1990. The Sandinistas were defeated but did not cling to office—an orderly transition of a kind took place. The bitter civil war in El Salvador, which had lasted for eleven years, came to an end with a peace accord signed in September 1991. Cynics and critics could not quite recognize in what was happening the 'democratic promise' that President Bush claimed to see spreading throughout the Americas, but the atmosphere was undoubtedly changing.

What was not clear was whether these changes, seen against the concurrent global developments, prefigured the cohering of 'the Americas', from Alaska to Argentina, in the light of the perceived economic consolidation of Europe and East Asia. In North America the US and Canadian governments had agreed in 1987 that they would eliminate tariffs and other trade barriers by January 1989 in a North American Free Trade Area. This had been contentious in Canada, partly for economic reasons but also because it touched perennially sensitive issues of identity. In 1982 Canada gave itself its own constitution, replacing the 'British' Acts of 1867 and 1949, as a further sign of its maturity. The relationship between Quebec and the rest of Canada remained difficult, and there was an underlying anxiety that Canada would be 'swallowed' by its southern neighbour. North American 'regionalism' therefore had its political limits. The British link remained important both economically and politically for this reason (in 1991 the UK was the second largest foreign investor in Canada as was Canada in the UK).

In June 1990 the Bush administration mooted a free trade zone for the western hemisphere. Negotiations on a free trade agreement had already begun with Mexico. A tripartite North American Free Trade Area (NAFTA) came into operation in January 1994 (perhaps it was symbolically significant that the second stage of economic and monetary union came into force on the same date). Supporters lauded NAFTA as a great step forward: critics believed that it was yet another example of American dominance. In South America, reviving notions of regional economic co-operation in the new political climate might be as much against as with North America. Two steps agreed at this time illustrate the ambivalence. In December 1994 the Presidents of Argentina, Brazil, Paraguay, and Uruguay created the Southern Common Market to come into force in January 1995. That same month, however, leaders of thirty-four countries agreed to create the Free Trade Area of the Americas by 2005. Such developments should also be seen in the context of population shifts within the United States itself. After the decade which ended in 1969, 'Europe' for the first time ceased to provide 30 per cent or more of the immigrant population. The main areas of origin of the immigrant population of some 10 million between 1970 and 1989 were Asia and the Americas. In California and elsewhere, use of Spanish became so general as to cast serious doubt on whether in the future English would be the only common language of the United States. In short, trends elsewhere in the world did suggest an American continentalism on a scale not hitherto contemplated. Although this was 'home ground'—and perhaps in an important new cultural sense—for the United States, there was, however, little suggestion in the 1990s that Washington should or could withdraw completely from the rest of the world.

Gulf Syndrome

In August 1990 Iraq invaded and then annexed Kuwait, the small oil-rich state which had been under British protection until 1961. The emir fled to neighbouring Saudi Arabia, on whose borders Iraqi forces also massed. The UN Security Council imposed sanctions, including an oil embargo, on Iraq. In the same month Iraq finally made peace with Iran, largely on Iranian terms. Certain Western hostages were taken by the Iraqis.

Everything depended on how the United States would react. Washington's considerable immersion in Middle Eastern affairs needs no rehearsal now. Its relationship with Saudi Arabia required a signal of support to be sent and US forces were indeed dispatched there. But what more should be done? Suddenly the Gulf crisis brought together a number of issues thrown up both by former policies in the region and by the tumultuous shifts considered earlier in this chapter. In the significant capitals of the world decisions of great import had to be taken which would demonstrate just what 'the world' really amounted to at this juncture. If the United States did nothing, there was a certain hollowness in being the 'solitary superpower'. Suddenly, even in sections of the French press, there was enthusiasm for the United States as 'gendarme du monde'. Yet the initial American public reaction was sceptical about intervention if not hostile to it. President Bush's depiction of Saddam Hussein as the embodiment of evil evoked little dissent but that by no means required the United States to go to war against him. The shadow of Vietnam would not go away. Of course, in general terms, safeguarding access to Gulf oil was important, as was protecting friends and preventing another Arab–Israeli war, but were these sufficient grounds for the United States to play the leadership card?

If it did not, 'the Europeans' could not and would not. The European Community failed to find a common strategy and lacked the power: Germany could not be a military player, while Britain and France had tangled relationships with Iraq (against the background of the war in which, on balance, Iran had been thought the most serious threat to Western interests), which added some sourness to their customary difficulty in co-operating. Psychologically, despite all the talk of European assertiveness and self-confidence, eyes looked to Washington for the lead. Jacques Delors, President of the European Commission, spoke subsequently of the EC's embarrassing ineffectualness. There would be a coalition (with European members who might find it necessary to strike some awkward poses of their own) led by the United States. Britain seemed head prefect, very much in tune with the headmaster's thinking: very professional. But, given the reality of the Middle East, the relief of Kuwait could not be a Euro-American enterprise. Could the 'Arab world' mobilize? Within eight days of the invasion, Egypt, Saudi Arabia, the Gulf states, Morocco, and Syria backed a resolution, passed by a majority, which permitted Arab states to join the multinational coalition being organized through the United Nations. Jordan, Libya, and the PLO, on the other hand, tried unsuccessfully to organize an Arab mediation plan. There was anxiety, particularly in Egypt and Syria, that Arab would fight

Arab in large numbers. The Arab League proved quite ineffective as a regional organization.

Anxiety that the war for Kuwait might prove protracted and
involve heavy casualties also weighed heavily in Washington (the
US Senate only supported the operation by 52 votes to 47). It
was for this reason that 'Operation Desert Storm' to liberate
Kuwait began in mid-January 1991 with a heavy air offensive.
By 27 February coalition forces entered Kuwait City and declared Kuwait liberated. The victory of the curious coalition
representing the 'world community' was complete, so far as it
went, but an unrepentant Saddam Hussein remained in power
and was able to suppress both a Kurdish and a southern rebellion.
His regime could still be subjected to sanctions but no one deemed
it wise to use force in a direct attempt to dislodge him. It was
likely that there would be periodic crises in the future in which
Saddam Hussein would seek to test the continued resolution and
unity of the erstwhile 'Gulf coalition' which had defeated him.

The position particular Middle East states adopted during the
crisis continued to have reverberations for some time to come.
The expulsion of Yemeni workers from Saudi Arabia and Pales-
tinians from Kuwait was an indication of the depth of division
produced by the war. Some observers felt that 'Arab unity' as a
concept had disappeared for good. It was perhaps replaced by
three Arab units: the Gulf, North Africa, and the Levant. These
forecasts did not prove to be altogether accurate. King Hussein
of Jordan, for example, after a period of penance for his
equivocation, was able to earn a passage back to respectability
reasonably quickly. It remained the general view of commentators, however, that underlying conditions in the Middle East
were as unstable as ever. A fresh layer of resentments and
hatreds had emerged to complicate the ample supply already in
existence. Iraq had been contained but it was questionable
whether any Iraqi regime would be content with the current
Iraq–Kuwait border—though the regime recognized the independent sovereignty of Kuwait in November 1994. It was
not inconceivable that it could restore for itself a role as the

embodiment of Arab nationalism. It was at least arguable that majority opinion in the Arab world, while not supporting the annexation of Kuwait, was not enamoured of the Western-dominated coalition. Then again, no adequate acceptable place had yet been found for Iran in the structure of the Middle East. The Ayatollah Khomeini had died in June 1989, but the spirit of his revolution proved much more enduringly intransigent than some commentators had thought likely. The long arm of Iran extended beyond the Gulf into the Levant, where there was ample discontent with the status quo.

It was above all argued that the question of Israel had to be returned to with fresh urgency. Arab commentators noted that the West, which had discovered a great principle in a particular conflict, might turn fresh attention to another. A protracted and uneasy 'peace process' began, orchestrated so far as possible by the Bush and Clinton administrations in the United States. There was, perhaps, a deal which could be made on the basis of peace for land. Distrust, however, remained deeply embedded in any discussion. In 1988 the PLO parliament in exile had declared an independent state of Palestine—a prospect entirely rejected by Israel. Nevertheless, at least the possibility of a meeting of minds began to appear. A renewed post-Gulf effort began with a conference under American auspices in Madrid (October 1991). In 1993 the Israeli parliament approved legislation which permitted contact between Israeli citizens and the PLO. Yasser Arafat, its leader, branded a terrorist, was interviewed on Israeli television for the first time. In Washington, in September 1993, Israel and the PLO made a 'Declaration of Principles' which provided for Israeli withdrawal from the Gaza Strip and Jericho. Rabin, the Labour Prime Minister, shook hands with Arafat. There appeared to be an Arab acceptance, if grudging, of Israel's right to exist. Israeli opinion hovered between a belief that this was a historic step and deep suspicion. Mutual trust edged forward over subsequent years, with King Hussein of Jordan playing an important role, yet there remained intractable issues of security and ownership, not least of which was Jerusalem itself. The assassination of Rabin by an Israeli and the subsequent electoral triumph of Netanyahu brought a stiffening of the Israeli position. Every step forward was perilous and precarious for the individuals and communities concerned, and was likely to remain so. The role of the United States was frequently of critical importance in the twists and turns of the 'peace process' after 1993, but it should not be overestimated. Peace would only prevail when the regional players and their communities were ready for it. Washington could not dictate, even though it had important technological and financial levers at its disposal.

Despite the conclusion drawn by some contemporaries, therefore, the pivotal role of the United States in the Gulf crisis and its aftermath did not presage a willingness on the part of Washington to act without question as global master-builder. From the outset, the issue of who should pay for the substantial costs of the war was given an unusual degree of public prominence. In particular, there was resentment in Washington, and perhaps even more amongst the American people, that Germany and Japan had no direct role to play, and their financial contributions towards the cost of the operation became a cause of some friction. The United States, it seemed, could be criticized freely, but was left with the task of doing the world's necessary work for it. Middle Eastern beneficiaries from its protection could not expect to be free-riders. It has been calculated that the Gulf states paid two-thirds of the cost of Operation Desert Storm. Egypt had its outstanding debt to the Gulf Co-operation Council states (Abu Dhabi, Bahrain, Kuwait, Oman, Qatar, and Saudi Arabia) cancelled. In other words, looked at in the round, if the United States was to be the world's mercenary, it now expected other states to have their chequebooks ready. There were Americans, however, who felt humiliated by the whole business: 'Rent-a-Superpower' did not appeal to them as a slogan to characterize America's new world role.

There were other lessons that could be drawn. The 'political insignificance of Europe' was widely remarked upon but, as has already also been noted in the case of the subsequent Yugoslav crisis, it was more easily remarked upon than remedied. The episode perhaps showed the hollowness of some of the much-vaunted regional identities emerging throughout the world. In the end, in the Yugoslav crisis, it was the well-tried structure of NATO which proved effective. The United States still continued to have a singular capacity for decision-making which could be vital in world affairs. US troops withdrew in 1994 from Somalia where they had been since 1992 on a mission optimistically described as 'Restore Hope'. In 1994 Boutros-Ghali, then Secretary-General of the United Nations, wrote that in the face of an enormously increased demand for international action there was a need to reach common understanding of where the comparative advantage lay between the use of universal and regional organizations in the maintenance of internal peace and security.

There was a major difference, however, between identifying a need and finding a means to meet it. From 1991 to 1993 the number of UN soldiers increased from 10,000 to 80,000 and the peacekeeping budget trebled, adding to the organization's already acute financial difficulties. When US troops invaded Haiti in September 1994, it was with the blessing of the Security Council—Boutros-Ghali conceded that he was willing to delegate responsibility to a 'lead country', the United States, because of the UN's financial straits (although the United States itself claimed that it was in no financial condition to fund a 'bloated' United Nations Organization!). It looked likely that in this sense there would be occasions when the United States would be 'world policeman' of the ragged 'New World Order' (though subject to monitoring and observation in the implementation of its brief). In the case of Haiti itself, a mixed UN force later took over from the Americans.

China

In June 1989, six months before the ceremonial opening of the Brandenburg Gate in Berlin, a good deal of world attention was fixed on events in Beijing. For several months there had been unrest in China, given most vocal expression by thousands of students. Such dissent was not without precedent. Two years earlier in Wuhan, Shanghai, and elsewhere there had been 'pro-democracy' demonstrations. The Party leadership had then reacted by arresting a few ringleaders and their supporters in high academic places. Hu Yaobang, Party General Secretary, was accused of being too sympathetic to the protesters and forced to resign. His replacement, Zhao Ziyang, was to suffer the same fate in 1989. When Hu Yaobang died in April 1989, students staged demonstrations in his honour and, amongst other things, demanded freedom of the press, and information on the assets and incomes of high-ranking leaders. Such requests, after they had been refused, became more radical, extending to seeking an end to Communist rule and the introduction of 'democracy'. In late April and May an estimated 100,000 demonstrators marched through Beijing. Hunger-strikers and their supporters occupied Tiananmen Square. There was embarrassment for the government in that Gorbachev visited Beijing in mid-May and was not able to enter the Great Hall of the People through the main entrance facing Tiananmen Square. Civilians also blocked routes to the city centre when soldiers tried to advance—an indication that the protesters could not be dismissed as merely students. A stand-off continued until 3 June when the army fired on a crowd assembled in central Beijing. The loss of life which ensued may have risen to as high as one thousand. Subsequently, the government took determined steps to arrest, imprison, and restrict those identified as leaders, and seemed to have done so with some success.

In arguing in March 1990 that the democracy movement had stemmed from infiltration and subversion by 'foreign hostile forces', Premier Li Peng seemed again seeking to seal China off from the outside world. Indeed, for a few years, there were restrictions on outside contacts, but it was also clear that there would be no reversal of the economic thrust of the previous decade. There was, therefore, an unresolved tension in China's position. Could China move—no doubt in its own way—to 'Western' democracy? In approving the events in Tiananmen Square, Deng Xiaoping demonstrated that he was no liberal. His overwhelming anxiety, stemming from his own experiences during the Cultural Revolution, would appear to be that China would dissolve into chaos if 'democracy' was let loose. It was necessary to retain firm central control to prevent the creeping assertion of economic warlordism. Stability was also threatened by crime and corruption. China had to deal with matters in its own way, however much outsiders disapproved of an apparent lack of concern for 'human rights'. The collapse of Soviet Communism appeared to give justification for the strong stand against anarchy that had been taken. Perhaps the system would have survived in Europe if in Poland or the German Democratic Republic state forces had been prepared to be as 'strong-minded' in dealing with unarmed protesters as the People's Liberation Army had been.

Outside powers, however, issued strong condemnations in public and some foreign loans were cut off. The Dalai Lama of Tibet received the 1989 Nobel Peace Prize on the thirtieth anniversary of the rebellion in his country in 1959—a sign that it was not only the lack of 'democracy' in China that caused external criticism. Strong voices in the US Congress repeatedly called for the ending of China's 'most-favoured nation' trade status. Both the Bush and Clinton administrations fluctuatingly contemplated such a threat as a means of altering the stance of the Chinese government. It was far from clear, however, that external pressure would have that result, and commercial advantages soon seemed irresistible. Indeed, Deng no doubt calculated that after a couple of years the attempt to treat China as a pariah would have run its course.

So, largely, it proved. By the middle 1990s, 'Tiananmen' was being pushed into the background as the country, or at least parts of it, hurtled forward in unsteady fashion. It was also clear, by 1997, that Moscow and Beijing were beginning to seek each other out. There was advantage, from both sides, in seeking a compatible relationship which might enable both to resist undue American pressure. Jiang Zemin had first visited Moscow in the 1950s—training at the ZIL car factory. In April 1997, as President of China, he came to sign agreements (which had been in negotiation since 1991) with Russia and other former Soviet republics which demilitarized the 5,000-mile border area, in places one of the most fortified frontiers in the world, and to take a further step forward in resolving boundary disputes. Both countries declared that they rejected claims by any country to the role of absolute leader—whom could they mean?—in fashioning the international order of the twenty-first century. Such gestures apart, however, it could not be disguised that both countries still needed Western money and expertise.

Commentators had often suggested that, despite his advanced age, it was still Deng Xiaoping who kept the structure together. However, when he died in 1997, his departure seemed to have been so long anticipated that it did not result in the internal breakdown so often predicted. It was, however, another matter whether, despite the roller-coaster pace of economic develop-ment in China, either the basis of its own internal order or its relationship with the outside world had been resolved. It was now the only major 'Communist' country, but beneath such a blanket label there existed a complex interplay of influences which emerged from the long Chinese past and the potent attraction of the West, particularly the English-speaking West. Familiar ideological concepts were still paraded, but it was obvious that the economic reforms were having a profound impact on both the social structure and societal values.

The fate of Hong Kong came to be seen as pregnant with implications for the future of China itself. Chris Patten, the last British governor, had controversially sought to root certain constitutional and representational principles in a system that came closer than ever before in Hong Kong to democratic government. However, after 1997 the Chinese government would be in control and it was not clear how the relationship between ruler and ruled would work out in practice; it is still too early to offer any judgement. There would be a sense in which Hong Kong would be a kind of 'world city' combining in its hectic life principles and practices often thought incompatible elsewhere.

Outside commentators could not decide what to make of these developments. No one could dispute the significance of the path followed by a country which, with a population of some 1,150 million in 1990, contained nearly one in five of the world's inhabitants. 'Late Dengism' seemed to legitimate authoritarian rule on the grounds that it provided the economic progress that China had yearned for, but was that enough? In September 1993, for example, Lady Thatcher, the former British Prime Minister, argued that democracy followed economic freedom sooner or later. China was clearly taking a different route to democracy from the former Soviet Union by giving priority to economic freedom, but she had no doubt that the end result would be greater political freedom. On the other hand, Fang Laizhi, the noted dissident, speaking in the United States in May 1993, argued that there was little substance in the belief that economic development automatically would lead to a democratic society. He noted that Deng Xiaoping and his associates had continued to rule in an autocratic way and that there had been no substantive changes in Chinese political life since the pro-democracy protests in 1989. This argument, specific though it was to China, was undoubtedly relevant to the consideration of the impact of economic development on political systems throughout East Asia.

And in late 1997 it became apparent that East Asia as a whole was in serious economic difficulty, with ramifications which might extend to the world as a whole. The 'tiger economies', so frequently contrasted in their dynamic growth with the ponder-ous over-regulated economies of the West, were in trouble. The fall from grace was most conspicuous in the case of South Korea, which had turned itself into the world's eleventh largest economy. The state was technically bankrupt and had to call dramatically and urgently for help from the International Mon-etary Fund. At the same time there was political uncertainty arising from the election to the Presidency of the opposition candidate in December 1997. The problems of economic and political management were seen to be closely allied. What was true in the case of South Korea also applied, to greater or lesser degree, elsewhere in East Asia. The value of local currencies fell erratically and stock markets oscillated bewilderingly. Malaysia, apparently so successful, ran into great difficulty and prompted

fresh criticism of the malign influence of Western-based speculators. In Indonesia, too, currency turbulence brought with it
renewed political uncertainty. It seemed, paradoxically, that only
a country like Burma, whose military leaders had long kept
detached from the frenzied 'modernization' to be observed in
other countries, retained its unenviable 'stability'. Such volatility
may only be a 'blip' in a continuing story of economic success
or may indicate that deep-seated politico-cultural issues need to
be resolved, and may take time to resolve, before stable expansion can resume.

India

India still constituted the other major Asian 'option', but the
decade after 1985 revealed a depressing catalogue of unresolved
problems. Population continued to grow rapidly (largely owing
to a fall in the death rate), reaching a figure of some 870 million
in 1990 (double what it had been in 1960). Life expectancy grew
dramatically—in 1991 it was over 62, whereas thirty years earlier
it had been 47. Yet it was evident, twenty years on, that Mrs
Gandhi's 1971 election slogan 'Abolish Poverty' was very far
from being realized. Millions, both urban and rural, continued
to live in poverty—by almost any definition. Health, education,
and welfare services were stretched to the limit. The position of
the 'Untouchables' remained almost as intractable in the 1990s
as it had been half a century earlier—despite the passage of
legislation and the symbolic elevation of some Untouchables to
high office. By the late 1980s, commentators continued to
observe that it was private industry which was efficient and
competitive and to argue that the sector as a whole was subjected
to excessive bureaucratic control (and some corruption). However, there seemed neither the will nor the capacity to 'unshackle
the Indian economy' before 1991 when near-bankruptcy forced
the government's hand. The 'privatization' of Indian industry,
however, was neither a smooth nor a rapid process, and its
benefits, though discernible, still did little to bring comprehensive

prosperity. Generalization is hazardous, but such progress as was made served often only to give added prominence to the disparities which characterized Indian life at almost every turn.

The paradoxes of Indian life therefore remained. At one level, in terms of the conduct of elections and turnout on the part of voters, the performance was impressive. However, violence was never far away. Rajiv Gandhi, whose Congress party had lost its majority in the 1989 general election, was assassinated by a Tamil suicide bomber during the 1991 general election campaign. Mother and son had therefore both met violent deaths. More fundamentally, doubts increased about the federal system and the capacity of parliamentary institutions, both centrally and at the state level, to provide effective decision-making. The fragmentation and decline of the Congress compounded the problems. By the later 1990s, it seemed almost inevitable that the country would be governed at the centre by coalitions whose durability was only temporary. In 1997, when Inder Kumar Gujral became Prime Minister, he was the seventh man in eight years to hold the office, and it did not seem likely that he would hold it for long.

It was also apparent, fifty years after Indian independence, that the fundamental 'identity' of the state remained to some extent problematic. It is not an unusual paradox to discover that Mr Gujral himself, it so happens, was born in what is now Pakistan and is fluent in Urdu. Islamicization in Pakistan fed the evident waxing of Hindu consciousness in India. The Janata Alliance, founded in 1980, had grown in strength and sought to portray Hindu values as a unifying national force. Such a policy naturally caused anxiety on the part of non-Hindus. The most explosive aspect was the campaign to 'liberate' from Muslim 'occupation' sites antecedently regarded as sacred by Hindus. In 1992 Hindu militants stormed a mosque in Uttar Pradesh built on the alleged birthplace of Ram. Perhaps 1,000 people were killed in riots elsewhere. Hindu–Muslim relations remained strained. It was also clear that 'Hindu values' did not bind non-Muslims together in 'national unity'. It was only in Hindi-speaking regions that this emphasis on Hindu values had a fundamental appeal. The 'new Hindu nationalism' thus gave a further twist to regional assertiveness. It also remained the case, despite everything, that English retained a place in important sectors of Indian life and continued to give an élite a strange consciousness of a Western strand amidst the many pluralities of Indian life.

'Religion' and 'Identity' naturally also continued to spill over into all issues in the subcontinent as a whole (including Sri Lanka, where Tamil aspirations continued to be unsatisfied and violence became endemic, intervention by the Indian army to try to lay the ground for a settlement having proved a failure). In Pakistan, the Zia regime had pushed for 'Islamicization' as much as anything to try to give the country coherence, but it scarcely did so. Democracy was restored in 1988 but could almost be equated with ungovernability. Karachi, the country's initial capital, was plagued by violence as the Mohajirs, descendants of refugees from India at the time of partition, forged an identity for themselves. In the north-west the Afghan crisis continued to have reverberations. Benazir Bhutto proved as controversial a political leader as her father had been. Defeated in 1990, she became Prime Minister in 1993 after an election which produced a hung parliament. She was not able to reconcile ethnic/linguistic differences and her personal behaviour led to her dismissal by the President. Argument raged as to whether this was a 'coup' or a proper action under the constitution.

Crisis in Kashmir in 1989/90 drew world attention to another unresolved subcontinental problem which seemingly bound India and Pakistan in perpetual antagonism. In fact, the uprising in Kashmir probably owed little to Pakistani prompting (though assistance was later provided). In 1990 Indian troops brought the area under direct rule following the resignation of the state government. The manner of doing so alienated the population and left the fundamental political problem unresolved. By the 1990s accession to Pakistan had lost some of its attractions for secessionists (partly a reflection of the ethnic tensions within Pakistan itself), and an independent Kashmir had to some extent replaced it as the rebel objective. In so far as this was the case, another attempt at Pakistani–Indian rapprochement might be more successful since neither New Delhi nor Islamabad would want such an outcome. Elsewhere, given that the objective of a Sikh 'Khalistan' had not faded away, it was apparent that fissiparous tendencies remained strong. It has been calculated that some 40 million people in India were living under military rule.

These internal preoccupations help to explain why India's world role remained modest. Its foreign policy, in a sense, grew out of, and was influenced by, internal events to an unusual degree. By the 1990s, the axioms of non-alignment seemed exhausted—a situation compounded by the collapse of the Soviet Union, for so long India's major external partner. It is perhaps instructive in this respect to contrast the ferociously critical stance of Nehru towards the 1956 Suez campaign and the Indian government's complaisant attitude towards the Gulf War in 1991. India maintained an army of over 1 million in the early 1990s, and defence consumed 15 per cent of its national budget. India was also making its own intermediate-range ballistic missiles, though in other respects the army was not well equipped. Viewed in this light, it was a major world power, but one somewhat handicapped in its external projection (should it ever wish to exercise it outside the context of war with Pakistan) both by its internal divisions and by logistical shortcomings. For the same reason, the 'option' that it offered in Asia was blurred and muted.

African Alternative?

The sense of foreboding which had long hung over southern Africa was unexpectedly lifted in 1989/90. It had been customary for decades to fear that change could only come in South Africa by violence and massive loss of life. Whatever else 'the world' disagreed about, there was a consensus, at least in public, that apartheid was evil and it was a duty to bring it to an end (though there was still no consensus as to whether 'sanctions' offered the best possibility or whether the African National Congress merited full support). The United States and Britain vetoed attempts by the UN to impose sanctions mandatorily. In September 1989 the National Party was returned with a reduced majority in the (whites-only) general election. F. W. de Klerk became President. Two months later, he announced the end of the Separate Amenities Act in South Africa. Change was in the air. In neighbouring Namibia, formerly South-West Africa, Sam Nujoma, the South-West African People's Organization (SWAPO) guerrilla leader, was elected President and the country became independent in February 1990. In that same month, however, even more momentous change began. President de Klerk, Afrikaner though he was, announced the end of the ban on the African National Congress which had lasted for thirty years; its leader, Nelson Mandela, was released after spending twenty-seven years in prison. In June 1990, except in the case of troubled Natal, de Klerk lifted the four-year state of emergency. In February 1991 he formally announced the intention to repeal the laws which underpinned apartheid. A year later the white electorate voted in favour of major constitutional reform—and the ANC embarked on a 'mass action' campaign. The 'world community' lifted sanctions against South Africa in October 1993.

Such a recital of important dates does not do justice to a sequence of events as dramatic and as unpredicted as the concurrent developments in the Soviet Union, China, or Eastern Europe. As South Africa moved through transitional arrangements to a general election in 1994 which made possible a government by the African National Congress, there was surprise at the relative smoothness of the process. Some interpreters supposed that at last sanctions and boycotts had had their effect. For once, 'the world' had been effective. Others stressed the extent to which there was also a genuine, if reluctant, change of mind amongst necessary sections of the white community. Archbishop Desmond Tutu could reach the hearts of many Christians across the racial divide. The part played by both Mandela and de Klerk was widely admired: personifications of racial reconciliation, without whose individual contribution the path to change would have been much more difficult. It seems likely that the old order had not been brought to its knees by the sanctions that were imposed (replacement suppliers were found elsewhere), but there was none the less a possibility that in time it would have been. The sporting boycott hit a white community devoted to its cricket and rugby. In these circumstances it is impossible to identify a single cause of the collapse of apartheid. These various factors came together to enable South Africa to avoid the predicted cataclysm.

Of course, the picture was not all light. The position to be occupied by Kwa-Zulu Natal remained problematic and a hor-rifying pattern of violence seemed deep-rooted. Formidable problems of social adjustment remained but there was a will to succeed. Many ANC leaders had been brought up to believe in command economies and reached power just at the point when they passed out of fashion. Commentators asked themselves what would happen 'after Mandela' but could give no clear answer. The example of India suggested that congress parties which delivered freedom could not endure indefinitely and, sooner or later, a new basis for democratic party politics would have to be found.

It was likely to be the case that the magnitude of its internal problems would limit South Africa's impact elsewhere on the continent and in the wider world. Distinguished visitors flocked to the country and Nelson Mandela was received ecstatically abroad, but such activities did not betoken a lasting major external role. Indeed, the ANC past posed problems for the South African government. Washington did not like, for example, the continuance under new circumstances of old links with Cuba, Libya, and Iran. In another instance, Pretoria had to make awkward choices between Beijing and Taipei. Rejoining the Commonwealth of Nations, however, posed no problems as its member states hastened to reconstruct old networks and relationships. South African foreign ministry officials dampened immediate expectations that their country could 'save' the Afri-can continent by transforming the Organization of African Unity into an effective body or resolve problems in Rwanda, Burundi, Liberia, Somalia, Nigeria, or Zaïre. Pretoria, it seems, was prepared to use 'good offices' in trying to provide a diplomatic framework for solutions—but initially was reluctant to go further. Nevertheless, by the very fact of its existence, South Africa offered encouragement and example in a continent in need of both. In 1997, however, its role in brokering the end of the Mobutu regime in Zaïre (now renamed the Democratic Republic of Congo) indicated a greater willingness to become Southern and Central Africa's 'core state'.

In the decade after 1985, it remained too often the case that the African continent largely only gained the attention of the world beyond in the context of natural disasters and political instability. In Nigeria, 1985 was the year of another military coup—by Major-General Ibrahim Babangida. A later brief period of civilian rule was followed in 1993 by another coup when General Abacha took over as head of state. Paths to civilian rule, sometimes promised, proved difficult subsequently to negotiate. The military regime found itself increasingly criticized by the outside world, an outside world which could seemingly do little about the situation. In another instance, Liberia was plagued by civil war. In 1990 West African states did send in a multinational force to end it but, although a peace settlement was signed in Ghana in December 1994, warfare both preceded and succeeded it. Violence and massive human rights abuses in Rwanda in 1994 precipitated both the intervention of French forces and an international relief effort. Conflict between Hutus and Tutsis seemed endemic and spilled over into other countries in Central Africa, once again, in the late 1990s, raising questions about borders, frontiers, and statehood, most notably in the case of Zaïre, ruled for so long by President Mobutu. In Mediterranean Africa, the struggle for supremacy between government and Islamic opposition took a gruesome turn and was a reminder that there too fundamental problems of alignment and identity had still not been resolved.

It is, no doubt, to fall victim, in these and other instances, to images of Africa which flashed on the world's television screens to suppose that the picture of the continent was invariably gloomy. However, in the mid-1990s, 'bad news' from Africa (not of course a new phenomenon) became so endemic that international agencies acknowledged a certain 'aid fatigue', as it was called in Europe and North America. On the other hand, such a washing of hands was regarded as hypocritical. It was argued by sympathizers that African states could never extricate themselves from their difficulties whilst they were compelled to service and repay debts which they had incurred. It was time to cancel and reschedule in order to give a fresh start but, although modest steps in this direction were agreed, the 'debt mountain' was still in existence. The countries that were relatively most heavily indebted were Mozambique, Tanzania, Somalia, Zambia, Congo, the Ivory Coast. It was difficult to envisage that their debts were ever likely to be repaid in full.

A combination of these circumstances therefore continued to mean that as a continent Africa lacked political weight in world affairs. A black African did become Secretary-General of the United Nations in 1997, but there was some irony in the fact that his mission was more to deal with the enormous bureaucratic and financial problems of the United Nations itself than to assist in healing the divisions within the African continent.

Pulling it All Together

Dag Hammarskjöld once spoke of 'the one world we have created before we were ready for it'. It is a remark which has even more pertinence at the end of the twentieth century. The changes that have been related in this chapter, indeed in this book, have been extraordinary in both their scale and unpredictability. The world of 1945 has come to seem very remote. It has been above all the scale of population growth which puts this half-century in a category different from any other in human history. The world of the year 2000 is likely to contain just over 6 billion human beings (as against some 2.4 billion in 1945)—a new London, as it were, added every three months. It is an expansion which contributed to expressions of gloom about the conditions in which human beings might live after a further half-century—and not only in those continents where poverty still abounds. Conferences on how these issues are to be tackled are almost as abundant—the 1994 Cairo UN Conference on Population and the 1995 Beijing UN Conference on Women being amongst the most notable. It is difficult to feel confident that solutions can be found.

Perhaps because it is a half-century that brings a millennium to a close that an apocalyptic note can be detected. It is sometimes said that the stark population crisis may never be reached because some major catastrophe will occur before it. There are many candidates being proposed, ranging from the collapse of the world monetary system to nuclear war, from accelerating global warming to the collapse of a major staple food crop, and from a global disease epidemic to changes in oceanic currents. It has already become apparent—dramatically in the case of the major accident at the Chernobyl nuclear power station in the former Soviet Union in 1986 which led to rises in radiation levels in countries beyond its borders—that pollution is no respecter of national sovereignty as classically defined. It is noted that international tourism on its massive scale—some 600 million travellers annually—together with global transport, takes new diseases across borders within hours and days with potentially dire health consequences. These anxieties have led to the emergence of political groupings in Europe with unconventional agendas. In Germany, in particular, in the 1980s 'Greens' combined socialist, liberal, and ecological ideals and, although divided between 'realists' and 'fundamentalists', became a substantial political force, appealing to the young and educated in particular with the message that the protection of the environment was more important than the relentless pursuit of economic growth. Contemporary 'Greens' urge a non-violent revolution which will 'overthrow our whole polluting, plundering, and materialistic industrial society'. They argue that it is still possible for human beings to live in harmony with the planet. Yet, even as attempts are made to 'think globally' the reality of conflicting interests in different parts of the world cannot be easily overcome. In 1992 the 'Earth Summit' which took place in Rio de Janeiro revealed how difficult it is to 'manage' global warming in a 'neutral' fashion. Industrialized countries looked to a stabilization and then reduction in overall carbon monoxide emissions—but how was such a cut to be dealt with equitably? Lesser industrialized countries saw hypocrisy in any arrangement which restricted their emissions but did not deal drastically with countries which had been polluting for two centuries.

It is impossible, therefore, to conceive of a 'global perspective' which has totally superseded the partial perceptions of nations, states, and countries. But it is equally impossible, with only very minor exceptions, for states and peoples to contract themselves out from the current of ideas and practices which sweep the globe. Intergovernmental organizations and international non-governmental organizations grow rapidly. The number of international agreements designed to cope with transnational activities likewise mushrooms. The number of international telephone calls constantly accelerates—outgoing international calls from the top twenty countries increased some threefold between 1983 and 1992. It scarcely needs to be added that in respect to telephones, telex, fax machines, and, latterly, the Internet, the pattern of transactions is not uniform but itself reflects and reinforces already well-established information flows and cross-country relationships.

Such globalization, however, coexists, as has already been noted frequently, with intense localism and a disposition to break up even existing state structures. Processes of integration and disintegration seem to coexist in an awkward dialectic. It is not satisfying (or perhaps even possible) to be a 'citizen of the world' *tout court*. Global awareness still seems to require a firm personal location in a particular place. Perhaps, after all, cultural diversity is not merely a quaint aspect of human organization but as essential to the survival of the human species as biodiversity. It can be argued that for every language that disappears a unique view of the world is lost with it—and there are some authorities who believe that the 6,000 or more languages in the world are reducing so sharply that in the twenty-first century there may only be some 200 which survive. Yet, politically, it is still only too apparent that cultural, linguistic, and religious diversity in so many parts of the world still leads frequently to conflict. Only in around thirty of the world's more than 190 states are there no ethnic problems. Indeed, some scholars see little prospect ahead but of a world locked into ethnic/religious conflicts for many decades to come. Half a century on, it remains the case that the United Nations, inaugurated with such hope in 1945, still offers little more than a framework for co-operation.

In short, the 'One World' dreamed of by Wendell Wilkie in 1943 has not come into existence, perhaps never can come into existence. 'World loyalty' and 'world government' remain, at best, distant prospects. Nevertheless, a rather different 'One World' has arrived. It is criss-crossed still by alliances and alignments among states but now also by a multiplicity of non-governmental organizations. It is brought alive by means of communication which did not exist in 1945. It remains, however, in many respects, still a world 'in crisis': whether it is a world hurtling to disaster, or primed for prosperity, or perpetually poised between these extremes is an engrossing speculation.

Afterword

Final comments on a constantly changing world scene cannot be conclusive. The shape of the future is as much contested as the interpretation of the past, though with rather less evidence available! That the future does currently generate such vigorous debate, however, is indeed testimony to the fact the decades considered in this book do have a kind of unity and are now 'the past'. The competition of the 'Cold War' penetrated everywhere and brought into a rather ragged line countries and cultures which are now no longer constrained by its dictates. The genie of globalization cannot be put back into the bottle. It plays havoc with the political and constitutional concepts inherited from the past: sovereignty, boundaries, frontiers, citizenship, political loyalty among them. The individual now presents his or her business card to the world—phone, fax, E-mail, Internet—without need, perhaps, for a mediating 'national' identity. We are told, too, that in the not-too-distant future people will be able to have their own lifelong number and a personal computer assistant will sort out the exchange of messages: place will lose its resonance.

Yet there also appears to be a loneliness at the heart of this enveloping and developing cybernetic universalism. The onrush of modernity is simultaneously welcomed and feared. A cosmopolitan global culture suffused with vibrant supranational ideals seems both desirable and threatening. Individuals and societies seek reassuring anchorage in ethnic heritages and invent new ones. Specialists in international relations and comparative politics, in political theory, in international economics, and even humble historians wrestle with this central paradox of our times.

The fact that the world at the end of the twentieth century does appear to be in this condition is an outcome which could not have been readily predicted in 1945. It is worth, therefore, briefly noting the concerns that have dominated this narrative. The half-century has a coherence as the 'era of the Cold War' in all its facets and phases. There were wars and rumours of wars, but a cataclysmic nuclear global 'Third World War' was avoided. It was an era apparently defined not by a utopian 'One World' but rather by clearly denominated partial worlds: 'Free', 'Communist', and 'Third'. Much of this book has been concerned to delineate their establishment, consolidation, and collapse. It was an era which witnessed the end of European colonization and with it the formal control of parts of different continents by one continent. Western Europe, and latterly perhaps Europe as a whole, embarked on an ambiguous process of integration in a manner likely to banish its previous history of periodic internecine war. The ideological construct which went under the name of 'Marxism-Leninism' and the structures which embodied it collapsed (the special case of China apart). By the end, therefore, there were 'victories'. The 'Free World', flawed though it unsurprisingly was, did 'win'. A justified satisfaction at this outcome has, however, been shot through with questioning.

For some authors, the story of the world is now a matter of 'endgames', where the progressive global agenda inherited from the European Enlightenment has exhausted itself. In its place cultural diversity will become, or has already become, axiomatic. The story of the world since 1945, it is said, is not a story of 'progress' because to believe in progress is to be willing to pass judgement on cultures or regimes and to categorize certain 'civilizations' as 'better' or 'higher' than others. Such a willingness offends a pervasive contemporary, though largely 'Western', relativism which appears to make 'toleration' the supreme virtue. It has been pointed out by a British philosopher, Gordon Graham, however, that since toleration is not a given but clearly emerges as desirable (patchily) over a long period of time, it is itself some measure of moral progress. Espousal of a general

cultural or political relativism by some writers still seems paradoxically to go hand in hand with a willingness to condemn
certain behaviour.

For other writers, therefore, cultural relativism, itself a European construct, is a dead end. Instead, the idea of a universal
and directional history leading up to liberal democracy, as
Fukuyama puts it, is both meaningful and desirable. The 'end of
history' is to be discerned in the evolving world since 1945. The
United States 'and other liberal democracies' have to get to grips
in a post-Communist world with the fact that old geopolitics is
dead. Universal and rational recognition, as he writes, has
replaced the struggle for domination. An author writing outside
the United States may not so readily recognize in the culture of
that country the culture of the world—though Fukuyama's own
Japanese-American ancestry is itself not an insignificant factor
in his thought. However, his general contention may become
more plausible if the events of recent decades continue in the
same broad pattern, though what exactly 'liberal democracy'
means, when viewed globally, is problematic.

Yet other writers, conscious of its brief time-span, regard
democracy, as understood in Euro-America, as a fleeting phenomenon doomed to destruction in the savagely unjust and
environmentally exhausted future that they envisage. Indeed, say
some, the clash of civilizations is already upon us and, no
surprise, the fault-lines of conflict, within each continent, have a
formidably *longue durée*. The 'secular', materialistic, gadget-
ridden, health-obsessed, fashion-absorbed society of the United
States is not, as it were, 'universalizable'. It may not know it, or
want to acknowledge it, but the United States is not the world-
in-becoming. It is in fact still essentially the heir to the Protestant
and Catholic traditions of Western Europe. So, says Samuel
Huntington, prepare for the clash of civilizations.

Others argue that the attempt to freeze the world back into
historically conditioned, regionally constituted 'civilizations' is
unpersuasive. It is precisely characteristic of our time that civilizations, cultures, and religions have been, at least to a degree,
emancipated from their geographical location. In short, perhaps

we are living in a world in which there is *both* clash *and* convergence of civilizations.

This confused picture seemed to be confirmed by the events that have followed the extraordinary attacks on New York and Washington on 11 September 2001. The ensuing determination of the United States in response to declare 'war' on terrorism was presented as something that would unite upholders of 'civilized values' across the world. The early phase of the response saw elaborate attempts to sew together a 'global coalition' to which would adhere states who had a history of mutual suspicion or hostility, but who could and would unite in a common endeavour to rid the world of a terrorism which would otherwise destabilize it. Thus presented, it could not be a 'clash of civilizations' for it would surely unite adherents of all the major religions and demonstrate a real convergence of values and intentions in defence of order and freedom. However, the targets of counter-terrorism did not see the issues in this light. They did think in terms of a 'clash of civilizations' and claimed that they had a hold on all followers of Islam in the struggle against the United States and its allies whose claims that they were not hostile to Islam as such were spurious. These words are written as the first military strikes into Afghanistan take place. How events unfold from this point on, one must suppose, will have a substantial bearing on whether a new and enduring meaning can be attached to the concept of a 'global community' or whether such a transcending aspiration is a flawed piece of hegemonic rhetoric which cannot in the end be mobilized.

The perusal of merely half a century offers no firm basis for forecasting the shape of the world in the new millennium. What is notable, however, at its conclusion, as this brief discussion shows, is that the question of whether there is a meaning and direction in history, whether even there is a God who both stands outside history yet is involved in it, and in some sense controls it, is back on the agenda.

In 1955, the English historian Arnold Toynbee, consummate producer of annual *Surveys of International Affairs* and at the time a world figure as author of the many-volumed *A Study of*

History, drew 10,000 people through deep snow to hear him lecture in the University of Minnesota on 'The New Opportunity for Historians'. In the years that immediately followed, however, he was simultaneously battered by professional historians in Britain and Europe for his visionary temerity and fêted by politicians across the globe for his prophetic and synoptic insight. The then King of Afghanistan even put a helicopter at his disposal to enable him to visit the Hindu Kush. Toynbee contended at the end of his life that 'we cannot verify whether the chart that we make of the mysterious universe corresponds to the elusive reality; but, in order to live, we have to make this chart, realizing that it is an act of faith which is also an act of self-preservation'. As a chart, rather than a revelation, or even an explanation, this book makes its contribution to understanding the world since 1945.

2001

Further Reading

A guide to further reading could be enormous but must necessarily be highly selective. What follows contains suggestions, but no more, both for the history of individual countries and for global developments. It enables the reader to follow up topics treated summarily, perhaps too summarily, in this volume but does not aim to repair omissions—that would make its length impossible. The compilation is strongly tilted in the direction of recent publications because they will normally also refer in their bibliographies to other relevant and earlier material. A few titles have been translated into English, but most books listed were written in English, either in Britain, North America, or some other part of the English-speaking world. Perhaps there is no other language which offers readers such a richly endowed entry into twentieth-century world history. At the same time, that language, given its home bases, may itself encapsulate certain priorities and assumptions about what is important in the world since 1945 which may not be shared by users of other major world languages. That point should be kept in mind. Place of publication is London unless stated otherwise.

Reference

P. Waller and J. Rowett, *Chronology of the 20th Century*, Oxford, 1995; C. Cook and J. Stevenson, *The Longman Handbook of World History since 1914*, 1991; A. Isaacs and E. Martin, *Longman Dictionary of 20th Century Biography*, 1985; A. Palmer, *The Penguin Dictionary of Twentieth-Century History 1900–1982*, 1983; B. Mitchell, *Global Historical Statistics 1750–1993*, 1997; C. Cook and D. Bewes, *What Happened Where: A Guide to Places and Events in Twentieth-Century History*, 1997; J. Grenville and B. Wasserstein, *The Major International Treaties of the Twentieth Century*, 1997, is an updated edition of an established reference work.

General Perspectives

J. Dunbabin, *International Relations since 1945: A History in Two Volumes*, 1994, concentrates respectively upon the dealings of the Great Powers with their allies and with the wider world: C. J. Bartlett, *The Global Conflict 1880–1990*, 1994; T. E. Vadney, *The World since 1945*, Harmondsworth, 1987; P. Calvocoressi, *World Politics since 1945*, 1996 edn., is a well-established text: R. Little and M. Smith, eds., *Perspectives on World Politics*, 1991, is a collection of readings; W. Keylor, *The Twentieth Century World: An International History*, Oxford, 1992 edn.; E. Hobsbawm, *Age of Extremes: The Short Twentieth Century 1914–1991*, 1994; P. Johnson, *A History of the Modern World from 1917 to the 1980s*, 1983; R. Bosworth, *Explaining Auschwitz & Hiroshima: History Writing and the Second World War 1945–1990*, 1993, is a penetrating assessment of the 'long second world war'; J. Mittelman, ed., *Globalization: Critical Reflections*, 1996; M. Albrow, *The Global Age*, Oxford, 1996, S. Latouche, *The Westernization of the World*, Oxford, 1996, and T. von Laue, *The World Revolution of Westernization: The Twentieth Century in*

Global Perspective, New York, 1987, offer perspectives on where, for better or worse, we are heading; P. M. H. Bell, *The World since 1945: An International History*, 2001; D. Reynolds, *One World Divisible: A Global History since 1945*, 2000; I. Clark, *Globalization and Fragmentation: International Relations in the Twentieth Century*, 1997; N. Woods, ed., *Explaining International Relations since 1945*, 1996; R. W. Bulliet, ed., *The Columbia History of the Twentieth Century*, 1998.

Long Views

J. Roberts, *The Pelican History of the World*, Harmondsworth, 1980; F. Gilbert, *The End of the European Era, 1890 to the Present*, 1984 edn.; E. Burns, P. Ralph, R. Lerner, and S. Meacham, *World Civilizations*, vol. C, 1986 edn.; H. Thomas, *An Unfinished History of the World*, 1979; W. H. McNeill, *A World History*, Oxford, 1979 edn., is only one of McNeill's 'world' volumes. He has also written *Arnold Toynbee: A Life*, Oxford, 1989—the celebrated or despised English historian of civilizations; J. Mayall, *Nationalism and International Society*, Cambridge, 1989; M. Howard and W. R. Louis, eds., *The Oxford History of the Twentieth Century*, 1998.

Encounters

D. C. Gordon, *Images of the West*, Savage, Md., 1989; E. Said, *Orientalism*, New York, 1978; J. MacKenzie, *Orientalism: History, Theory and the Arts*, Manchester, 1995; J. Clarke, *Oriental Enlightenment: The Encounter between Asian and Western Thought*, 1997.

Transnational Interactions

E. Hanson, *The Catholic Church in World Politics*, Princeton, 1987; P. Kent and J. Pollard, *Papal Diplomacy in the Modern Age*, 1994; J. de Gruchy, *Christianity and Democracy: A Theology for a Just World Order*, Cambridge, 1995; R. Keohane and J. Nye, eds., *Transnational Relations and World Politics*, 1971; V. Mastny, *Helsinki, Human Rights and European Security*, 1986; D. Armstrong, *The Rise of the International Organisation: A Short History*, Basingstoke, 1982; A. Iriye, *Cultural Internationalism and World Order*, Baltimore, 1997; D. Crystal, *English as a Global Language*, Cambridge, 1997; J. McCormick, *The Global Environment Movement*, 1989; J. Carroll, ed., *International Environmental Diplomacy*, Cambridge, 1988; J. Bale and J. Maguire, eds., *The Global Sports Arena: Athletic Talent Migration in an Interdependent World*, 1994; D. Willey, *God's Politician: John Paul at the Vatican*, 1992; O. Chadwick, *The Christian Church and the Cold War*, 1992.

Power and Peace

L. Freedman, *The Evolution of Nuclear Strategy*, 1989 edn.; M. Mandelbaum, *The Nuclear Question: The United States and Nuclear Weapons, 1946–1976*, Cambridge, 1979; D. Holloway, *Stalin and the Bomb: The Soviet Union and Atomic Energy, 1939–1956*, New Haven, 1994; E. Luard, *The Blunted Sword: The Erosion of Military Power in Modern World Politics*, 1988; K. J. Holsti, *Peace and War: Armed Conflicts and International Order 1648–1989*, Cambridge, 1991; A. Carter, *Peace Movements: International Protest and World Politics since 1945*, 1992; F. Barnaby and D. Holdstock, eds., *Hiroshima and Nagasaki*, 1995; G. Best, *War and Law since*

1945, Oxford, 1994; B. Heuser, *NATO, Britain, France and the FRG: Nuclear Stategies and Forces for Europe, 1949–2000*, 1997; B. Heuser, *The Bomb: Nuclear Weapons in their historical, strategic and ethical context*, 2000.

Cold War: Commencement, Course, and Conclusion

M. McCauley, *The Origins of the Cold War 1941–1949*, 1995 edn.; J. Mayall and C. Navari, *The End of the Post-War Era: Documents on Great-Power Relations 1968–1975*, Cambridge, 1980; J. Smith, *The Cold War 1945–1965*, Oxford, 1997 edn.; M. Dockrill, *The Cold War 1945–1963*, 1988; J. Gaddis, *The United States and the Origins of the Cold War 1941–1947*, New York, 1972, and *The Long Peace: Inquiries into the History of the Cold War*, New York, 1987; B. Heuser and R. O'Neill, eds., *Securing Peace in Europe, 1945–1962: Thoughts for the Post-Cold War Era*, Basingstoke, 1992; J. W. Young, *The Longman Companion to Cold War and Detente 1941–1991*, 1993; S. Ball, *The Cold War: An International History, 1947–1991*, 1997; D. Reynolds, ed., *The Origins of the Cold War in Europe: International Perspectives*, New Haven, 1994; M. J. Hogan, ed., *The End of the Cold War: Its Meaning and Implications*, Cambridge, 1992; M. Bowker and R. Brown, eds., *From Cold War to Collapse: Theory and World Politics in the 1980s*, Cambridge, 1993; J. L. Gaddis, *We Now Know: Rethinking Cold War History*, 1997; G. Donaghy, *Canada and the Early Cold War, 1943–1957*, 1998.

World Economy

A. Milward, *War, Economy and Society 1939–1945*, Harmondsworth, 1987; H. van der Wee, *Prosperity and Upheaval: The World Economy, 1945–1980*, Harmondsworth, 1987; J. Spero, *The Politics of International Economic Relations*, 1992 edn.; B. Tew, *The Evolution of the International Monetary System 1945–1977*, 1977; I. Wallerstein, *The Politics of the World-Economy: The States, the Movements and the Civilizations*, Cambridge, 1984; S. Strange, *The Retreat of the State: The Diffusion of Power in the World Economy*, Cambridge, 1996; B. Nossiter, *The Global Struggle for More: Third World Conflicts with Rich Nations*, New York, 1987; W. Greider, *One World, Ready or Not*, 1997; R. Skidelsky, *The World after Communism*, 1995.

Power Struggle?

H. Morgenthau, *Politics among the Nations: The Struggle for Power and Peace*, New York, 1961 edn.; W. Olson and A. Groom, *International Relations Then & Now: Origins and Trends in Interpretation*, 1991; H. Bull and A. Watson, eds., *The Expansion of International Society*, Oxford, 1984; P. Kennedy, *The Rise and Fall of the Great Powers*, 1988.

Geopolitical and Other Theoretical Perspectives

I. Wallerstein, *Geopolitics and Geoculture: Essays on the Changing World System*, Cambridge, 1991; R. Johnson and P. Taylor, eds., *A World in Crisis? Geographical Perspectives*, 1989 edn.; P. Taylor, ed., *Political Geography of the Twentieth Century: A Global Analysis*, 1993; C. Williams, ed., *The Political Geography of the New World Order*, 1993; J. Anderson, C. Brook, and A. Cochrane, eds., *A Global World?*,

Oxford, 1995; P. Knox and P. Taylor, eds., *World Cities in a World-System*, Cambridge, 1995; B. Evans, D. Rueschmeyer, and T. Skocpol, eds., *Bringing the State Back In*, New York, 1985; R. Jervis, *Perception and Misperception in International Politics*, Princeton, 1976; R. Neustadt and E. May, *Thinking in Time: The Uses of History for Decision-Makers*, New York, 1986; G. Graham, *The Shape of the Past: A Philosophical Approach to History*, Oxford, 1997.

Global Communications

K. Ward, *Mass Communications and the Modern World*, 1989; A. Smith, *The Geopolitics of Information: How Western Culture Dominates the World*, Oxford, 1980; A. Smith, ed., *Television: An International History*, Oxford, 1995; E. Said, *Covering Islam: How the Media and the Experts Determine How We See the Rest of the World*, 1981; M. Macluhan and G. Fiore, *The Medium is the Message*, New York, 1967; P. Taylor, *Global Communications and International Relations*, 1997; P. Golding and P. Harris, eds., *Beyond Cultural Imperialism: Globalization, Communication and the New International Order*, 1996; L. Friedland, *Covering the World: International Television News Services*, 1992.

The United Nations and International Organization

B. Rivlin and L. Gordenker, *The Challenging Role of the UN Secretary-General*, 1993; A. Roberts and B. Kingsbury, eds., *United Nations, Divided World: The UN's Roles in International Relations*, Oxford, 1993 edn.; H. Wiseman, ed., *Peacekeeping: Appraisals and Proposals*, New York, 1983; D. Armstrong, L. Lloyd, and J. Redmond, *From Versailles to Maastricht: International Organisation in the Twentieth Century*, 1996; C. Archer, ed., *International Organizations*, 1992; A. Parsons, *From Cold War to Hot Peace: UN Interventions 1947–1994*, 1995; R. Righter, *Utopia Lost: The United Nations and World Order*, 1995.

European Enterprise

R. Vaughan, *Post-War Integration in Europe*, 1976, is an early collection of documents; D. Urwin, *Western Europe since 1945*, 1997 edn., is standard; P. Calvocoressi, *Resilient Europe 1870-2000*, 1991, is general; D. Buchan, *Europe: The Strange Superpower*, 1993; J. Young, *Britain and European Unity, 1945–1992*, 1993; M. Hogan, *The Marshall Plan: America, Britain and the Reconstruction of Western Europe, 1947–1952*, Cambridge, 1987, is the best account; J. Young, *Cold War Europe 1945–1989: A Political History*, 1991; A. Milward, *The Reconstruction of Western Europe, 1945–1951*, 1984, and *The European Rescue of the Nation-State*, 1992, which challenges simple notions; R. Brubaker, *Nationalism Reframed: Nationhood and the National Question in the New Europe*, Cambridge, 1996, notes nationalism's endurance; K. Middlemas, *Orchestrating Europe: The Informal Politics of European Union 1973–1995*, 1995, is a conducted tour inside the concert hall; A. Deighton, *Building postwar Europe, 1948–1963*, 1995.

Great Britain

D. Reynolds, *Britannia Overruled: British Policy & World Power in the 20th Century*, 1991; P. Taylor, *Britain and the Cold War: 1945 as Geopolitical Transition*, 1990;

V. Rothwell, *Britain in the Cold War, 1941–1947*, 1982; K. Robbins, *The Eclipse of a Great Power: Modern Britain 1870–1992*, 1993.

France

R. Gildea, *France since 1945*, Oxford, 1996; F. Costigliola, *France and the United States: The Cold Alliance since World War II*, New York, 1992; R. Aldrich and J. Connell, eds., *France in World Politics*, 1989; P. Cerny, *The Politics of Grandeur: Ideological Aspects of de Gaulle's Foreign Policy*, Cambridge, 1980; J. Chipman, *French Power in Africa*, Oxford, 1989; P. M. H. Bell, *France and Britain, 1940–1994: The Long Separation*, 1997.

East-Central Europe

J. Rothschild, *Return to Diversity: A Political History of East Central Europe since World War II*, New York, 1994 edn.; N. Davies, *Heart of Europe: A Short History of Poland*, Oxford, 1986; H. G. Skilling, *Czechoslovakia's Interrupted Revolution*, Princeton, 1976; D. Rusinow, *The Yugoslav Experiment 1948–1974*, Oxford, 1977; I. Berend, *Central and Eastern Europe 1944–1993*, Cambridge, 1996; G. Litvan, ed., *The Hungarian Revolution of 1956: Reform, Revolt and Repression 1953–1963*, 1996; R. Tokes, *Hungary's Negotiated Revolution*, Cambridge, 1996; R. Crampton, *Eastern Europe in the Twentieth Century*, 1997 edn.; D. Dyker and I. Vejvoda, *Yugoslavia and After*, 1996; D. Pryce-Jones, *The War that Never Was: The Fall of the Soviet Empire, 1985–1989*, 1995; V. Meier, *Yugoslavia: A History of its Demise*, 1999; R. H. Ullman, *The World and Yugoslavia's Wars*, 1996.

Germany

D. Cesarani, *The Final Solution*, 1993; L. Kettenacker, *Germany since 1945*, Oxford, 1997; P. Pulzer, *German Politics 1945–1995*, Oxford, 1995; M. Fulbrook, *Anatomy of a Dictatorship: Inside the GDR 1949–1989*, Oxford, 1995; A. Tusa, *The Last Division: Berlin and the Wall*, 1996; A. J. Nicholls, *The Bonn Republic: West German Democracy, 1945–1990*, 1997.

Italy

P. Ginsborg, *A History of Contemporary Italy: Society and Politics 1943–1988*, Harmondsworth, 1990; D. Sassoon, *Contemporary Italy: Politics, Economy and Society since 1945*, 1986; N. Doumanis, *Inventing the Nation: Italy*, 2001.

European Decolonization

R. F. Holland, *European Decolonization 1918–1981: An Introductory Survey*, 1985; P. Cain and A. Hopkins, *British Imperialism: Crisis and Deconstruction 1914–1990*, 1993; J. Darwin, *The End of the British Empire: The Historical Debate*, Oxford, 1991; M. Kahler, *Decolonization in Britain & France*, Princeton, 1984; F. Ansprenger, *The Dissolution of the Colonial Empires*, 1989; J. M. Brown, *The Oxford History of the British Empire: Volume IV The Twentieth Century*, 1999; N. MacQueen, *The Decolonization of Portuguese Africa*, 1997.

United States of America: Superpower

A. Schlesinger, *The Disuniting of America: Reflections on a Multicultural Society*, New York, 1992, treats of the cooling of the melting pot; G. Martel, ed., *American Foreign Relations Reconsidered 1890–1993*, 1994; C. Kegley and E. Wittkopf, *American Foreign Policy: Pattern and Process*, 1987 edn.; S. Ambrose, *Rise to Globalism: American Foreign Policy since 1938*, Harmondsworth, 1985 edn.; P. Duignan and L. Gann, *The Rebirth of the West: The Americanization of the Democratic World 1945–1958*, Oxford, 1992; P. Boyle, *American–Soviet Relations from the Russian Revolution to the Fall of Communism*, 1993; R. Crockatt, *The Fifty Years War: The United States and the Soviet Union in World Politics, 1941–1991*, 1994; W. LaFeber, *America, Russia and the Cold War, 1945–1990*, New York, 1991 edn., is a standard perspective; J. Harper, *American Visions of Europe*, Cambridge, 1996—distinguished visionaries; M. White, *The Cuban Missile Crisis*, 1996; C. Bell, *The Reagan Paradox: American Foreign Policy in the 1980s*, 1989; M. J. Hogan, *America in the World: The Historiography of American Foreign Relations since 1941*, Cambridge, 1995, is an invaluable collection of essays; R. L. Garthoff, *The Great Transition: American–Soviet Relations and the End of the Cold War*, 1994.

Latin America

E. Williamson, *The Penguin History of Latin America*, Harmondsworth, 1992; P. and S. Calvert, *Latin America in the Twentieth Century*, Basingstoke, 1990; H. Thomas, *Cuba or the Pursuit of Freedom*, 1971; S. Balfour, *Castro*, 1995 edn.; T. Skidmore, *The Politics of Military Rule in Brazil, 1964–1985*, Oxford, 1988; L. Schoultz, *Human Rights and United States Policy towards Latin America*, Princeton, 1981; L. Bethell and I. Roxborough, *Latin America between the Second World War and the Cold War*, Cambridge, 1996; S. Collier and W. F. Sater, *A History of Chile, 1808–1994*, Cambridge, 1996; N. Miller, *Soviet Relations with Latin America, 1959–1987*, 1989; S. Balfour, *Castro*, 1994; T. E. Skidmore and P. H. Smith, *Modern Latin America*, 1997; G. Smith, *The Last Years of the Monroe Doctrine, 1945–1993*, 1994; T. Donghi, *The Contemporary History of Latin America*, 1993.

Soviet Union/Russia: Superpower and After

G. Hosking, *A History of the Soviet Union 1917–1991*, 1992, is standard; N. Melvin, *Russians beyond Russia: The Politics of National Identity*, 1995; P. Dukes, *World Order in History: Russia and the West*, 1995, reflects on options; E. Acton, *Russia: The Tsarist and Soviet Legacy*, 1995 edn., is standard; M. McCauley, *The Soviet Union 1917–1991*, 1993 edn.; G. Gorodetsky, ed., *Soviet Foreign Policy 1917–1991: A Retrospective*, 1994, is a useful collection of essays; J. H. L. Keep, *Last of the Empires: A History of the Soviet Union 1945–1991*, Oxford, 1995, is a good internal history companion; G. A. Hosking, J. Aves, and P. Duncan, *The Road to Post-Communism: Independent Political Movements in the Soviet Union 1985–1991*, 1992, is useful on the final phase of Soviet history; M. McCauley, *Gorbachev*, 1998; S. White, *After Gorbachev*, 1994; V. Tolz, *Russia*, 2001; I. Bremner and R. Taras, eds., *New States, New Politics: Building the Post-Soviet Nations*, 1997.

India

J. M. Brown, *Modern India: The Origins of an Asian Democracy*, Oxford, 1994 edn.; B. R. Tomlinson, *The New Cambridge History of India*, vol. iii, pt. 3: *The Economy of Modern India, 1860–1970*, Cambridge, 1993; S. Wolpert, *Roots of Confrontation in South Asia: Afghanistan, Pakistan, India and the Superpowers*, 1982, and *A New History of India*, 1993 edn.; A. Vanaik, *The Furies of Indian Communalism: Religion, Modernity and Secularization*, Oxford, 1997; I. Talbot, *Inventing the Nation: India & Pakistan*, 2000.

South-East Asia

A. Bowie and D. Unger, *The Politics of Open Economies: Indonesia, Malaysia, the Philippines and Thailand*, Cambridge, 1997; F. Godement, *The New Asian Renaissance*, 1996; R. Cribb and C. Brown, *Modern Indonesia: A History since 1945*, 1995; R. Murphey, *East Asia*, 1996.

China

I. Hsu, *The Rise of Modern China*, New York, 1995 edn., is standard, as is J. Gray, *Rebellions and Revolutions: China from the 1800s to the 1980s*, Oxford, 1990; G. Chang, *Friends and Enemies: The United States, China and the Soviet Union 1948–1972*, Stanford, Calif., 1990; J. Gittings, *China Changes Face: The Road from Revolution 1949–1989*, Oxford, 1989; E. Moise, *Modern China*, 1994 edn., is standard; J. Spence, *The Search for Modern China*, 1991; G. Hicks, ed., *The Broken Mirror: China after Tiananmen*, 1990; R. Benewick and P. Wingrove, eds., *China in the 1990s*, 1995; W. L. Cohen, *America's Response to China: A History of Sino-American Relations*, 1990; H. Harrison, *Inventing the Nation: China*, 2001.

Australia

G. Stokes, ed., *The Politics of Identity*, Cambridge, 1997; J. Rickard, *Australia: A Cultural History*, 1996 edn.

Japan

A. Iriye, *The Cold War in Asia*, Englewood Cliffs, NJ, 1974; M. Schaller, *The American Occupation of Japan: The Origins of the Cold War in Asia*, New York, 1985; R. Buckley, *Occupation Diplomacy: Britain, the United States, and Japan 1945–1952*, Cambridge, 1982, and *US–Japan Alliance Diplomacy 1945–1990*, Cambridge, 1992; K. Newland, ed., *The International Relations of Japan*, Basingstoke, 1990; P. Bailey, *Postwar Japan: 1945 to the Present*, Oxford, 1996—an introduction; P. Duus, ed., *The Cambridge History of Japan*, vol. vi: *The Twentieth Century*, Cambridge, 1988; J. Dower, *Japan in War and Peace*, 1995—interpretative essays: T. McGraw, ed., *America versus Japan*, Cambridge, Mass., 1987; D. Smith, *Japan since 1945: The Rise of an Economic Superpower*, 1995; R. Buckley and W. Horsley, *Nippon: New Superpower*, 1997; A. Iriye, *Japan and the Wider World: From the Mid-Ninteenth Century to the Present*, 1997; J. Babb, *Tanaka*, 2000.

Korean War

P. Lowe, *The Origins of the Korean War*, 1997 edn.; C. Macdonald, *Korea: The War before Vietnam*, 1986; B. Cuming, *The Origins of the Korean War*, 2 vols., Princeton, 1981–90; S. N. Goncharov, J. W. Lewis, and X. Litai, *Uncertain Partners: Stalin, Mao and the Korean War*, Stanford, Calif., 1994; W. Stueck, *The Korean War: An International History*, 1995.

Middle East/Near East

Fawaz Gerges, *The Superpowers and the Middle East: Regional and International Politics, 1955–1967*, Boulder, Colo., 1994; D. Gilmour, *Lebanon: The Fractured Country*, 1983; M. E. Yapp, *The Near East since the First World War*, 1996 edn.; R. Ovendale, *The Origins of the Arab-Israeli Wars*, 1992 edn.; K. Kyle, *Suez*, 1991; L. Freedman and E. Karsh, *The Gulf Conflict, 1990–1991: Diplomacy and War in the New World Order*, 1993; Y. Sayigh and A. Shlaim, eds., *The Cold War in the Middle East*, 1997; A. Shlaim, *The Iron Wall: Israel and the Arab World*, 2000; M. Gilbert, *A History of Israel*, 1998.

North Africa

A. Horne, *A Savage War of Peace: Algeria, 1954–1962*, 1987 edn.; K. J. Perkins, *Tunisia: Crossroads of the Islamic and European Worlds*, Boulder, Colo., 1986.

Islamic Dimensions

A. Dawisha, *Islam and Foreign Policy*, Cambridge, 1983; J. Piscatori, *Islam in a World of Nation-States*, Cambridge, 1986; D. F. Eickelman and J. Piscatori, *Muslim Politics*, Princeton, 1996; J. L. Esposito, *The Islamic Threat: Myth or Reality?*, New York, 1992; F. Halliday, *Islam & the Myth of Confrontation*, 1996; J. M. Landau, *The Politics of Pan-Islam: Ideology and Organization*, Oxford, 1990; M. E. Marty, *Accounting for Fundamentalisms*, Chicago, 1994; G. Keppel, *The Revenge of God: The Resurgence of Islam, Christianity, and Judaism in the Modern World*, University Park, Pa., 1994.

Iran

N. Keddie, *Iran and the Muslim World, Resistance and Revolution*, 1995; B. Rubin, *Paved with Good Intentions: The American Experience in Iran*, New York, 1980; J. Bill, *The Eagle and the Lion: The Tragedy of American–Iranian Relations*, 1988.

Africa

J. Iliffe, *Africans: The History of a Continent*, Cambridge, 1995; P. Calvocoressi, *Independent Africa and the World*, 1985; Y. El-Ayouty, *The Organization of African Unity after Thirty Years*, 1994; H. and J. C. Kitchen, *South Africa: Twelve Perspectives on the Transition*, 1995; C. Clapham, *Africa and the International System*, Cambridge, 1996; S. Dubow and W. Beinart, eds., *Segregation and Apartheid in Twentieth Century South Africa*, 1995; J. Barber and J. Barratt, *South Africa's Foreign Policy: The Search for Status and Security, 1945–1988*, Cambridge, 1990; P. Gifford and W. R. Louis, eds., *The Transfer of Power in Africa:*

Decolonization 1940–1960, New Haven, 1982; T. Ranger and O. Vaughan, eds., *Legitimacy and the State in Twentieth Century Africa*, 1993; J. Hargreaves, *Decolonization in Africa*, 1996 edn.

Futures

F. Fukuyama, *The End of History and the Last Man*, 1992, and *Trust: The Social Virtues and the Creation of Prosperity*, 1995; T. Burns, ed., *After History: Francis Fukuyama and his Critics*, 1994; H. Williams, D. Sullivan, and G. Matthews, *Francis Fukuyama and the End of History*, Cardiff, 1997; S. P. Huntington, *The Clash of Civilizations and the Remaking of World Order*, 1996; Z. Brzezinski, *Out of Control: Global Turmoil on the Eve of the Twenty-First Century*, New York, 1993; C. de Alcantara, *Social Futures, Global Visions*, Oxford, 1996.

Index